HISTORY OF
HIGHER EDUCATION
ANNUAL

On the Cover:
Henrie Monteith Treadwell and Robert Anderson register for classes.

History of Higher Education Annual

2003-2004

Volume Twenty-Three

Roger L. Geiger

EDITOR

LONDON AND NEW YORK

First published 2005 by Transaction Publishers

Published 2017 by Routledge
2 Park Square, Milton Park, Abingdon, Oxon OX14 4RN
711 Third Avenue, New York, NY 10017, USA

Routledge is an imprint of the Taylor & Francis Group, an informa business

ISSN: 0737-2698
ISBN 13: 978-0-7658-0839-4 (pbk)

Contents

Higher Education and Civil Rights:
South Carolina, 1860s–1960s

Peter Wallenstein

Higher education, underemphasized in the literature on civil rights, can in fact be considered a key indicator of the texture of public policy and the nature of black opportunity in America. A case study of a single state, this article takes an approach that addresses change in black access to higher education across five generations—before emancipation, during Reconstruction, and in the 1890s, the 1940s, and the 1960s—in a conceptual context that relates the roles of black Carolinians, white Carolinians, and the federal government. Beginning in the 1860s, black Carolinians had some possibility, and white Carolinians some need, to take into account federal policies in shaping their own behavior regarding higher education. Each set of policies, state and federal, placed limits on what the other level of government could do. The interplay of the three forces, two of them within South Carolina, the other outside, dynamically shaped the changing policy outputs at every step of the way.

Increasingly during the past generation, scholars have redefined the Civil Rights Movement—or what such writers as Richard Kluger and Harvard Sitkoff have called African Americans' "struggle for equality"—as something that had its origins well before the decisions in *Brown v. Board of Education* (1954 and 1955) or Rosa Parks' arrest and the Montgomery Bus Boycott (in 1955–56), let alone the Greensboro and other sit-ins of February 1960 and after. One alternative is to go back into the 1940s—for example, to A. Philip Randolph's March on Washington Movement—or the 1930s. Another might be to pick up the story in the era that, in general terms, Rayford Logan referred to as "the nadir," marked in South Carolina by a state constitutional convention, in 1895, that punctuated a post-Civil War era of greatly expanded black opportunity in electoral politics and higher education. Yet another, and the approach adopted here, is to go back to slavery times and the beginnings of black freedom in the South in the 1860s.[1]

History of Higher Education Annual 23 (2004): 1-22.
©2004. ISBN: 0-7658-0839-0

The struggle for black freedom can be seen as encompassing every dimension of resistance to any and all markers of "the nadir," to every facet of Jim Crow's constellation of concepts and laws and attitudes and behavior—political disfranchisement, economic subservience, social proscription, and institutional segregation, together with the ever present prospect of violence to enforce the whole affair. Wherever we start the story, one significant feature is higher education. This essay does not seek to delineate in detail the developments in racial policy and higher education during the 1860s, the 1890s, the 1940s, or the 1960s. Rather, it seeks to pull those periods together; see how they fit; outline ways to understand them; and suggest that doing so for one state has the additional benefit of sketching an approach that could be applied to every state, across the South.

Higher education provides a significant marker of public policy and racial identity, a marker that has not been particularly prominent in the literature, either across the Age of Segregation or in the changes that began in every segregated state at some point between the 1930s and the 1960s. In earlier work, I have surveyed the South to create a context for exploring the beginnings of black access to so-called "white"[2] institutions of higher education as a dimension of the civil rights movement between the 1930s and about 1970.[3] This essay gives equal emphasis to a black institution, and it works with a longer time line.

Mentioned but not dwelt upon in this essay are two markers profoundly connected to some aspects of the history of segregation and desegregation, *Plessy* v. *Ferguson* (1896) and *Brown* v. *Board of Education*. Those Supreme Court rulings, although often incorporated in historical treatments of education, are best understood as symbolic markers, not explanations for change in school policy and practice. By no means did *Plessy* mark a beginning of segregated schools, at any level. And—aside from Texas, Arkansas, and North Carolina—*Brown* brought a quick end to racial segregation and black exclusion perhaps nowhere in the former Confederate South in the 1950s, though indeed it had an immediate effect in the Border South. The South Carolina story of higher education had a lot to do with federal policy, but relatively little to do with the Supreme Court's decisions in those two leading cases on civil rights.

Black Access to Schools before Emancipation

Before the Civil War, there was scarcely space for a discourse in South Carolina that brought together the concepts of black Carolinians, civil rights, and higher education. Most black Carolinians were slaves, and most slaveholders were committed to the proposition that no slaves should learn to read or write, let alone advance in knowledge to any higher branches. Surely, for example, there would be no black lawyers and no occasion for black access to law school. The federal government, if it played any role in these matters, did so in the sense that, in the Nullification Crisis of the early 1830s, the leading nullifiers were the white Carolinians most outspokenly and uncompromisingly supportive of strengthened legislation and other use of white power to close down black schools and foreclose black literacy. A new law, enacted in 1834, targeted black schools for extinction.[4]

Yet even in the final decades of the antebellum period, a triangle of social forces was at work, in that some white Carolinians, working from various motives, opposed such legislation, even sought its repeal; they supported some kind of schooling for black children, at least for free black children in Charleston; or they permitted, even ensured, that some of their own slaves learn to read or write. Some Afro-Carolinians found space within their unpromising social and political environment, in other words, to gain access to the gift of literacy. But it was not many. In an interview in the 1930s, one former slave named Sylvia Gannon insisted: "De white folks didn' never help none of we black people to read en write no time. Dey learn de yellow chillun, but if dey catch we black chillun wid a book, dey nearly bout kill us."[5]

Ned Walker, eighty-five years old when interviewed in the late 1930s near Winnsboro, recalled the huge plantation owned there by the Gaillard family in the late antebellum years. He told how, among the countless slaves on the place, his own father came to be, at the moment when freedom came, "de only one dat could read and write": "De young white marsters break de law when they teach daddy to read and write. Marse Dick say: 'To hell with the law, I got to have somebody dat can read and write 'mong de servants.'"[6]

As that story suggests, Ned Walker's father, Tom, was most unusual, in fact unique on that large plantation. Other elderly black South Carolinians, also interviewed in the 1930s, offered representative observations on the matter, particularly as it stood on plantations in the pre-Civil War era. Nellie Boyd, born about 1846, recalled, as her words were reported: "De slaves never learned to read and write." Adeline Jackson, a couple of years younger and speaking of her own experience, declared: "I never learned to read or write." Mary Jane Kelley, who was about thirteen when freedom came, said of her master that he "never let us learn to read and write."[7]

Al Rosboro, who had been about eighteen in 1865, pointed out that black Carolinians "never learned to read and write. It was 'ginst the law." Law or no law, some slave owners made it clear that slaves put themselves at grave risk should they demonstrate literacy or efforts to become literate. A woman born in Laurens County about 1845 reported: "We didn't have a chance to learn to read and write, and master said if he caught any of his slaves trying to learn he would 'skin them alive.'" Charlie Davis explained about schools and slavery: "Didn' 'low you to go to school cause if you was to pick up a book, you get bout 100 lashes for dat."[8]

From Slavery to Freedom: The 1860s

Then came the 1860s. Even during the war, as Union soldiers took control of some areas, teachers from the North—black teachers like Charlotte Forten; white teachers like Laura Towne—came to the Sea Islands and opened schools for former slaves. In 1865 and 1866, across the state, the Freedmen's Bureau fostered schools, as did people from the American Missionary Association and some other groups.[9]

Not all slaves entered the post-slavery world entirely illiterate, and many free people of color did not. So, although it would be misleading to assume a literacy rate of zero among Afro-Carolinians at the time slavery ended in one place or another, the figures were surely very low, and the public policy environment in South Carolina underwent tremendous change in the 1860s—in fact, the environment went through one tremendous change after another in the 1860s and 1870s. Those changes began with elementary schooling, but they soon raced ahead to include higher education as well.

In 1867, South Carolina history veered off in a radically new direction, even when compared with the first postwar years, themselves reflecting great change. Congress suspended the white state government that year and directed new elections, elections in which black Carolinians as well as white Carolinians would participate. The new electorate chose delegates to a state constitutional convention, where they wrote into the new organic law a provision enfranchising black men, and they directed the state legislature, when it should be formed under the new constitution, to create a system of public schools—with space for black Carolinians as well as for whites. That moment brought a new baseline from which black Carolinians could push for expanded educational opportunity.[10]

The remainder of this article explores a few periods in the century between the 1860s and the 1960s, as white Carolinians, black Carolinians, and the federal government participated in a three-way conversation about what educational opportunities black Carolinians might have and what kinds of institutional arrangements would make those opportunities available. Never again would the prewar regime return, with its ban on black Carolinians' being taught reading and writing.

Open to negotiation in the post-Civil War world were various matters that presupposed a right to learn to read and write. Yet the new dispensation reflected no reliable consensus as to whether some schools would be designated all-black and others non-black; how much public money, if there were segregation, would go into black schools relative to the funds offered white schools; or what should be done to ensure an expansion of educational opportunity by black Carolinians that might more or less match an expansion of educational opportunity for white Carolinians—whether in elementary schools, at the secondary level, or in higher education. Recognizing the agency of black citizens and white citizens alike gives essential texture to the continuing contest in South Carolina over educational policy, and the changing role of the federal government provides the other core dynamic to the conversation.

Emancipation, Reconstruction, and Higher Education

During Reconstruction, the South Carolina legislature did more than act regarding elementary schooling. Two key measures were related to higher education. One stemmed from the 1862 Morrill Land-Grant College Act, a federal law that supplied South Carolina, as it did every other state, with a fund designed to support some form of higher education, in particular agricultural and mechanical programs of study. South Carolina, like some other southern states but not most, divided its fund to make the benefits available to black as well as white citizens. In 1872, the legislature established the South Carolina Agricultural College and Mechanics Institute in Orangeburg, in close association with a private black school, Claflin University, and provided the school with funds from the 1862 Morrill Act.[11]

The other initiative in South Carolina regarding higher education for black citizens represented the Reconstruction era's greatest break with the racial past in higher education anywhere in the former Confederacy. In 1873, the state established a normal school in Columbia to train black teachers for black elementary schools. More significantly, the entire state university in Columbia was opened that year to black as well as white students, and—for four years—black students, in considerable numbers, took classes there and took degrees as well, not only undergraduate degrees but law degrees. In 1877, the end of substantial black political power and of Republican Party domination brought an absolute end to the pattern of integrated higher education at the school, and the state university resumed its status as an exclusively white institution. After 1877, although black Carolinians were by no means barred from access to higher education, they were categorically excluded from the state university. Segregation became absolute.[12]

Then came a particularly murky period in the history of higher education in South Carolina. The institution in Columbia suspended operations. The black school at Orangeburg continued operations, and some black students from the university at Columbia transferred there to continue their studies. New legislation in 1878 divided the university into two branches, one each in Orangeburg and Columbia, both to derive some support from Morrill Act funds. The Agricultural College and Mechanics Institute would be known as Claflin College, to distinguish it from Claflin University, with which it would continue to be associated. Reserved for white students would be a reopened institution in Columbia, to be known as the South Carolina College of Agricultural and Mechanical Arts.[13] Thus the state lurched into the post-Republican years with some sort of public institution of higher education set up for white Carolinians, at Columbia, and for black Carolinians, at Orangeburg.

With regard to education at any level, the differences between slavery and what came after could be subtle or stark. Like many former slaves, Solomon Caldwell broke history at before and "atter de war," and he noted: "We never had schools den, not till later. I never had a chance to go a-tall." Washington Dozier, who was born a slave in Florence County in 1847, split history in a similar manner: "Dey ain' n'er hab no schools fa de colored peoples no whey 'bout whay I stay 'fore freedom come heah. Won' long a'ter de war dat free schools wus open up dere." Samuel Boulware, who had been ten years old in 1865, answered his interviewer some seventy-two years later: "Does I 'member much about slavery times? Well, dere is no way for me to disremember, unless I die." He obliged his visitor by recounting his long life, and as for schooling, he observed: "Us slaves had no schoolin', 'cause dere was no teacher and school nigh our plantation. I has learnt to read a little since I got grown."[14]

Mary Wright was born a slave during the Civil War, so she grew up at a time when she could go to school, and in fact, in contrast to Samuel Boulware, she managed far more than learn "to read a little." She attended Claflin in the 1870s for a year. She taught school for more than a half century, and she sent her seven children through the Spartanburg public schools and some of them to college.[15]

Rev. James H. Johnson recalled in 1937 that he was nine years old in 1865 when "we learned we were free," and the next year his father moved the family to Camden, where young James "went to the public schools" with "teachers from the North." James Johnson, like Mary Wright, exemplified the transformation of opportunity that emancipation brought some black Carolinians. He "finished all the grades," he said, and then in October 1874 he "entered the University of South Carolina," where he studied until the "change in government in 1876," after which "Negroes were excluded from the university in 1877," when he was in his junior year. After that he taught school for ten years before becoming a minister.[16]

Thomas Ezekiel Miller was living in Charleston in the 1930s when he told an interviewer about his long life since being born free in Charleston in 1849. An 1872 graduate of Lincoln University in Pennsylvania, he then "studied law at South Carolina College, and was graduated in the last class before Negroes were barred." One of his "first political fights," in which he proved successful, was "to put Negro teachers in the City public schools" in Charleston. He served in the 1870s in the state House of Representatives, in the 1880s in the state Senate. Later he served in Congress and also, as we shall see, in the 1895 state constitutional convention.[17]

The 1890s

Regarding civil rights and higher education in South Carolina throughout the Age of Segregation, a three-way conversation took place among black Carolinians, white Carolinians, and the federal government. The imperatives of white Carolinians and the federal government offered opportunities as well as obstacles to black Carolinians, and, albeit under the rules of the Jim Crow regime, the three groups collaborated as well as clashed. An early development in higher education illuminated the post-Reconstruction world and, in its own way, demonstrated how much had changed—and how much had not—since slavery times.

Key markers of the post-1877 era—after the end of the biracial experiment at the University of South Carolina—include an important piece of federal legislation, the Morrill Land-Grant College Act of 1890. That Act reflected the Fourteenth Amendment's equal protection clause and also a brief moment when Republicans controlled both houses of Congress as well as the presidency. The Morrill Act of 1890 offered the states more money for higher education than had the Morrill Act of 1862, but it did so on the express condition that black citizens have access to an institution that received some of those funds—though the new money could be "equitably divided," in the language of the law, between "a college for white students" and "an institution for colored students." The 1890 Morrill Act embodied congressional validation, six years before *Plessy* v. *Ferguson*, of what came to be known as "separate but equal" (although the *Plessy* decision did not mention the Morrill Act).[18] Thus there emerged in 1896, as the black counterpart to what grew into Clemson University, what came to be known as South Carolina State University—though with even less state support and an even narrower curriculum.

South Carolina State University is characterized as a "college of 1890," a term that is understood to refer to black public institutions of higher education in the South that emerged in the aftermath of the Morrill Act of 1890. Every southern state has two land-grant institutions, a "college of 1862" and a "college of 1890"—such as today's Clemson University and South Carolina State University.[19] Though most "colleges of 1890" originated with the 1890 Morrill Act, not all did. Beginning about 1872, Virginia, Mississippi, and Georgia each apportioned land-grant money to a black school as well as a white one.[20] And, though South Carolina State University conventionally dates its origins to 1896, in fact, as we have seen, South Carolina had acted in 1872 much as those three other states did.

The groundwork for the change in 1896 was laid in the 1895 constitutional convention—in which six African American delegates served. One of them, Thomas E. Miller, urged that a new institution be established, entirely separate from Claflin University and with only "Southern men and women of the Negro race" on its faculty. There would, under this plan, be no whites on the faculty, nor could there be any black northerners, and it would be a secular school, not associated, as Claflin was, with the Methodist Church. White supremacist Benjamin Tillman embraced this move, and it was agreed to.[21]

The next year, the same Thomas E. Miller—as a member of the state legislature—proposed the measure that established (this was its full name) the Colored Normal, Industrial, Agricultural and Mechanical College of South Carolina, also in Orangeburg. Claflin College was "severed" from Claflin University and reorganized and renamed. Miller then resigned his seat in the legislature to accept appointment as the new school's first president, a position he held for the next fifteen years.[22]

In short, both races had an interest in the new regime, and black Carolinians were not entirely bereft of a voice in the convention or the legislature that inaugurated the new school. The new school had its origins in an arrangement that dated from a quarter-century earlier, yet the 1890 Morrill Act was a vital part of the reckoning that led to South Carolina State's establishment, just as the 1862 Morrill Act had played a vital role in the support of its predecessor. Developments in higher education in a Deep South state in the late-nineteenth century—developments related to black access as well as white opportunity—were dependent on legislation by the U.S. Congress.

What became of the school in the years to come was by no means in all respects salutary. A central explanation is that the new state constitution did as it was intended to and virtually ended black enfranchisement. The defeat of John W. Bolts for reelection to the state legislature in 1902 punctuated thirty-five years of black office holding in South Carolina, and not until 1970 was another African American elected to the South Carolina legislature.[23]

The term "separate but equal" provided a constitutional bulwark against racial integration, but it did not, by any measure, guarantee anything approaching equality. This can be seen in various ways. The state legislature could, and did, increase the funding for the white institutions—while leaving the black institution with little or nothing more than the federal money. The 1890 Morrill Act provided that the amount of new money would grow each year through the 1890s. In 1894, before the Morrill Act money was transferred from Claflin to South Carolina State, Tillman had declared that, as the black school "gets each year a larger and larger amount from the Morrill fund, its appropriation from the State can be diminished."[24] The state supplied black residents far less per capita by way of public money than it supplied their white counterparts.

Abysmal funding of elementary education for black Carolinians diminished the prospects for black teachers who took their degrees at South Carolina State; and it diminished the preparation of black youngsters to do undergraduate work in any discipline. John E. Swearingen, the state superintendent of education, asked a bit plaintively in 1915: "Is it too much to hope for a minimum of $25 per white child and $5 per negro child?" His query came after a fifteen-year period during which total expenditures on public schools in South Carolina had been multiplied by four—and during which the proportion of that money going to black schools had dropped from 21 percent to 11 percent. And it came at a time that a mere 5 percent of state spending in South Carolina on higher education went to a black institution.[25] This in a state that continued past 1920 to have a black-majority population.

By the 1920s and 1930s, South Carolina State was drawing more support from the state legislature than previously, and it was able to upgrade its facilities and curricula. It dropped its elementary school in 1923 and its high school in 1933. Various members of the faculty took leave to pursue graduate degrees at such schools as Columbia University, Kansas State, Ohio State, and Hampton Institute. By shortly after World War II, students could earn bachelor's degrees in English, social science, mathematics, chemistry, business administration, elementary education, and secondary education. Even some graduate programs were in prospect by that time—as a consequence of the emergence of new performance standards set by federal authority as a consideration in state policymaking. In the 1940s, South Carolina State College was not the University of South Carolina, or even Clemson, but it offered black Carolinians far more than any public institution had offered since at least 1877.[26]

The 1930s and 1940s

A 1938 decision by the U.S. Supreme Court—*Gaines* v. *Canada*, a case from Missouri regarding black access to the law school at the state university—was a key event in prompting South Carolina in the 1940s to develop an engineering curriculum, master's programs, and a law school at South Carolina State College, so as to provide a basis for deflecting black applicants away from Clemson or the University of South Carolina. The ruling in *Gaines* declared that a state did not fulfill its constitutional responsibility under the Fourteenth Amendment to provide equal protection of the laws if, having denied a black resident access to a "white" program that the state supported, it gave that black resident financial assistance to take classes outside the state.[27]

Yet *Gaines* not only spurred some states to create a parallel system of segregated programs, it also spurred some states to enact just the kind of out-of-state scholarships that *Gaines* would have appeared to decry. South Carolina took both actions in the 1940s. During what might be called the pre-history of desegregation, some black applicants tried to gain admission to the so-called "white" schools. As early as 1938, Charles B. Bailey applied to the law school at the University of South Carolina, and Rollin P. Green applied to graduate school there. Though unsuccessful, they reflected changing conditions, and created conditions that eventually brought about new programs at the black school. Black Carolinians seized greater equality within the old framework; "separate but equal" had to be far more equal than before. Segregation itself, however, could—and did—persist. Comparable efforts by black southerners emerged in the 1930s in various states. Litigation in North Carolina, seeking black access to the state university's school of pharmacy, failed, for example, but litigation in Maryland, seeking black access to the state law school, succeeded. In the years that followed, *Gaines* v. *Canada* reverberated across the South.[28]

In this shifting context, the South Carolina legislature acted in the mid-1940s to beef up the curricular offerings at South Carolina State College. White Carolinians acted to insulate the University of South Carolina from black applicants in law or graduate studies, and Clemson from black applicants in engineering. In 1945, the legislature created—on paper—graduate programs, a law school, and even a medical school at South Carolina State for black Carolinians. The gesture in 1945 required no new funding right away, and it created no new programs, but it laid the legislative groundwork, and in fact State College soon had master's programs in education, as well as a school of engineering, and then even a law school.[29] These developed because of actions taken by black Carolinians, in a context that the Supreme Court had changed with its ruling in *Gaines*.

In the mid-1940s, John H. Wrighten, a World War II veteran, twice sought admission to the College of Charleston, but rather than wait for something to develop when the college stonewalled his application, he enrolled at South Carolina State College. In 1946, as he neared graduation from that school, he applied to the University of South Carolina to study law. Also in 1946, Cleveland M. McQueen sought entry as a graduate student in education at the University of South Carolina. To deflect Wrighten's attempt to gain entry to the University, as well as McQueen's attempt and those of other black Carolinians who would no doubt follow, the legislature appropriated funds to support the establishment of a law school and a graduate school at State College.[30]

Having been rejected because of his racial identity, and unwilling to accept the legislature's attempt at compromise, Wrighten brought suit in federal district court. At trial, the state's attorneys argued that nobody had ever sought admission to the black law school, so it had not been thought necessary to have it up and running. Wrighten's attorneys insisted that he should have immediate access to an in-state law school, and the only one was in Columbia. Judge J. Waties Waring would not go so far as to order the University to admit Wrighten, but he did note that, in accordance with *Gaines* v. *Canada*, the state had only three options—to admit Wrighten to the white law school, open a black law school for him, or close the white school. Judge Waring was scarcely convinced that the Orangeburg school measured up as equal to the Columbia school, but when he ruled, the U.S. Supreme Court had not yet raised the bar on segregated schools (as it did in 1950) in such a way that full equality in tangible qualities—and intangibles too—would be required under "separate but equal." Regardless, the state demonstrated that it was prepared to fund an extravagant building to house a redundant program that would continue to insulate the state university from any black enrollment. Eventually, by 1949, a new law school had opened with its own elegant building at the Orangeburg campus, and Wrighten enrolled there. He graduated in 1952.[31]

Nor were McQueen and Wrighten the only black South Carolinians to seek admission to the state's "white" institutions in the years following World War II. In 1948, Spencer M. Bracey was a student at South Carolina State Agricultural and Mechanical College when he inquired of Clemson Agricultural College regarding the prospect of his transferring from the black school to the white one to study architectural engineering. In June that year, Clemson president R. F. Poole, having consulted with his board of trustees, wrote to inform Bracey that, in view of the post-World War II glut of students at Clemson, the school had no space to accommodate him.[32]

President Poole went on, though, to say: "Inasmuch as you are now attending a land-grant college where comparable facilities are available for taking the Architectural Engineering course, which you desire, your application for admission to The Clemson Agricultural College would not be favorably considered even at a later date." Poole explained the state policy requiring racial segregation and concluded: "As long as this policy is maintained[,] the Board of Trustees of this institution does not feel that it has the right to consider the application of a Negro student for admission to a white institution."[33] In short, "separate but equal" was alive and well. The state had taken preemptive measures against initiatives by black Carolinians like Spencer Bracey and, when it insisted on upholding the "separate," it could point toward what might pass for "equal."

The 1960s

Black Carolinians challenged the new version of the old system. In fact, in the late 1950s and early 1960s, students at South Carolina State protested against many facets of the very segregation that had led to the establishment, maintenance, and development of their own school. Moreover, in April 1960, a teenager in Charleston named Harvey Gantt and some of his classmates at all-black Burke High School were arrested for conducting a sit-in at a department store lunch counter.[34]

South Carolina was the only southern state where black students enrolled at a "white" university in the 1870s; South Carolina was the last state for that to be accomplished during the so-called "Second Reconstruction"—after court orders led to change in Georgia in 1961 and in Mississippi in 1962. In the late 1950s and early 1960s, black Carolinians made various attempts to enroll at the University of South Carolina, but none gained admission.[35]

Eventually, Charleston native Harvey Gantt broke through at Clemson. As early as July 1959, before his high school senior year, Gantt requested information from Clemson about its architecture program. But he enrolled in 1960 at Iowa State, funded in part with a South Carolina scholarship for black students who studied in other states, a program that had originated in the 1940s. Then in 1961 he applied to Clemson as a transfer student in architecture. Regarding his desire to transfer, Gantt pointed to Iowa's winters (too cold); demography (too white); and distance from home (too great). He had found, moreover, that Iowa was no interracial promised land. The dominant points were clear, though: Clemson had a fine program in architecture, and he had a right to enroll in it. Repeatedly rebuffed, Gantt went to federal court. Finally, in January 1963, he won his case at the Fourth Circuit Court of Appeals, and Clemson admitted him that month for the spring semester. "It's time we stepped out to claim some of our rights," Gantt explained during the litigation. "It's not that we want to take these things to the courts," he said, "but that seems to be the only away to get anything done."[36]

Clemson's second black student, math major Lucinda Brawley, enrolled that fall, and then a third, Larry Nazry, a year later. Gantt and Brawley very visibly attended home football games together; and during his senior year, Gantt shared a dormitory room at first with Nazry but then moved off campus when he married Brawley.[37] In 1965, Gantt graduated, and the school he left behind continued to enroll black Carolinians. What's more, the Gantts returned to Clemson in 2000 for the dedication of the Harvey and Lucinda Gantt Office of Multicultural Affairs in the campus student center.

Meantime, the University of South Carolina had admitted its first black students in 1963, too, and undergraduate Henrie Monteith also graduated in 1965—the school's first black graduate since 1877. In 1966, The Citadel enrolled its first black cadet, Charles D. Foster, and South Carolina State began admitting white students. In 1967, Jasper M. Cureton and John Lake—who in 1965 had transferred from the law school at South Carolina State College to the law school at the University of South Carolina—graduated there. The law school at State was no longer effective in entirely preventing black access to the "white" University, so the state closed it.[38]

In the 1960s as in the 1940s, black Carolinians, and white Carolinians, too, had worked with the materials at hand; timing was everything. Officials in white South Carolina made no concessions to desegregation until, as the saying went, they had simply run out of courts. Governor Ernest F. "Fritz" Hollings sought to console constituents and smooth the way for peaceful change when he explained, as he prepared to leave office in January 1963: "South Carolina is running out of courts." Hope died hard, however. A legislative committee observed, some days later: "We have not yet run completely out of courts." But when the U.S. Supreme Court, on January 21, turned down a request from Clemson for a delay in admitting Gantt, the game was over.[39] No longer would it be possible to prevent any black Carolinians from enrolling at all at South Carolina's non-black public institutions of higher education.

Nobody in authority at Clemson was prepared to risk the wrath of the state legislature by permitting a black student to enroll, until the federal judiciary directed the school to do so. Harvey Gantt was a fully qualified candidate—except for his racial identity—and he proved persistent. He also happened to press the issue in the early 1960s rather than in the 1940s. Until the Fourth Circuit spoke in 1963, Clemson was prepared to continue forever to tell Gantt—and any other black applicant to study architecture or engineering—what it had told Spencer Bracey back in 1948, when Harvey Gantt was a child in Charleston.

Clemson Agricultural College was renamed Clemson University in 1964. One could say that the school's new designation reflected a collection of major changes of the 1950s and 1960s. One was a surge in enrollment, another a greater emphasis on research. Dramatic changes in policy led to the enrollment of females as well as males, and blacks as well as whites, so that something approaching a universe of South Carolina's high school graduates—no longer categorically excluded by race or gender—could earn degrees there. Moreover, the curriculum was expanded from undergraduate technical subjects to include the gamut of liberal arts and a wide range of graduate programs, so that something approximating a universe of academic subjects could be studied there, and at both the undergraduate and graduate levels. When the change of name came in 1964, of course, the school had barely begun the process of desegregation.

In the years to come, although Clemson continued to be heavily white, and State largely black, none of the three schools remained exclusively black or nonblack. By the 1990s, moreover, the University of South Carolina's record of recruiting black faculty and black students was one of the best among historically white universities in the South.[40] Black Carolinians made a home there, and—in sharp contrast to the 1870s—white students did not flee the institution, and the multiracial experiment showed no indications that it might prove evanescent.

Higher Education and Civil Rights, 1860s–1960s

Emphasizing developments peculiar to South Carolina, but suggesting a much broader context, this article explores how black citizens of the Palmetto State made their way—especially in the Reconstruction years, the 1890s, the 1940s, and the 1960s—toward enhanced access to public higher education. In prewar South Carolina, a law prohibited schools for black residents. Hence, having any schools for black South Carolinians at all in the 1860s reflected a revolution in public policy as a consequence of emancipation. For a few years during Reconstruction, moreover, black students took classes and earned degrees at the University of South Carolina.

From the late 1860s on, at least some black Carolinians had access to some kind of formal higher education within the state. It might be said that white Carolinians set whatever restrictions seemed possible, and black Carolinians, at least at some times and places, resisted those restrictions. Across the Age of Segregation, black Carolinians were effectively displaced from participation in policymaking within the state, but they could rely on federal legislation for some benefits in higher education and could call upon the federal courts for possibly enhancing those benefits. From the 1860s to the 1960s, the continued presence of federal authority framed a set of changing conditions that shaped the outcome of every struggle between whites and blacks. During that hundred years, the system of public higher education for black Carolinians went from nonexistent to segregated; then desegregated, at least at the state university; then utterly separate and radically unequal; then a bit less unequal; and then formally desegregated again.

In the 1870s—after the federal government ended slavery, enfranchised black men, and supplied some funding under the 1862 Morrill Act—black electoral power in South Carolina produced state legislation to direct some of the benefits of public funding to black higher education. Some remnants of black electoral power persisted into the 1890s, when an arrangement with white Carolinians led to establishment of South Carolina State College. One perceived benefit to white Carolinians was a thorough institutionalization of segregation, with the bonus that the education offered at the black school was in multifarious ways inferior to what the white schools offered. Another was white access to the enhanced funds that came with new federal legislation, the 1890 Morrill Act.

In the 1940s, black electoral power had long since vanished, but the federal judiciary proved to be a tool that black Carolinians could employ to secure some of the "equal" in the world of "separate but equal." In the early 1960s—still with no electoral power to speak of—black Carolinians called on federal judicial power again, this time to obtain the beginnings of desegregation in higher education. In the years to come, the process of desegregation continued to unfold, as could be seen in the emergence—at Clemson; at the University of South Carolina—of black faculty, black athletes, black members of boards of trustees, and rising numbers of black students, far beyond the solitary soul, like Harvey Gantt, whose enrollment is so often taken to mark a conclusion rather than a beginning.[41] The beginnings of desegregation at Clemson Agricultural College and the University of South Carolina, in 1963, ended the absolute exclusion of black students from "white" institutions but opened new questions about the role of black schools and the degree of desegregation that would take place in the state's dual system of public higher education.

In the 1960s, not all black Carolinians were on the same page—one great divide often separated students from the administration at South Carolina State College. Not all white Carolinians were on the same page, then or earlier—as Judge Waring demonstrated.[42] And the federal government's role went through considerable changes between the 1890 Morrill Act and the judicial decisions of 1938 through 1950, let alone *Brown* v. *Board* and the decisions that followed, including the court order that brought Harvey Gantt's enrollment at Clemson.

Nonetheless the idea of a three-way conversation across the generations—with black Carolinians, white Carolinians, and the federal government each pursuing their own agendas and tugging history their own way—can help integrate, into one narrative, the varied developments on the racial front in higher education in one state. And the story of black access and black exclusion in public higher education in South Carolina offers one variant of a pattern that held across the South in the century after the Civil War, as black citizens sought to expand their civil rights in general, and pursue access and equity in higher education in particular, against all manner of obstacles.[43]

Notes

1.   Richard Kluger, *Simple Justice: The History of Brown v. Board of Education and Black America's Struggle for Equality* (New York: Random House, 1976); Harvard

Sitkoff, *The Struggle for Black Equality, 1954–1980* (New York: Hill and Wang, 1993 [1981]); Rayford W. Logan, *The Negro in American Life and Thought: The Nadir, 1877–1901* (New York: Dial Press, 1954). For the most generous definition, see *Civil Rights since 1787: A Reader on the Black Struggle*, eds. Jonathan Birnbaum and Clarence Taylor (New York: New York University Press, 2000); the introduction, "It Didn't Start in 1954," points back to the dawn of the colonial era in the New World but then settles on the Constitution of 1787 as the place to begin their account.

2.   I use "white" in quotation marks in this paragraph for two reasons. One has to do with my skepticism regarding the use of terms that assume some clear demarcation; see my *Tell the Court I Love My Wife: Race, Marriage, and Law—An American History* (New York: Palgrave Macmillan/St. Martin's Press, 2002). More directly relevant to the topic at hand, I object that the conventional use of the term "white" is generally—and understandably, though often erroneously—taken to mean that only Caucasians could attend such schools. For much of the twentieth century, people of Asian ancestry could enroll in many "white" schools; a telling example is the presence of Chinese cadets at The Citadel in the 1920s and 1930s. Therefore a division is better made between "black" and "nonblack" institutions than between "nonwhite and "white" ones; see my discussion in Peter Wallenstein, "Black Southerners and Non-Black Universities: Desegregating Higher Education, 1935–1967," *History of Higher Education Annual* 19 (1999): 125; and see Jian Li, "A History of the Chinese in Charleston," *South Carolina Historical Magazine* 99 (January 1998): 58–64. Mixing an absolute notion with a general tendency just promises to confuse the matter; despite the utter exclusion of people identified as African American, calling an institution "white" (especially without the quotation marks) might appear, in the modern context, to connote just a tendency, a preponderance, as in the current term, "predominantly white institution."

3.   Wallenstein, "Black Southerners and Non-Black Universities," 121–48. See also Wallenstein, "Naming Names: Identifying and Commemorating the First African American Students on 'White' Campuses in the South, 1935–1972," *College Student Affairs Journal* 20 (fall 2000): 131–39, and Wallenstein, "Higher Education and the Civil Rights Movement: Desegregating the University of North Carolina," in *Warm Ashes: Issues in Southern History at the Dawn of the Twenty-first Century*, eds. Winfred B. Moore Jr., Kyle S. Sinisi, and David H. White Jr. (Columbia: University of South Carolina Press, 2003), 280–300. I take a stab at addressing the current literature in "*Brown* v. *Board* and Segregated Universities: From Kluger to Klarman—Toward Creating a Literature on King Color, Federal Courts, and Undergraduate Admissions," a paper presented at an annual meeting of the Organization of American Historians, Boston, Mass., March 2004.

4.   Janet Duitsman Cornelius, *"When I Can Read My Title Clear": Literacy, Slavery, and Religion in the Antebellum South* (Columbia: University of South Carolina Press, 1991), 37–45. See also Marina Wikramanayake, *A World in Shadow: The Free Black in Antebellum South Carolina* (Columbia: University of South Carolina Press, 1973), 85–87, 167–68; Thomas Holt, *Black over White: Negro Political Leadership in South Carolina during Reconstruction* (Urbana: University of Illinois Press, 1977), 52–54; Norrece T. Jones Jr., *Born a Child of Freedom, Yet a Slave: Mechanisms of Control and Strategies of Resistance in Antebellum South Carolina* (Hanover, N.H.: Wesleyan University Press/University Press of New England, 1990), 56–57. The law of 1834 did not necessarily restrict private tutoring.

5.   Cornelius, *When I Can Read My Title Clear,* 45–58; George P. Rawick, gen. ed., *The American Slave: A Composite Autobiography*, vol. 2, *South Carolina Narratives, Parts 1 and 2* (Westport, Conn.: Greenwood Publishing Company, 1972),

part 1: 192. See also Holt, *Black over White*, 52–54; Jones, *Born a Child of Freedom*, 118, 125, 140–41; Bernard Edward Powers, *Black Charlestonians: A Social History, 1822–1885* (Fayetteville: University of Arkansas Press, 1994), 52–54.

6. Rawick, *American Slave*, vol. 3, *South Carolina Narratives, Parts 3 and 4* (Westport, Conn.: Greenwood Publishing Company, 1972), part 4: 176, 178.

7. Ibid., part 3: 2, 89; Rawick, *American Slave*, supplement, series 1, vol. 11, *North Carolina and South Carolina Narratives* (Westport, Conn.: Greenwood Press, 1977), 64.

8. Rawick, *American Slave*, vol. 2, part 1: 63, 246; vol. 3, part 4: 40.

9. Willie Lee Rose, *Rehearsal for Reconstruction: The Port Royal Experiment* (Indianapolis: Bobbs-Merrill, 1964), 85–89, 229–35, 372–74; Luther Porter Jackson, "The Educational Efforts of the Freedmen's Bureau and the Freedmen's Aid Societies in South Carolina, 1862–1872," *Journal of Negro History* 8 (January 1923): 1–40; Martin Abbott, *The Freedmen's Bureau in South Carolina, 1865–1872* (Chapel Hill: University of North Carolina Press, 1967), 82–98.

10. Francis B. Simkins and Robert H. Woody, *South Carolina during Reconstruction* (Chapel Hill: University of North Carolina Press, 1932), 416–43; Joel Williamson, *After Slavery: The Negro in South Carolina during Reconstruction, 1861–1877* (Chapel Hill: University of North Carolina Press, 1965), 209–39.

11. George Brown Tindall, *South Carolina Negroes, 1877–1900* (Baton Rouge: Louisiana State University Press, 1966 [1952]), 226–29; John F. Potts Sr., *A History of South Carolina State College, 1896–1978* (Orangeburg: South Carolina State College, 1978), 1–8, 180–83.

12. Williamson, *After Slavery*, 227–33; Daniel Walker Hollis, *University of South Carolina*, vol. 2, *College to University* (Columbia: University of South Carolina Press, 1956), 61–79; W. Lewis Burke Jr., "The Radical Law School: The University of South Carolina School of Law and Its African American Graduates, 1873–1877," in *At Freedom's Door: African American Founding Fathers and Lawyers in Reconstruction South Carolina*, eds. James Lowell Underwood and W. Lewis Burke Jr. (Columbia: University of South Carolina Press, 2000), 90–115; Pamela Mercedes White, "'Free and Open': The Radical University of South Carolina, 1873–1877" (M.A. thesis, University of South Carolina, 1975).

13. Hollis, *College to University*; 80–97; Potts, *History of South Carolina State College*, 8–11. It can further confuse matters that Claflin University spent most of the twentieth century as Claflin College. It recently took back its original name.

14. Rawick, *American Slave*, vol. 2, part 1: 65, 68, 170, 335.

15. Rawick, *American Slave*, supp., series 1, vol. 11: 319–21.

16. Rawick, *American Slave*, vol. 3, part 3: 45–46.

17. Rawick, *American Slave*, supp., series 2, vol. 1, *Alabama, . . . South Carolina, Washington Narratives* (Westport, Conn.: Greenwood Press, 1979), 392–96; Maurine Christopher, *America's Black Congressmen* (New York: Thomas Y. Crowell Company, 1971), 113–18.

18. Jean L. Preer, *Lawyers v. Educators: Black Colleges and Desegregation in Public Higher Education* (Westport, Conn.: Greenwood Press, 1982), 7–8; Peter Wallenstein, *Virginia Tech, Land-Grant University, 1872–1997: History of a School, a State, a Nation* (Blacksburg, Va.: Pocahontas Press, 1997), 74–77, 283–87.

19. Preer, *Lawyers v. Educators*, 5–30; Joel Schor, *Agriculture in the Black Land-Grant System to 1930* (Tallahassee: Florida A&M University, 1982), 47–150. A different treatment—an important cultural study that pays little attention, however, to the opportunities or mandates that came with the 1862 or 1890 Morrill Acts—is James D. Anderson, *The Education of Blacks in the South, 1860–1930* (Chapel Hill: University of North Carolina Press, 1988).

20.   Preer, *Lawyers v. Educators*, 7; Peter Wallenstein, *From Slave South to New South: Public Policy in Nineteenth-Century Georgia* (Chapel Hill: University of North Carolina Press, 1987), 160–69; David G. Sansing, *The Troubled History of Higher Education in Mississippi* (Jackson: University Press of Mississippi, 1990), 63–64; Wallenstein, *Virginia Tech*, 44–46, 74–78.

21.   Tindall, *South Carolina Negroes*, 229–30; Potts, *History of South Carolina State College*, 11–12. As for Thomas Ezekiel Miller, who had served in 1890–91 in the U.S. House of Representatives—virtually the identical time served by another mixed-race Republican, John Mercer Langston of Virginia, who also successfully contested his being declared defeated in the 1888 elections—Miller is described in binary terms as "black" but in genealogical terms as perhaps one-sixty-fourth black. See the brief biography (and an illustration) in Eric Foner, *Freedom's Lawmakers: A Directory of Black Officeholders during Reconstruction* (New York: Oxford University Press, 1993), 149–50.

22.   Tindall, *South Carolina Negroes*, 230–31; Potts, *History of South Carolina State College*, 12–35; Frank C. Martin et al., *South Carolina State University* (Charleston: Arcadia Publishing, 2000).

23.   I. A. Newby, *Black Carolinians: A History of Blacks in South Carolina from 1895 to 1968* (Columbia: University of South Carolina Press, 1973), 43.

24.   Stephen Kantrowitz, *Ben Tillman and the Reconstruction of White Supremacy* (Chapel Hill: University of North Carolina Press, 2000), 217–19, 353–54 note 45.

25.   Louis R. Harlan, *Separate and Unequal: Public School Campaigns and Racism in the Southern Seaboard States, 1901–1915* (Chapel Hill: University of North Carolina Press, 1958), 170 (quotation), 205 (table 9), 208 (table 11).

26.   Newby, *Black Carolinians*, 106–14, 258–73; Potts, *History of South Carolina State College*, 35–86.

27.   Mark V. Tushnet, *The NAACP's Legal Strategy against Segregated Education, 1925–1950* (Chapel Hill: University of North Carolina Press, 1987), 82–166; Preer, *Lawyers v. Educators*, 31–62; Michael J. Klarman, *From Jim Crow to Civil Rights: The Supreme Court and the Struggle for Racial Equality* (New York: Oxford University Press, 2004), 148–52, 160–63.

28.   Henry H. Lesesne, *A History of the University of South Carolina, 1940–2000* (Columbia: University of South Carolina Press, 2001), 68–69; Tushnet, *The NAACP's Legal Strategy against Segregated Education*, 52–58. See also J. Douglas Smith, *Managing White Supremacy: Race, Politics, and Citizenship in Jim Crow Virginia* (Chapel Hill: University of North Carolina Press, 2002), 244–48.

29.   Pauli Murray, comp., *States' Laws on Race and Color* (Athens: University of Georgia Press, 1997 [1951]), 410; Howard H. Quint, *Profile in Black and White: A Frank Portrait of South Carolina* (Westport, Conn.: Greenwood Press, 1958), 11; Potts, *History of South Carolina State College*, 74–75. See also Frank A. DeCosta, "Negro Higher and Professional Education in South Carolina," *Journal of Negro Education* 17 (summer 1948): 350–60. DeCosta was a member of the State College faculty; he also served as acting dean of the graduate school and, in 1948–49, acting president of the college (Potts, *History of South Carolina State College*, 72, 73, 92).

30.   Tinsley E. Yarbrough, *A Passion for Justice: J. Waties Waring and Civil Rights* (New York: Oxford University Press, 1987), 58–59. For a similar account—disconcertingly similar in places—see Nadine Cohodas, *Strom Thurmond and the Politics of Southern Change* (Macon, Ga.: Mercer University Press, 1994 [1993]), 104–5, 112. See also Edmund L. Drago, *Initiative, Paternalism, and Race Relations: Charleston's Avery Normal Institute* (Athens: University of Georgia Press, 1990), 231–33.

31.   Yarbrough, *Passion for Justice*, 58–60; Cohodas, *Strom Thurmond*, 112–14; *Wrighten v. Board of Trustees of University of South Carolina*, 72 F. Supp. 948 (1947). For glimpses of Wrighten as a lawyer in the Civil Rights Movement, see Drago, *Initiative, Paternalism, and Race Relations*, 272–73 (on the 1950s) and 278 (on the April 1960 sit-ins in Charleston, in which Harvey Gantt was a participant).

32.   William D. Workman Jr., *The Bishop from Barnwell: The Political Life and Times of Senator Edgar A. Brown* (Columbia: R. L. Bryan, 1963) 297. See also *Tradition: A History of the Presidency of Clemson University*, ed. Donald M. McKale (Macon, Ga.: Mercer University Press, 1988), 197 note 41, and Maxie Myron Cox Jr., "1963—The Year of Decision: Desegregation in South Carolina" (Ph.D. diss., University of South Carolina, 1996), 14–15, 15 note 2.

33.   Workman, *The Bishop from Barnwell*, 297–98.

34.   Newby, *Black Carolinians*, 346–49; Potts, *History of South Carolina State College*, 145–46, 148; Levona Page, "Gantt Takes Clemson," *The State* (Columbia), 23 January 1983: 12B; Bob Dunn, "Moment of Truth," *Anderson Independent Mail*, 29 May 1985: 7A.

35.   Quint, *Profile in Black and White*, 122–23; Lesesne, *University of South Carolina*, 138; Robert A. Pratt, *We Shall Not Be Moved: The Desegregation of the University of Georgia* (Athens: University of Georgia Press, 2002); William Doyle, *An American Insurrection: The Battle of Oxford, Mississippi, 1962* (New York: Doubleday, 2001).

36.   Newby, *Black Carolinians*, 351; Lesesne, *University of South Carolina*, 143; Cox, "1963," 14–69; George McMillan, "Integration with Dignity," *Saturday Evening Post*, 16 March 1963: 15–21, reprinted in *Perspectives in South Carolina History: The First 300 Years*, eds. Ernest M. Lander and Robert K. Ackerman (Columbia: University of South Carolina Press, 1973), 381–92; Wright Bryan, *Clemson: An Informal History of the University, 1889–1979* (Columbia: R. L. Bryan, 1979), 153–62; McKale, *Tradition*, 196–202; M. Ron Cox Jr., "'Integration with [Relative] Dignity'—Clemson's Desegregation and Georgia McMillan's Article at Forty," paper presented at The Citadel Conference on Civil Rights in South Carolina, Charleston, S.C., March 2003; "Harvey B. Gantt" biographical file, University Archives, Special Collections, Strom Thurmond Institute Building, Clemson University. See also John G. Sproat, "'Firm Flexibility': Perspectives on Desegregation in South Carolina," in *New Perspectives on Race and Slavery in America: Essays in Honor of Kenneth M. Stampp*, eds. Robert H. Abzug and Stephen E. Maizlish (Lexington: University Press of Kentucky, 1986), 164–84. The quotations are from Nancy Anderson, "'Hard to Explain,' Says Harvey Gantt," *Iowa State Daily*, 27 September 1962: 1. Gantt turned twenty in January 1963. To register and begin classes at Clemson, he drove up from Charleston with his father, Christopher Gantt; his minister, Rev. A. R. Blake; and his lawyer, Matthew J. Perry (Page, "Gantt Takes Clemson," 12B). A native of Columbia, Perry embodies the transformation of black Carolina in the twentieth century. A veteran of World War II, he graduated from South Carolina State College in 1948 and earned his law degree there in 1951. President Carter nominated him as a federal district judge in 1979. A new federal court building, dedicated in Columbia in April 2004, carries his name.

37.   John McCarter, "Harvey Gantt to Wed Coed Lucinda Brawley," *Greenville News*, 10 October 1964.

38.   Lesesne, *University of South Carolina*, 137–51; Cox, "1963," 69–101; Alexander S. Macaulay Jr., "Black, White, and Gray: The Desegregation of The Citadel, 1963–1973," in Moore, Sinisi, and White, *Warm Ashes*, 320–36; Thomas E. Sebrell II, "Black Integration into the South's Two Most Prominent Military Schools: The

Virginia Military Institute and The Citadel," undergraduate paper written at VMI for HI 487-W, December 2000; Newby, *Black Carolinians*, 351; W. Lewis Burke and William C. Hine, "The School of Law at South Carolina State College: Its Creation and Legacy," paper presented at The Citadel Conference on Civil Rights in South Carolina, Charleston, S.C., March 2003—see *Matthew J. Perry: The Man, His Times, and His Legacy*, eds. William Lewis Burke and Belinda Gergel (Columbia: University of South Carolina Press, 2004).

39.   Bryan, *Clemson*, 158; Cox, "1963," 37; McKale, *Tradition*, 199.

40.   Peter Wallenstein, "Model Universities and Racial Diversity: Undergraduate Enrollment in 24 Public Universities in the South," *Diversity News* 7 (fall 2000): 10–11.

41.   Desegregation as a "process" rather than an "event" is one of the core concepts underlying my "Black Southerners and Non-Black Universities." Lesesne, *University of South Carolina*, 149–50, adopts the concept and applies it to USC.

42.   Also demonstrating white dissenters from mainstream opinion were graduate students Dan Carter, Charles Joyner, Hayes Mizell, and Selden Smith in the history department at the University of South Carolina in the early 1960s (Lesesne, *University of South Carolina*, 139–40).

43.   For a book-length study of another state, see Amilcar Shabazz, *Advancing Democracy: African Americans and the Struggle for Access and Equity in Higher Education in Texas* (Chapel Hill: University of North Carolina Press, 2004).

In Pursuit of Excellence:
Desegregation and Southern
Baptist Politics at Furman University

Courtney L. Tollison

Among southern colleges and universities over the course of the 1950s and 1960s, desegregation became a litmus test for an institution's commitment to progress. At Furman University in Greenville, South Carolina, desegregation was but one aspect of a clearly articulated campaign to achieve "academic excellence by national standards." Adherents to this vision confronted hostility from the university's denominational affiliate and parent institution, the South Carolina Baptist Convention; this conflict reflected an increasing ideological disparity between the university and convention. From November 1963 to December 1964, the ensuing desegregation debate purged conflicting values and forced a reevaluation of the university's institutional identity. Furman defied the convention and implemented token desegregation in January 1965. Resentment of convention governance grew among other southern Baptist affiliated colleges and universities over the next several decades as well. Throughout the 1990s, many of the Southern Baptist Convention's preeminent academic institutions, including Furman, accepted the fundamental nature of these conflicts and severed all relations. Southern Baptist ideology ultimately proved fundamentally irreconcilable with institutions seeking national prominence.

From a prison cell in Birmingham in April 1963, Martin Luther King wrote a letter in which he appealed to the white churchgoing people of the South, the so-called "white moderates," or, perhaps more appropriately, those King thought ought to feel a moral imperative to support the civil rights movement.[1] As president of the Southern Christian Leadership Council, King believed that white churchgoers, whom he labeled the white moderates, must lead white southerners in support of the movement's aims. He expressed his disappointment regarding their lack of support, and noted that he had "almost reached the regrettable conclusion that the Negro's great stumbling block in his stride towards freedom is not the White Citizen's Counciler or the Ku Klux Klanner, but the white moderate,

History of Higher Education Annual 23 (2004): 23-48.
©2004. ISBN: 0-7658-0839-0

who is more devoted to 'order' than to justice; who prefers a negative peace which is the absence of tension to a positive peace which
is the presence of justice...."[2]

Many southern white religious leaders, however, were uncom-
fortable with King's insistent pleas for support; the religious right
was particularly opposed. In his book *Southern Civil Religions in
Conflict: Civil Rights and the Culture Wars*, Andrew Manis writes,
"From Richard Furman's defense of slavery and the Lost Cause evan-
gelism . . . to the mid-century segregationists, preachers have sought
to give divine sanction to the southern social order and maintain its
socially constructed world."[3] Having been heavily indoctrinated into
a society that viewed African Americans as inferior, many southern
white churchgoers thus feared the increasingly assertive rhetoric of
the civil rights movement.

Token desegregation of southern, predominantly white denominationally affiliated colleges and universities forced the white church-
going people of the South to confront changes introduced by the
civil rights movement; the desegregation of Southern Baptist affiliated colleges and universities forced a reevaluation of institutional
identity and, in the case of Richard Furman's namesake, Furman
University in Greenville, South Carolina, ironically furthered the
increasingly disparate ideologies espoused by the university and its
Southern Baptist Convention (SBC) state affiliate, the South Carolina Baptist Convention (SCBC).[4]

Throughout the 1950s and 1960s, National Association for the
Advancement of Colored People (NAACP) attorneys strategically
instigated suits against state-supported universities in the southern
states. Court-ordered desegregation became the primary means of
desegregating the South's public universities. Until the 1964 Civil
Rights Act, however, private institutions could, with few exceptions,
avoid such changes if they so wished. State-supported institutions
thus tended to desegregate earlier than the majority of the South's
private institutions. For various reasons, however, some private and
denominationally affiliated colleges and universities hastened to
implement desegregation before the 1964 Civil Rights Act financially forced most institutions to do so.[5] Denominationally affiliated
institutions that desegregated before and after the congressional
mandate confronted concerns and even opposition within their respective denominational affiliates. Largely because of the hierarchi-
cal structure of the Catholic Church, the few colleges and universi-

ties in the South that were associated with the Catholic Church tended to be somewhat progressive in their efforts to desegregate.[6] State Methodist and Presbyterian bodies usually issued an official statement of support, articulating their trust and faith in the actions of an institution's board of trustees; behind these formal endorsements, however, often lay unresolved tensions.[7] Southern Baptist affiliated institutions faced not only a lack of support but often outright opposition to the implementation of such change.[8]

Consequently, desegregation often contributed to existing tensions and thus forced some Southern Baptist affiliated universities to reexamine their value systems, goals, and, eventually, their long relationships with state denominational bodies. By the late 1990s, at institutions such as Wake Forest (N.C.), Furman (S.C.), Stetson (Fla.), Meredith (N.C.), and the University of Richmond (Va.), these increasingly tenuous relationships ceased to exist.

The desegregation of predominantly white denominationally affiliated colleges and universities is a story of educational politics, of clashes between student activism and student conservatism, of the relationship between the federal government and denominationally affiliated higher education, and between the state's religious bodies and their affiliated institutions. For many colleges and universities, it is also the story of how race became a litmus test of progress. Colleges and universities who implemented, or attempted to implement desegregation before the passage of the 1964 Civil Rights Act often viewed desegregation as a condition necessary for and indicative of a commitment to institutional progress. At Furman, desegregation was but one aspect of a clearly articulated campaign by President Gordon Blackwell to achieve "academic excellence by national standards." Racial issues purged underlying issues and tensions and thus provided an impetus for intense discussion of the university's identity. The university had become increasingly secular, and no longer derived the majority of students from the SCBC; by the early-1960s Furman had outgrown the purposes for which she had been founded.

The desegregation debate at Furman University was a widely publicized and controversial story involving the SCBC and the students, faculty, administrators, supporters, and trustees of Furman University. The story, which sporadically occupied newspapers across the state for almost one year and a half, resulted in the matriculation of Joseph Vaughn into the university in January 1965. Motivated by an ideological commitment to institutional distinction that viewed segregation as an impediment to their vision, many members of the Furman community welcomed the decision after nearly thirteen months of uncertainty created by segregationists within the SCBC.

Furman was not the first college or university in South Carolina, state-supported or private, to desegregate; the university did not begin the implementation process until 1963. The significance of Furman's history lies in the way in which the university community approached desegregation as a necessary aspect of a strategic plan to achieve academic prominence. Excepting the 1968 Orangeburg Massacre, South Carolina's history of race relations and higher education and specifically desegregation is less dramatic than other deep South states.[9] No one threw bricks into dorm room windows as did mobs at the University of Georgia when Charlayne Hunter and Hamilton Holmes arrived on campus in January 1961; no federal marshals were required to calm the violent mobs as they were at the University of Mississippi on 30 September 1962; and no governor stood in the doorway to prevent desegregation as Alabama Governor George Wallace did at the University of Alabama in June 1963. South Carolina's colleges and universities implemented desegregation with relatively little commotion. In 1962, Our Lady of Mercy Junior College in Charleston, South Carolina, quietly admitted ten African American students into its student body. Supported by a court order, Harvey Gantt matriculated at Clemson College on 28 January 1963. Certainly, Gantt's entrance into Clemson attracted the most national media attention. Reporters present, however, described it as a "non-event."[10] After the lengthy court battle that resulted in Gantt's admittance, the state government maintained its policy of massive resistance by obstructing desegregation at the University of South Carolina; a judge ultimately ordered the university to admit Henrie Montieth and two others into the university in September 1963. Later that fall, Furman University laid the foundation for its desegregation, only to have their efforts delayed by the SCBC. In the spring of 1964, President Charles Marsh of Wofford College in Spartanburg, South Carolina, announced its newly passed desegregated admissions policy; Wofford integrated when Albert Gray began his studies in the fall of that year, while Furman and the SCBC debated the desegregation question. Furthering the dynamic nature of higher education and race relations in the upstate, Bob Jones University

(BJU), located about five miles from Furman's campus and about thirty miles from Wofford, maintained the attention of national media as it both defended itself against the Department of Health, Education, and Welfare and sued the Internal Revenue Service throughout the 1970s and 1980s.[11]

Racial desegregation of Furman University was a necessary component of a deliberate campaign by Furman administrators to seek "academic excellence by national standards."[12] At various stages throughout the desegregation process, state-supported and private institutions across the South appealed to the morals and pragmatism of their supporters. Beyond this, however, Furman administrators strategically and successfully appealed to the Furman community's vision of a nationally esteemed liberal arts college.

Furman University: Origins and Development

Furman University was established by the SCBC as an "academy-seminary," named for noted Baptist leader Richard Furman after his death in 1825. It served as a regional institution for white Baptist education throughout the 1800s. In 1845, the split between northern and southern Baptists resulted in the formation of the Southern Baptist Convention (SBC), and for many years Furman served as the training ground for the denomination's white ministry. In 1859, the SBC formally established the Southern Baptist Theological Seminary in Greenville. During the Civil War, the all-male student body fought for the Confederacy. The Greenville Baptist Female College (f. 1854), which later changed its name to Greenville Woman's College and merged with Furman University, remained open, and was instrumental in assisting in the reconstruction of the university after the war's end.[13] In 1877, the seminary moved to Louisville, Kentucky, and soon thereafter disagreements grew between Furman and the SBC.

In the late 1800s and early 1900s, Furman grew slightly more independent from the SBC, and began to test the SBC's power in what would become the first of many conflicts. In the early 1870s, when most southern institutions were highly skeptical of the new biblical scholarship, Furman hired an Old Testament scholar, Crawford H. Toy, who had recently returned from Europe where he had studied the latest historical-critical methods of Biblical study. Toy spent one year on the Furman faculty, transferred to a faculty position in the seminary, and moved to Louisville when the seminary changed locations.[14] In his years at the Southern Baptist Theological Seminary, he was, according to former Furman University Professor of Religion Jeffrey Rogers, "considered the 'pearl' of the faculty." In the late 1870s, a dispute arose over his, as Rogers states, "doctrine of the inspiration of Scripture, not because he didn't have one, mind you, but because he developed one that was consistent with his historical-critical investigation of the nature and origin of the Bible." The Seminary fired Toy and he accepted a position at Harvard University, where he became one of the most "respected and influential pioneers of American critical Old Testament scholarship." Although the denomination shunned Toy, Furman audaciously offered, before he assumed his position at Harvard, a professorship and the presidency of the university. Clearly, an ideological gulf existed as early as the late nineteenth century.

By the early 1900s, Furman University had become much more than a Baptist institution, and in the 1920s, Furman began to promote its image as an *academic* institution situated within a Christian environment. In 1925, the Scopes trial that posited Christian beliefs against the theory of evolution garnered national attention. In contrast to the religious fervor that many brought to the debate, David Ramsey, president of the Greenville Woman's College, suggested that religion and science are not irreconcilable, and that "it seems to me that we should get better results if we allowed both religion and science to pursue the even tenor of their ways in an earnest and relevant search for truth." At the meeting of the Baptist Assembly at Furman in the summer of 1925, Furman President William J. McGlothlin echoed similar thoughts and assurances.[15] In 1933, the SCBC and administrators of Furman University and the Greenville Woman's College cemented the close relationship between the institutions when Furman assumed administrative and financial control of the College.[16] At mid-century, Furman University had 1200 students and remained under the direction of the SCBC. In the mid-1950s and early 1960s, Furman constructed a new campus north of the city, and, for the first time in its history, became a fully coeducational university.

Furman University: Campus Attitudes towards Civil Rights

As early as January 1950, Furman President John L. Plyler actively surveyed the changes occurring in race relations, often contacting university presses and the Carnegie Foundation with requests for written material about discrimination and private colleges.[17] Plyler wanted Furman to be a place of academic freedom and, in his efforts to improve the quality of instruction, recruited professors from respected graduate programs who exhibited progressive social ideals.[18] Plyler was careful to maintain a subtle approach, however. When the Southern Conference Educational Fund contacted President Plyler and asked him to join others in sponsoring a Southwide Conference on Discrimination in Higher Education in April 1950, Plyler politely declined.[19]

Five years later a small but influential group of students created a community and statewide controversy when they publicly opposed racial segregation in *The Echo*, a university newspaper. In May 1955, student editor Joan Lipscomb's article "No Way Back" supported the *Brown* v. *Board of Education* decision. Lipscomb disagreed with the lack of respect with which southern politicians had responded to this ruling and emphasized the inconsistencies between the opinions of Baptist students and the Baptist Convention. She wrote of the Supreme Court ruling as "a fact which all the emotionalism of Southern politicians cannot alter with their oratorical eloquence." She encouraged leaders to "lead the way, not backward, by adding to already existing prejudice, but forwards by promoting a program of adjustment to the situation as it stands."[20] She noted the success of the integrated annual convention of the South Carolina Baptist Student Union (BSU), an organization to which significant numbers of Furman students belonged. Lipscomb quoted a convention delegate: "The spirit of the group was wonderful. Democracy prevailed, and Negroes were elected to top positions in the regional group."[21]

This issue of *The Echo* also included an article by Charles King, "Perversion of the Baptist Heritage," that criticized the SCBC's approach to race relations.

Thus, while the majority of white South Carolinians supported delaying tactics to avoid implementation of *Brown*, a group of students at Furman University inadvertently furthered student opposition to the conservative SCBC. Because of disputes between student opinion and the Baptist Convention regarding race, dormitory visitation hours, on-campus dancing, and a fraternity system, Furman administrators were hesitant to provoke the convention. Vice President Frank Bonner and a faculty committee examined *The Echo* at the printers and, deciding that the antagonistic articles would exacerbate relations between the university and convention, ordered the destruction of all 1,500 copies. In response, King submitted proofs of the articles to *The Greenville News Piedmont*, which printed excerpts from the articles and a story on the incident in the next morning's newspaper. A report of the incident also appeared in an article several months later in the *Journal of Negro Education*. When questioned about the event, Furman officials replied, "No comment."[22] Largely because of previous unhappiness with the convention's limitations on student behavior, Furman students rallied behind the student editors and effectively created a campus atmosphere that furthered student resentment of interference from the SCBC.

In the late 1950s, Furman University decided to channel its energy over the next few years into a campaign to improve Furman's national reputation. Soon after the newspaper incident, Furman faculty and administrators grew increasingly frustrated with the SCBC's limitations, which curtailed their efforts to elevate Furman from a regionally recognized institution into a nationally esteemed liberal arts university. Most frustrating to the faculty was the *Statement of Principles of Academic Freedom and Tenure* that contained a limitations clause in the terms and conditions of the contract for employment at Furman University. Passed in 1940, this clause required that professors "avoid making or approving any statements which run counter to the historic faith or present work of Baptists," and that employees of Furman lead a Christian lifestyle that advanced the aims of the denomination. By the late 1950s, Furman administrators became increasingly anxious about the effects that such a limitation on academic freedom was having on faculty morale and the university's ability to recruit professors.[23] Just as Furman students rallied together behind *The Echo* incident, Furman faculty and administrators rallied together against the convention's censorship and in support of progress and academic excellence.

The results of *The Echo* incident and the convention's attempts to regulate intellectual freedom had immediate and long-lasting influences that contributed to student and faculty support for Furman and its policies, especially those that generated opposition from the convention. Student and faculty critics of the convention's limitations on free speech and extreme caution in regard to social progress articulated ideals of freedom and growth and would greatly contribute to the future success of Furman University.

The decision to elevate Furman's status included the recruitment of students from outside the southern United States, an emphasis on academic freedom, a campaign to increase the university's endowment, and the founding of a Phi Beta Kappa chapter on campus. Since 1924, Furman had applied for a chapter during the organization's evaluation of schools every three years, and was repeatedly denied. Each time the university applied throughout the 1950s, the governing committee of Phi Beta Kappa informed Furman that the high percentages of students majoring in home economics, the low percentage of faculty with doctoral degrees, and continued segregation reduced Furman's chances of approval. In the late 1950s and early 1960s, the implementation of Phi Beta Kappa was chief among the administration's goals for elevating Furman's national reputation.[24]

Throughout the early 1960s, the Furman University Advisory Council was another important element of Furman's campaign towards progress, and a reflection of the growing divide between the university and the SCBC. Established in 1960, the Advisory Council's purpose was to suggest ways to advance Furman's programs, facilities, and policies, thus enabling Furman to be placed on a par with nationally recognized liberal arts colleges and universities. Although the council had no official power, its recommendations for improvement fundamentally altered the future of the university. In reaction to increased hostility from the SCBC and its obstacles to growth, Furman administrators recruited influential men and women from across the country without regard for their denominational views to serve on the council. As more and more institutions across the nation and especially the South, including Clemson College and the University of South Carolina, admitted African American students, the Advisory Council, void of any affiliation with the convention, emphasized the necessity of desegregation if Furman hoped to realize its full potential for growth and recognition.

Student and faculty opinion continued to be more progressive than mainstream political sentiment in South Carolina, and certainly more progressive than most members of the SCBC. In December 1961, student members of the Baptist Student Union passed by a vote of 117-25 a resolution to "suggest that the Trustees of the institutions of our convention give careful study to this responsibility to open the door of knowledge and service to all students, regardless of race or creed." Students also adopted a resolution that was in direct contrast to a resolution taken at the November 1961 annual SCBC meeting. The resolution stated that, "We, the Baptist Student Union of the South Carolina Baptist institutions of higher learning . . . should accept all qualified applicants regardless of race."[25]

Across the state, newspaper headlines publicized the students' act with headlines that read: "S.C. Baptist Student Vote in Favor of Integration" and "SC Baptist Students Ask Study of De-Segregation."[26] Faculty support for desegregation coincided with student sentiment. In a poll taken in 1961, soon after the BSU vote, almost 90 percent of faculty members polled supported a non-racially discriminatory admissions policy.[27] Another article in *The Paladin* warned students of future relations with the SCBC: "The battle . . . is just beginning, and the struggle for power over this university, which now straddles the two worlds of a narrow, denominational school and a leading educational institution, will be bitterly fought."[28]

Desegregation: A Necessary Condition

Meanwhile, across town, Joseph Vaughn, a native of Greenville raised in an impoverished neighborhood by his single mother, served as the president of the student body at Sterling High School, Greenville's African American high school.[29] In the early 1960s, Sterling High students participated in protests that succeeded in desegregating the city's airport, main library, skating rink, and lunch counters.[30] Joe Vaughn came to Furman from a socially and politically active and organized environment. The influence of these events on Vaughn taught him that people, especially young people such as himself, could effectively promote change.

In their attempts to lay a foundation for students such as Joe Vaughn, Furman trustees, aware of the opposition the convention had posted to past university attempts to progress, questioned the power relationship of the Board of Trustees to the convention. Alester G. Furman Jr., a member of the Board of Trustees and grandson of Richard Furman, wrote United States Circuit Judge and Furman supporter Clement F. Haynsworth Jr. and inquired as to the legal constructs of this relationship. In May 1962, after examining Furman's charter, Haynsworth noted, in his ten-page analysis:

> it is apparent that all governmental powers are vested exclusively in the Board of Trustees and the Convention has no legal right or power to issue directions to the Trustees affecting their managerial authority. It is further apparent that the Convention has the right to elect successor trustees, but it has neither the right nor the power to remove duly elected trustees or to vacate the offices of elected trustees.[31]

Although Furman did not pass a racially non-discriminatory admission policy for another year and a half, its administrators and trustees were aware of the opposition that desegregation would generate from the convention and wanted to be knowledgeable as to the legal relationship between the two before acting.

Throughout the early to mid-1960s, Furman administrators, the Board of Trustees, and the Advisory Council officially focused their energies on molding Furman into an institution that could compete with other liberal arts universities across the nation. Furman constantly evaluated its standing among other institutions, specifically southern colleges and universities and other Baptist institutions. In early 1963, Furman hosted a meeting of administrators from institutions with ties to the Southern Baptist Convention. Academic freedom and desegregation were primary concerns among administrators. The limitations on academic freedom were increasingly becoming problematic for institutions that aimed to recruit talented students and professors. On 10 May 1963, one administrator remarked at the Southern Baptist Convention's Education Commission that these limitations by Baptists presented "a mortal enemy to learning." He emphasized that southern Baptist colleges and universities could lose their accreditation if nothing was done to abolish these limitations.[32] Additionally, Furman administrators realized that Furman's segregated status lagged behind other institutions in the Southern Baptist Convention, including Mercer University in Georgia, Wake Forest University and Meredith College in North Carolina, Stetson University in Florida, and Oklahoma Baptist University.

Other colleges and universities affiliated with their state's respective Baptist Conventions had already taken steps within their respective state conventions to operate under non-racially discriminatory admissions policies. Trustees at Wake Forest University, affiliated with the North Carolina Baptist Convention, voted on 27 April 1962 to open its doors to students of all races.[33] At Stetson University, an institution of the Florida Baptist Convention, President J. Ollie Edmunds quietly chose a transfer student, Cornelius Hunter, to desegregate the school in the fall of 1962.[34]

Mercer University had emerged only weeks prior to the administrators' meeting from a heated battle over the admission of Sam Jerry Oni, a young man from Ghana who had been christianized by missionaries from the Georgia Baptist Convention and wanted to study at Mercer in hopes of returning to preach in his native country. The debates among Georgia Baptists, as Oni noted in 1994, forced "our Southern Baptist brothers and sisters in America to confront gross contradictions in their Christian witness at home and abroad." On

18 April 1963, Mercer's Board of Trustees voted to drop its racial barriers.[35] Oni desegregated the college in the fall of 1963. Oni lived on campus, while two other African-American students, Cecil Dewberry and Bennie Stephens, attended as day students.[36]

From observations of Mercer's experience and from the discussions that arose at the conference, Furman administrators were convinced that prestige and nationally competitive standards of scholarship were simply impossible if the university continued to abide by SCBC policies. Furman had little choice but to challenge the convention's convictions. Months after Clemson University and weeks after the University of South Carolina admitted African Americans, both by court order, Furman trustees passed a racially non-discriminatory admissions policy on 8 October 1963. Although many trustees were somewhat reluctant, only one member dissented from supporting Dr. Bonner and President John Plyler's decision, which favored desegregation on the basis that it was in Furman's best interests.[37] The Advisory Council overwhelmingly supported the decision, although one member, a southerner and former president of the American Bar Association, slammed his fists on the table and declared that the day that Furman admitted an African American student was the day that he ended all associations with the university.[38] Nevertheless, Furman University had achieved a momentous step in its history.[39]

Days after the trustees' vote on the admissions policy, an editorial from a prominent white South Carolinian encouraged support for Furman and applauded its initiative. On 11 October 1963, Wayne Freeman, editor of *The Greenville News* and, more importantly, a member of State Senator Marion L. Gresette's Segregation Committee, the primary vehicle for massive resistance in the state, wrote "Wisdom Seen in Decision of Trustees." He saw Furman's voluntary acquiescence as a "smart move" designed "to meet a situation that is almost inevitable."[40] By accepting a policy of desegregation before it was forced upon them, he said, Furman administrators and the board of trustees took control of the situation and were thus able to desegregate according to their own timetable. Many white South Carolinians, especially those with connections to Furman, respected its reception of this inevitable occurrence.[41]

Furman and the SCBC: A Year of Contention

Upon hearing the news of the board of trustees' intentions, the SCBC was shocked and troubled by Furman's abrupt display of independence. As a preventive measure, Alester G. Furman Jr. wrote to Dr. Horace Hammett, General Secretary-Treasurer of the SCBC, explaining the decision of the Board of Trustees was not based upon "liberalism" but a mission in line with orthodox Christianity. Furman encouraged Hammett to use his "great influence to undergird the great world missionary program by proper action as to our denominational colleges in the convention."[42] Nevertheless, at their 1963 annual meeting in Charleston, the convention voted to ask board members to delay implementation for one year so the convention's General Board could study the issue.[43] Eager to move forward but reluctant to disturb relations with the convention further, Furman administrators acquiesced to the waiting period.

Furman students immediately and angrily reacted to the convention's delay tactics. In the 26 October 1963, issue of *The Paladin,* one article recounted the convention's reaction and another called on Furman students to "Support Our Trustees."[44] In this article, one Furman student wrote,

Judging from past action of the Convention, the Furman trustees' resolution will be raked over coals. The final result of the vote is about as unpredictable as the campus weather.... Furman's continuing progress in the academic world should not be curtailed for the sake of other Baptist institutions which don't have as much foresight as Furman.

Two weeks later, a student poll revealed that Furman students supported the admissions policy four to one. Showing a disregard for convention opposition, 214 of the 365 students polled answered that the policy should be implemented immediately. Although tensions had long existed between Furman administrators and students and the SCBC, never before had they become as strong as they did during Furman's quest to maintain their racially non-discriminatory admissions policy. *The Paladin* articles reveal much about the growing tensions. The 16 November 1963 issue ran a front page headline, "S.C. Baptists Adopt Wait and See Policy; Mystical Bride is Practical Divorcee." This article, laden with heavy sarcasm, read,

In the three short days of the South Carolina Baptist Convention, that unquiet segment of the mystical bride of Christ succeeded in obtaining a Nevada-style divorce.... Some of the good messengers in Charleston seemed anxious to get the "real" issue settled and to forget about such minor concerns as propagation of the gospel, overcoming the world and loving one's neighbor.... It was indeed inspiring to see such staunch dedication and such a clear vision in our leaders, the honored keepers of our storied religious heritage.

The article closes, "Piety and alarm are no excuses for ignorance, and the whole tone of the meetings was one of zealous piety and impassioned ignorance. The messengers were anxious to do what was 'right' for Furman; but somehow neglected to ask administrative officials of the University what was, in reality, best for the institution."[45] Another student wrote his opinion, "Once again the many messengers to the South Carolina Baptist Convention got the only 'kicks' of their usually drab lives by attacking Furman University and its policies with sadistic glee." The student commented on the convention's closed minded approach: "All of Right and Truth have been crucified and are buried in a Cave, covered by a rock too big to be rolled aside for a second coming."[46] Throughout the fall of 1963 and the spring of 1964, student articles criticized the Baptist Convention and generated support for desegregation.

During this waiting period, Furman confronted the retirement of its president and increasing reasons that it must desegregate. On 28 January 1964, President Plyler announced his intentions to retire effective August 1964. Plyer wanted to pass the position to someone younger, but more importantly, someone equally as committed to aggressively pursuing growth and academic advancement.[47]

As Furman's board began to search for a suitable candidate, Vice President Bonner began to take over more and more duties from President Plyler, and among his first acts was the search for an appropriate African American student to admit. Bonner and Alumni President Claude Sapp Funderburk decided that, although they would still comply with the convention's request for a delay, desegregation was an absolute necessity, and thus they began the search. Funderburk visited one of Greenville's segregated high schools, Sterling High School, and hand-selected senior Joseph Allen Vaughn. Vaughn held a position on the school's student government and membership in the National Honor Society. Vaughn excelled academically, ultimately graduated third in his class, and was a Baptist.[48]

After Bonner met with Vaughn, Bonner and Funderburk arranged for him to spend one semester at Johnson C. Smith University in Charlotte, North Carolina. Pending convention approval, Vaughn would transfer to Furman in the winter of 1965.[49] Although the university could not implement desegregation until the Baptist Convention's annual meeting in November 1964, Funderburk and Bonner believed in the necessity of desegregation for the future success of the university.

* * *

In August 1964, the board of trustees filled the vacant presidency with a successful scholar and nationally respected administrator who, with his progressive ideals and high hopes for Furman, ushered in a new era for the school.[50] The board convinced Gordon W. Blackwell, Furman graduate and then president of Florida State University, to accept the presidency of his alma mater. Blackwell shared the Furman community's hopes for growth and was willing to endorse practical advances. Throughout negotiations with the Board of Trustees, Blackwell maintained that integration was "a condition of my coming to Furman." He admitted that initially, the trustees "gulped a little" in response to his non-negotiable demand, but eventually they agreed, although they knew that this promise might bind them to defy the Baptist Convention.[51] Blackwell assured the trustees that, during his presidency, he would operate under the goal of "excellence by national standards." As the slogan behind a financial campaign drive, the phrase initially appeared soon after Blackwell's acceptance and continued for several years in his speeches and in Furman literature.[52] Under Blackwell's leadership, Furman aggressively sought measures to achieve this clearly articulated vision of the Furman of the future.[53]

In the fall of 1964, the Department of Health, Education, and Welfare (HEW) issued a warning to administrators at southern educational institutions that encouraged immediate compliance with federal law and further contributed to the need for desegregation. The Civil Rights Act of 1964 required that institutions receiving any amount of federal aid must be in compliance with federal law. Furman's drive towards excellence included increased reliance upon federal grants needed for faculty research and the improvement and building of new facilities on campus. Although a private institution, Furman was in the process of applying for a federal grant for construction of a science and technology facility under the Higher Education Facilities Act of 1963.[54] It was also conducting a feasibility study to determine the establishment of a medical school, for which the federal government would contribute two-thirds of the cost. On 23 November 1964, A. W. Boldt of HEW's southern regional office met with educators from southern colleges and universities to discuss the possibility of discontinuing federal money to institutions that remained segregated. The threat of the loss of federal funding contributed to the urgency of desegregation at Furman and other private colleges and universities.

Furman's desire to grow had long provoked disagreement with the SCBC, and thus the argument that desegregation was a necessary component to growth took no priority over southern racism. At its annual meeting in Columbia on 10–12 November 1964, the convention's General Board proposed passage of a statement the Executive Committee had composed in May 1964.

> Furman University has rendered a splendid service in training for the ministry and church related vocations. It is now faced with the tremendous task of trying to relate itself to a changing world and its ministry to the realities of a world in revolution. The question of admission has always been, and we feel must continue to be, a matter for the administration through its trustees to decide.... We feel sure these servants of the Lord will act with wisdom.[55]

Leaders of the convention understood the negative implications that continued segregation would bring to its institutions. Members, however, allowed racial prejudices to thwart educational and social progress. Convention members rejected the Board's statement by only a slim margin, 943–915, due to hesitation by a significant number to reject their governing board's study and recommendation. Immediately after the vote, a minister called for another vote. The results were more indicative of social attitudes towards dismantling Jim Crow. In a simple yes-no vote on whether the convention favored integration in its institutions, it voted "no" 905–575.[56] In the final stages of Furman's grand plan, racist sentiment from white South Carolinians provided another obstacle to freedom of growth and observance of federal law. Furman students prayed that the image of the convention would change from a "'Circus of Fools' to a Christian Convention dedicated to true Christian ideals."[57] As late as the mid-1960s, some white South Carolinians continued to resist any change to their segregated way of life.

Immediately, Furman administrators recognized the challenge before them. Gordon Blackwell was only months away from assuming the presidency with the expectation that Furman would soon desegregate. Administrators had to convince the trustees, all South Carolina Baptist appointees, to reinstate the previously passed admissions policy. Although it could not legally obstruct implementation of these policies once passed, the vote of the SCBC presented an enormous challenge to desegregation. Trustees were weary of acting against the organization that had placed them in these roles. Upon hearing that the board was wavering in its commitment, Blackwell wrote to J. Wilbert Wood, chairman of the Board of Trustees, on 17 November 1964, stating that he was deeply troubled by recent developments and encouraged the trustees to implement a policy of desegregation immediately: "I accepted the Presidency with the understanding that the position of the Trustees on this aspect of admission had been determined and would not be revoked."[58] As the primary organizer of Furman's push to desegregate, Bonner stood before the board and, with forceful eloquence, urged them to support desegregation.[59] On 8 December 1964, the trustees voted to reinstate the previously passed policy of racial non-discrimination. Joseph Vaughn would enter Furman at the beginning of the next semester.

Members of the SCBC immediately voiced their disapproval of Furman's defiance. The temporary chairman of the South Carolina Baptist Laymen's Association expressed his shock at Furman's decision and felt it "a tragedy.... If they integrate it, our objective will be to disintegrate it."[60] Members of the convention felt that Furman trustees did not have the authority to make such a decision in light of convention disapproval.[61]

In an attempt to calm the opposing sides, Wood wrote letters to convention president Robert W. Major and to alumni explaining the "historical facts which make it improper for the convention to direct the trustees of Furman to take any specific action" and emphasizing the duty of the trustees to vote, above all else, in the best interests of the university. He wrote that Furman voted to desegregate because it was the "right" and "Christian" decision, and that further delay of the policy would be "gravely injurious." Continued segregation, he said, would endanger Furman's accreditation, hamper the university financially, and would negatively affect Furman's recruitment of talented professors and students.[62] Segregation was simply antithetical to the university's aims.

Furman Desegregates

Furman's public defense of its decision set the tone for acceptance of desegregation on campus. Furman students took pride in their university's decision and in Joe Vaughn.[63] On 29 January 1965, the Furman community welcomed Vaughn and Gordon Blackwell, each man a tangible representation of hope and progress for Furman.

Many factors, including the luxury of hand selecting a student to desegregate, contributed to Furman's successful desegregation. The premeditated act of selecting and grooming a student specifically to bear the momentous mantle of token desegregation offers an example that contrasts with the court-ordered desegregation of many southern state-supported institutions by the also highly qualified NAACP-supported plaintiffs. "Our being private allowed us to be selective," said Bonner. "Joe Vaughn had enough maturity and intelligence to be an excellent student regardless of color."[64] Vaughn's personality, talents, and tolerance quelled any racist sentiments that members of the Furman community may have harbored against him after his arrival and greatly contributed to the continued success of desegregation.[65]

Vaughn made friends easily, involved himself in campus activities, such as cheerleading, BSU, and the Southern Students Organizing Committee (SSOC), and was academically motivated. Vaughn did not attempt to downplay his interest in African-American affairs: as vice-president for the first campus SSOC chapter in the state, Vaughn organized and led, in mid-February 1968, a rally in support of students at South Carolina State University soon after the Orangeburg Massacre. Several months later, he again organized and led a march to honor the recently assassinated Martin Luther King Jr.[66] Furman administrators felt that Vaughn easily surpassed the high expectations that the Furman community had of him.[67] In Vaughn's opinion, he and Furman were a match "made in heaven."[68] Privately, however, Vaughn experienced a great deal of pressure to perform academically and struggled to exhibit ease in public.

Conclusion

Between the late 1950s and mid-1960s, desegregation and progress became synonymous on the Furman campus; Furman's desire to achieve "academic excellence by national standards"[69] prevailed over conservative southern racism. Its desire to avoid the threat of the loss of monetary support and academic prestige rallied support for desegregation at a time when many white South Carolinians wished to preserve the days of Jim Crow.

Desegregation at Furman University furthered the ideological gap between the university and the SCBC. The desegregation process forced administrators and others to address fundamental questions about the university's character and institutional goals. Increasingly in the decades before, during, and after the civil rights movement, differences in societal values became evident. The inerrancy move-

ment, based upon the fundamentalist belief that the Scripture is iner-
rant and should be perceived in literal terms, had gained momentum
within the Southern Baptist Convention, and Furman administrators
and moderates within the SCBC became increasingly alarmed over
Southern Baptist Convention statements regarding homosexuality,
religious pluralism, and the role of the church in an academic environment. Fundamentalists assumed control of the board of the South-
eastern Seminary, located in North Carolina, and subsequently voted
to hire as faculty members only those who believed and taught the
inerrancy of the scripture. In 1988, Furman officials became aware
that

> fundamentalists were working to gain seats on this and other boards connected with the
> convention. When six were named to Furman's 25-member board, the school was
> understandably concerned about eventual loss of academic independence to individuals
> whose primary allegiance is to a narrow religious agenda rather than to the university
> itself.[70]

Thus, the university hired a legal team to research the relationship
between the SCBC and Furman; it dispelled notions of the SCBC's
perceived ownership of the university, and on 15 October 1990,
Furman trustees, all SCBC appointees, voted to amend the charter to
allow the board of trustees of Furman to become a self-perpetuating
body, thus abolishing the SCBC's power to appoint trustees to the
university.[71] Aware of the fundamentalists' ambitions towards Furman
and other Southern Baptist affiliated universities, Furman's trustees
passed this preemptive measure. Moderate Baptists who constituted
the majority of the board in 1990 decided to take measures to "preserve its values in a religious atmosphere that had become highly
combative and increasingly restrictive."[72]

The convention, of course, was extremely disturbed by the trustees' action. One month after the vote, the convention voted to enter
into negotiations with the university and placed Furman's funding
into an escrow account until the parties reached some sort of compromise. They soon reached an agreement that allowed for Baptist
input but not complete control over the trustees' selection process.
In November 1991, however, the convention was no longer content
with the compromise, and voted to take legal action against the university. Almost immediately, thirty-four ministers and leaders within
the convention signed a statement that called for a special meeting
in hopes that the SCBC and Furman would sever all legal and financial ties. Furman President John E. Johns, the son of a southern Bap-

tist preacher, desperately hoped for an end to almost a century of increasing conflict. After 166 years of cooperation, convention members voted to sever ties between Furman and the SCBC and to discontinue all financial support of the university.

As with Furman, obtaining complete control of institutional governance was the primary concern for other academically prominent SBC affiliated institutions. Furman thus successfully distanced itself from denominational politics. It joined Wake Forest University, which disaffiliated from the North Carolina Baptist Convention in 1986 following a series of ideological conflicts that began in the 1920s.[73] Baylor University loosened its association with the Texas Baptist Convention in 1990.[74]

Stetson University and the Florida Baptist Convention and Meredith College and the North Carolina Baptist Convention followed Furman and severed ties in 1995 and 1997, respectively. The University of Richmond experienced conflicts in the early decades of the twentieth century and began to slightly but significantly alter the relationship between the University of Richmond and its Southern Baptist Convention affiliate, the Baptist General Association of Virginia. In 1970, E. Claiborne Robins offered a fifty million dollar gift to the university with one stipulation: the university's charter must be amended so as to liberate the university from the Baptist General Association. While the charter did not entirely dissolve the relationship, it sufficiently altered the terms of this relationship. Continued discord resulted in a complete break between the university and the Baptist General Association in 1999. Across the South, conflicts including but not limited to the teaching of evolution, on-campus dancing, desegregation, and religious pluralism reflected the growing dissonance between these academic institutions and their southern Baptist affiliates.[75]

Free from the restraints of the SCBC, Furman has flourished. The university has steadily risen in national rankings and is considered one of the top fifty liberal arts colleges in the nation. President David E. Shi's emphasis on engaged learning, a "problem-solving, project-oriented, experience-based approach to the liberal arts," has proven highly successful; in its undergraduate research category in 2002, *U.S. News and World Report* ranked Furman fourth among all institutions of higher education in the country.[76] Although the university has expended considerable effort in the recruitment of minorities, Furman has struggled to attract substantial numbers of African American students and thus remains engaged in the desegregation process.[77]

Because its primary emphasis was on institutional growth, Furman University was able to overcome the southern racism that tainted implementation of desegregation at other southern institutions. Desegregation, in sum, was an obstacle to Furman's efforts towards progress. Those institutions that maintained elements of racial discrimination, such as Bob Jones University, delineated a course that differed greatly from institutions such as Furman.

Tensions between southern Baptist affiliated universities and their denomination were not limited to the desegregation debate. Over the next several decades, frustrations and resentment felt by Furman and other Southern Baptist universities resulted in the acceptance of the insurmountable nature of their conflicts with the Southern Baptist Convention. The social values of the Southern Baptist Convention had become fundamentally irreconcilable with those of academically prominent universities of the late twentieth century. Throughout the 1980s and 1990s, these universities asserted their commitment to institutional growth, and ended their relationships with the denomination that conceived them.

Notes

1.   This article is a modified version of a chapter from the author's dissertation. Courtney L. Tollison, "Moral Imperative and Financial Practicality: Desegregation of South Carolina's Denominationally-Affiliated Colleges and Universities" (Ph.D. diss., University of South Carolina, 2003).

2.   "Letter From Birmingham City Jail," The Martin Luther King Jr. Papers Project at Stanford University. www.stanford.edu/group/King/.

3.   Andrew M. Manis, *Southern Civil Religions in Conflict: Civil Rights and the Culture Wars* (Macon, Ga.: Mercer University Press, 2002), 131. Richard Furman, a South Carolina minister, was a well-known and well-respected leader on the national Baptist scene in the late 1700s and early 1800s who provided a biblically based defense of slavery. Elected in 1814 and reelected in 1817, he served as the first president of the Baptist Triennial Convention, the first national gathering of Baptists in the United States, held in Philadelphia. In the early 1820s, Richard Furman was instrumental in the establishment of the South Carolina Baptist Convention, and was elected its first president. Furman died in 1825; the next year, Furman University opened. Alfred Reid, *Furman University: Toward a New Identity, 1925–1975* (Durham, N.C.: Duke University Press, 1976), 4–5; Colyer Meriwether, *History of Higher Education in South Carolina with a Sketch of the Free School System* (Washington, D.C.: Government Printing Office, 1889), 93–94; Samuel Hill, ed., *The Encyclopedia of Religion in the South* (Macon, Ga.: Mercer University Press, 1997), 783–84.

4.   Denominationally affiliated colleges and universities are defined as those institutions that maintained a formal relationship with the denomination that founded them.

The state denominational bodies affiliated with these institutions appointed some or all of the institutions' trustees, and also contributed financially to these institutions. These denominationally affiliated colleges and universities are distinguished from seminaries and institutions whose purpose is strictly to train its students for the ministry, priesthood, or order.

5.   In January 1965, the federal government mailed an "Assurance of Compliance with Department of Health, Education, and Welfare Regulation Under Title VI of the Civil Rights Act of 1964" form to most southern institutions of higher education. Non-compliance with the Civil Rights Act rendered these institutions ineligible to receive any federal funding.

6.   See, for instance, Charles Stephen Padgett's work on Spring Hill College in Alabama. Additionally, the first substantial desegregation of an institution of higher education in South Carolina was not, as is most frequently assumed, Clemson College, but the now defunct Our Lady of Mercy Junior College in Charleston. Charles Stephen Padgett, "Schooled in Invisibility: The Desegregation of Spring Hill College, 1945–1963" (Ph.D. diss., University of Georgia, 2000); Charles Padgett, "'Without Hysteria or Unnecessary Disturbance': Desegregation at Spring Hill College, Mobile, Alabama, 1948–1954," *History of Education Quarterly* (summer 2001); C. Joseph Nuesse, "Segregation and Desegregation at The Catholic University of America," *Washington History* (spring/summer 1997); Tollison, "Moral Imperative and Financial Practicality."

7.   Tollison, "Moral Imperative and Financial Practicality."

8.   In South Carolina, conflicts that erupted over desegregation in a denomination's colleges and universities were directly proportional to the extent that power was diffused in the denomination. Mark Newman, *Getting Right with God: Southern Baptists and Desegregation, 1945–1995* (Tuscaloosa: University of Alabama Press, 2001).

9.   For more on the Orangeburg Massacre, see Jack Bass, *The Orangeburg Massacre*, 2d ed. (Macon, Ga.: Mercer University Press, 1996).

10.   George C. McMillan, "Integration with Dignity: The Inside Story of How South Carolina Kept the Peace," *Saturday Evening Post*, 16 March 1963. A reporter from New Jersey was overheard saying of Harvey Gantt's uneventful matriculation at Clemson College, "I expected blood, and all I got was cream puff."

11.   From 1965 to 1971, Bob Jones University's (BJU) tumultuous experience with the federal government resulted from its refusal to admit African American students. In 1971, it allowed Willie Thompson, a married, African American employee, to register for classes. After 1971, BJU unsuccessfully sued the Internal Revenue Service (IRS) when the IRS revoked its tax-exempt status as a result of BJU's formal prohibition of interracial dating and marriage. "Civil Rights Ruling Affirmation Asked," 28 February 1967. College/University Vertical Files, Box 2, University of South Carolina, South Caroliniana Library; Daniel L. Turner, *Standing Without Apology: The History of Bob Jones University* (Greenville: Bob Jones University Press, 1997), 225; Mark Taylor Dalhouse, *An Island in the Lake of Fire: Bob Jones University, Fundamentalism, and the Separatist Movement* (Athens: University of Georgia Press, 1996), 106; *Religious Freedom Imperiled: The IRS and BJU* (Bob Jones University, 1982), 41; *The Bomb and Its Fallout: Bob Jones University v. United States, U.S. Supreme Court Decision, May 24, 1983* (Bob Jones University, 1983), 3.

12.   Gordon W. Blackwell, interview by Courtney Tollison, 12 April 2000; A.V. Huff, interview by Courtney Tollison, 8 March 2001, Greenville. Although Furman University administrators and trustees decided to push for growth and elevated aca-

demic standards in the late 1950s and early 1960s, this formal campaign was not articulated until President Gordon Blackwell assumed the post in August 1964. Blackwell coined the phrase "academic excellence by national standards."

13. Judith Bainbridge, *Academy and College: The History of the Woman's College at Furman University* (Macon, Ga.: Mercer University Press, 2001).

14. Jeffrey S. Rogers, "Breaking Up is Hard to Do: Baptists and Furman," an unpublished speech given at Furman University, 16 April 2002, as part of Furman's 175th anniversary celebration.

15. A. V. Huff, *Greenville: The History of the City and County in the South Carolina Piedmont* (Columbia: University of South Carolina Press, 1995), 327. For more on the Scopes trial, see Edward J. Larson, *Summer for the Gods: The Scopes Trial and America's Continuing Debate Between Science and Religion* (Cambridge, Mass.: Harvard University Press, 1998).

16. Bainbridge, *Academy and College*.

17. John L. Plyler to Columbia University Press, requesting a copy of "Prevention of Discrimination in Private Educational Institutions;" John L. Plyler to The Carnegie Foundation for the Advancement of Teaching requesting, "The Colleges and the Courts 1941–1945," Baptist Controversies, Race Relations (#1) file, Furman University Archives, James Buchanan Duke Library, Greenville. Hereafter cited as FUA.

18. Huff, interview.

19. John L. Plyler from James A. Dombrowski of the Southern Conference Educational Fund; James A. Dombrowski from John L. Plyler, Baptist Controversies, Race Relations (#1) file, FUA.

20. "Student Releases Articles from Seized FU Echo," *The Greenville News Piedmont*, 19 May 1955; "Newspaper Comment," and "'Echo' Editors Resign," *Southern School News*, 8 June 1955, p. 11.

21. "Student Releases Articles from Seized FU Echo," *The Greenville News Piedmont*, 19 May 1955.

22. Ibid. Frank Bonner, interview by Courtney Tollison, 16 February 1999, Greenville; B. R. Brazeal, "Some Problems in the Desegregation of Higher Education in the 'Hard Core' States," in *The Journal of Negro Education: Desegregation and the Negro College* (summer 1958), 371–72; Preston Valien, "Desegregation in Higher Education: A Critical Summary," in *The Journal of Negro Education: Desegregation and the Negro College* (summer 1958), 379. Valien identified Furman as one of four segregated universities in the South in which the students are "far ahead of the governing boards and administrators in their acceptance of desegregation."

23. Reid, *Furman University*, 106–07.

24. Ibid.

25. "State BSU Convention Meets in Greenville: Delegates Pass Resolutions on Integration," *The Paladin*, 8 December 1961, FUA; "News from the South Carolina Student Council on Human Relations," South Carolina-Student Council on Human Relations, 1960–62, Papers of the United States National Student Association, Box 30, The Martin Luther King Jr. Center for Non-Violent Social Change Library and Archives, Atlanta, Ga.

26. *News and Courier*, 3 December 1961; *Record*, 6 December 1961; Amy McCandless, *The Past in the Present: Women's Higher Education in the Twentieth Century American South* (Tuscaloosa: University of Alabama Press, 1999), 336.

27. "Faculty Votes Indicate Heavy Support of Issue," *The Paladin*, 15 December 1961.

28. "Fight Goes On; But Candidly, is Finished," *The Paladin*, 19 May 1962.

29. David Shi, *The Greenville News*, 10 February 2002.

30.   Stephen O'Neill, "Facing Facts: The 'Voluntary' Desegregation of Greenville, South Carolina," unpublished paper given at the Citadel Conference on the Civil Rights Movement in South Carolina, 5–8 March 2003.
31.   Alester Furman Jr. from Judge Clement Haynsworth, 14 May 1962. Papers of Frank Bonner, Judge Haynsworth's opinion on relationship of Furman to the South Carolina Baptist Convention file, FUA.
32.   The individual state southern Baptist Conventions were under the auspices of the Southern Baptist Convention. "Are Baptist Colleges Crying Wolf?" *The Furman University Magazine* (autumn 1963): 14; "Furman Trustees Adopt Policy on Applications," *Baptist Courier*, 17 October 1963, p. 5.
33.   Bynum Shaw, *The History of Wake Forest College, Vol. IV, 1943–1965*. Wake Forest University Archives, Z. Smith Reynolds Library, Wake Forest; Courtney Tollison, e-mail communication with Julia Bradford, Special Collections Assistant, Wake Forest University, 8 June 2001.
34.   Courtney Tollison, e-mail communication with Gail Grieb, Archivist, Stetson University, 19 June 2001.
35.   Alan Scott Willis, "A Baptist Dilemma: Christianity, Discrimination, and the Desegregation of Mercer University," *Georgia Historical Quarterly* LXXIX (fall 1996): 595–615.
36.   Courtney Tollison, e-mail communication with Arlette Copeland, Special Collections Assistant, Mercer University, 8 June 2001.
37.   "All Qualified Students May Apply at Furman University," *Greenville News*, 9 October 1963, Integration file, FUA.
38.   Ernie Harrill, interview by Courtney Tollison, 15 February 1999, Greenville.
39.   Desegregated-Segregated Status of Institutions of Higher Learning in the Southern United States, United States Commission on Civil Rights, 15 November 1963, Papers of Frank Bonner, FUA.
40.   "Wisdom Seen In Decision of Trustees," *The Furman University Magazine* (autumn 1963): 13. This was an editorial reprinted from the *Greenville News*.
41.   Ibid.; Maxie Myron Cox, "The Year of Decision: Integration in South Carolina Education in 1963" (Ph.D. diss., The University of South Carolina, 1996), 74; Harry Shucker, interview by Courtney Tollison, 13 April 2000.
42.   Dr. Horace Hammett from Alester G. Furman Jr., 5 November 1963, F file, papers of Horace Greeley Hammett, Baptist Historical Collection, Furman University Special Collections, James Buchanan Duke Library, Greenville. Hereafter cited as BHC.
43.   Minutes of the South Carolina Baptist Convention, 1963 Convention *Annual*, 12–14 November 1963, Charleston. BHC; "Furman Trustees Adopt Policy on Applications," *Baptist Courier*, 17 October 1963, 5.
44.   "Baptist Board Challenges Trustee Integration Policy," *The Paladin*, 26 October 1963; "Support Our Trustees," *The Paladin*, 26 October 1963, FUA.
45.   "Mystical Bride is Practical Divorcee," *The Paladin*, 16 November 1963, FUA.
46.   "Group Attacks School Gleefully," *The Paladin*, 16 November 1963, FUA.
47.   Nowhere have I found any indication that Plyler retired due to the university community's support for desegregation. Two years earlier, President Plyler entertained notions of retiring, but the trustees dissuaded him. Plyler served as president for twenty-five years and was in his 70s when he retired.
48.   Harrill, interview; Bonner, interview; Shucker, interview; Blackwell, interview; Lillian Brock Fleming, interview by Courtney Tollison, 16 February 1999; "Furman Enrolls First Negro Undergraduate," *Baptist Courier*, 11 February 1965, p. 18.

49. Bonner, interview; "Racial Integration at Furman Twenty-One Years Later," Greenville, 16 April 1986, FUA; Frank Bonner Comments to the Furman University Board of Trustees, courtesy of Jim Stewart, in author's possession.

50. Blackwell admits that he was somewhat of a "radical." Under Blackwell's leadership, the Greensboro Women's College and Florida State University desegregated. Blackwell, interview; "Dr. Blackwell: Man of Ideas," *The Furman University Magazine* (autumn 1964), FUA.

51. Blackwell, interview.

52. "Remarks to South Carolina Baptist Convention," given by Gordon W. Blackwell, President-elect of Furman University, 10 November 1964, *Baptist Courier*, 3 December 1964, 11; Blackwell, interview.

53. Bonner, interview; Blackwell, interview; Reid, *Furman University*.

54. Baptist Colleges and the Higher Education Facilities Act; Statement of the Executive Committee of the Board of Trustees of Furman University. Baptist Controversies, Furman University-Integration, Federal Aid, 1955 Echo incident (#3) file, FUA.

55. Statement issued by the (South Carolina Baptist Convention) Executive Committee of the General Board, Columbia, S.C., 4 May 1964, Integration file, FUA.

56. *Baptist Courier*, 19 November 1964, p. 2; "Furman Trustees Maintain Stand," *Southern School News*, January 1965; Chairman of Furman Trustees Explains Action," *Baptist Courier*, 28 January 1965, pp. 5–6.

57. Editorial, *The Paladin*, 20 November 1964, FUA.

58. Reid, *Furman University*, 198.

59. He emphasized the rightness of this act, both in principle and for the future advancement of the school. Bonner reminded the Board of its obligation to support incoming President Blackwell and of its commitment, as trustees, to vote, above all, in the best interests of Furman University. Unpublished remarks of Frank Bonner to the Furman University Board of Trustees, in author's possession.

60. "Furman Trustees Maintain Stand," *Southern School News* (January 1965).

61. Harrill, interview. Members of the Baptist Convention threatened to discontinue funding for the schools, but Furman dismissed these threats. The Convention contributed only 6 percent of Furman's annual budget at the time. This potential loss was insubstantial compared to the threat of lost funding from the federal government.

62. "Chairman of Furman Trustees Explains Action," *Baptist Courier*, 28 January 1965, pp. 5–6; "Reaffirmation of the Admissions Policy: A Letter to Alumni From J. Wilbert Wood, Chairman of the Board of Trustees," *The Furman University Magazine* XIV (winter 1965), 4:4–5.

63. Bonner had also approved the admission of three African-American graduate students to degree programs in education. They matriculated at the same time as Vaughn. Furman has always emphasized its role as and identified itself as an undergraduate institution, however, and the admission of the three graduate students is rarely mentioned and probably went somewhat unnoticed by the majority of the undergraduate students.

64. Bonner, interview.

65. Shucker, interview. Shucker remembered that "Vaughn probably had the ideal demeanor to be placed in this situation."

66. Gregg Laurence Michel, "'We'll Take Our Stand': The Southern Student Organizing Committee and the Radicalization of White Southern Students, 1964–1969" (Ph.D. diss., University of Virginia, 1999), 403, 407, 464, 478, 481, 489.

67. Bonner, interview; Fleming, interview.

68.   "Furman Was Ready; Baptist Were Not," *The State*, Columbia, 4 February 2000. The publicly expressed feelings of those students whose presence indicated token desegregated often differed from the reality of their experiences, especially among those who were hand-selected. Vaughn was under a great deal of pressure, not only as the first African American student at the university, but also because some friends believe he struggled with his sexual orientation. These pressures weighed on Vaughn; some friends intimated private and excessive alcohol use. Vaughn died in 1991.
69.   "Remarks to South Carolina Baptist Convention," given by Gordon W. Blackwell, 10 November 1964, FUA.
70.   *The State* (Columbia, S.C.), 7 April 1992, p. 6A.
71.   Ibid.; Mark Allan Taylor, "Religious Identity on a Slippery Slope: Furman University and Mercer University During the 1990's" (Ph.D. diss, Florida State University, 2000).
72.   www.furman.edu/personnel/vpaa.htm.
73.   I thank Professor Edwin Hendricks of Wake Forest University for his comments. Bynum Shaw, *The History of Wake Forest College* (Winston-Salem, N.C.: Wake Forest University, 1988).
74.   Baylor's Board of Trustees voted to amend the university's charter to allow for self-perpetuation, effectively abolishing the Texas Baptist Convention's authority to appoint trustees. Mark Allan Taylor, "Religious Identity on a Slippery Slope," 6.
75.   For discussion on what many view as an impending break between the Georgia Baptist Convention and Mercer University, see Mark Allan Taylor, "Religious Identity on a Slippery Slope." Harry C. Garwood, *Stetson University and the Florida Baptists: A Documentary History of Relations Between Stetson University and the Florida Baptist Convention* (Deland: Florida Baptist Historical Society, 1962); Gilbert L. Lycan, *Stetson University: The First 100 Years* (Deland, Florida: Stetson University Press, 1983); Reuben E. Alley, *History of the University of Richmond, 1820–1971* (Charlottesville: University Press of Virginia, 1977), 206–07, 240–59.
76.   "Engaged Learning at Furman University," www.engagefurman.com/engaged/index.html; *U.S. News and World Report*, 23 September 2002, p. 104.
77.   In 2002–2003, the university received a record number of applications from minorities for admittance into the Class of 2007; minorities comprise 11 percent of the Class of 2007. African American students comprise 6.25 percent of the university's student body for the 2003–2004 academic year. Courtney Tollison, e-mail communication with Idella Glenn, Director of the Office of Multicultural Affairs, Furman University, 15 May 2003; Inside Furman Online (May 2003), www.furman.edu/if/may03/class.htm.

"Quacks, Quirks, Agitators, and Communists": Private Black Colleges and the Limits of Institutional Autonomy

Joy Ann Williamson

Private black colleges and their students played a vital role in the Civil Rights Movement of the middle twentieth century. The colleges' corporate structure shielded the colleges and their students from direct state intervention, and students took advantage of the liberal campus climate. Private philanthropic support and control enabled a more active form of participation in the movement, but insecure economic situations, internal dissention, and other convenient liabilities left the colleges vulnerable. State agencies found creative ways to interfere in campus affairs and capitalize on institutional weaknesses. This piece examines the battle for institutional autonomy as it played out in the state of Mississippi. It offers a picture of the lengths to which racists would go to crush the Civil Rights Movement, an evaluation of the public role of private institutions, and a window into the role of higher educational institutions in society.

The end of the Civil War forced the nation to grapple with integrating freedmen and freedwomen into the social order. Benevolent societies and denominational bodies created what are now labeled private, historically black colleges and universities (HBCUs) throughout the South to train African American leaders to uplift the race. These private institutions depended on private donations, tuition, and philanthropic gifts to sustain them and remained outside the state's purview. The campuses were tiny islands that promoted racial equality but rarely challenged the existing Southern social order. Racist state officials paid little attention to the internal affairs of private HBCUs until the middle twentieth century when students joined the campaign for black liberation. Private HBCUs enjoyed political and economic autonomy not shared by their state-supported counterparts, and students took advantage of the liberal campus climate. The corporate structure of private HBCUs buffered them from

History of Higher Education Annual 23 (2004): 49-81.
©2004. ISBN: 0-7658-0839-0

the most intense forms of state interference and allowed them and their students to play an active role in the Civil Rights Movement. But, their private status did not shield them completely from state pressures, particularly when college aims collided with state interests. Private HBCUs battled with state legislatures, racist citizen's organizations, and other groups hostile toward the colleges' role in the black freedom struggle. The public role of the private colleges made them enemies of the state.

This piece examines the battle between the state of Mississippi and private HBCUs and its consequences for institutional autonomy during the civil rights era. Mississippi, more than any other state, aggressively attacked all sources of activism. Its agency of choice, the Mississippi Sovereignty Commission, vowed to preserve and defend racial segregation at any cost. It targeted three private HBCUs in particular: Campbell College, Tougaloo College, and Rust College. Other private HBCUs existed in the state, but the Commission considered these three institutions the greatest threat to Mississippi laws and customs. The Commission never succeeded in destabilizing any of the colleges by itself, but it created conditions under which private HBCUs weighed the benefits and costs of remaining involved in civil rights. Its success hinged on its ability to act as a parasite that capitalized on institutional vulnerabilities. The weakest institutions suffered dire consequences, and none of the colleges were immune to the Commission's agenda. The colleges fought back, and in some ways were successful, but the tug-o-war for ultimate control of campus affairs exacted a toll. The experience of the three colleges demonstrates the value of civil society in an oppressive state and the price private HBCUs paid for assuming an active role in the Civil Rights Movement.

The Mississippi Context

Mississippi, like other Southern states, created public HBCUs to insure social stability, to create a separate black professional class, and to keep African Americans from attending historically white institutions.[1] Public college curricula taught respect for the racial order and the proper limits of black aspirations. The all-white Board of Trustees of Institutions of Higher Learning, the state legislature, and campus administrators carefully controlled the institutions to thwart radical notions of black equality. Religious philanthropists created a separate set of private HBCUs. Rather than fit African Americans to the racial status quo, these institutions educated African Americans for full political and civic equality. Religious philanthropists argued that a classical curriculum, paired with religious training, equipped future leaders in the black community with the skills and knowledge necessary for full citizenship. The campuses maintained an uneasy agreement with the surrounding white community: they instilled racial pride, a sense of entitlement, and leadership skills but accepted the segregated Southern reality.[2]

The growth of the Civil Rights Movement dissolved the compromise between the private colleges and hostile whites. The state aggressively attacked individuals and institutions sympathetic to the movement. The high rate of HBCU student participation, particularly by those at private campuses, marked HBCUs as prime targets. The use of campus facilities for integrated events and civil disobedience planning sessions infuriated segregationists. The state completely controlled the public HBCUs and felt confident about its control of some private HBCUs. The state, however, encountered resistance at Campbell College, Tougaloo College, and Rust College. In 1960, the three colleges, combined, educated 1,300 students total. An even smaller number participated in active protest. The number of students meant less than the colleges' private status, role in the movement, and key geographic locations in the state. Mississippi racists increasingly monitored events at private campuses as civil rights activism escalated.

The state of Mississippi organized its anti-desegregation efforts after the Supreme Court's 1954 *Brown* v. *Board of Education* decision, which declared racial segregation unconstitutional. The state legislature passed a parade of bills that ranged from repealing the state's compulsory education laws to an interposition resolution. It also created the Mississippi Sovereignty Commission, a tax-supported implementation agency and "a permanent authority for the maintenance of racial segregation."[3] Incorporated on 29 March 1956, the Commission sought to "do and perform any and all acts and things deemed necessary and proper to protect the sovereignty of the state of Mississippi, and her sister states, from encroachment thereon by the Federal Government or any branch, department, or agency thereof."[4] The Commission hired informants, conducted investigations on suspected integrationists, and distributed segregationist propaganda to defend Mississippi's racial hierarchy. It also allocated funds to the White Citizens' Council, a private citizen's organization whose agenda paralleled that of the Sovereignty Commission.[5] The Commission and the Council became part of an extensive network of racist public officials who closed ranks to protect the racial hierarchy.

Meanwhile, students at HBCUs across the South joined the Civil Rights Movement and inaugurated a period of sustained mass activism beginning in 1960. Their brand of activism broke with the past and shifted civil rights agitation from the courts to the streets. Four students from North Carolina A&T, a public HBCU, staged a sit-in at the local Woolworth's to protest segregation and discrimination in eating establishments (1 February 1960). Other HBCU students in North Carolina followed their example, and HBCU students in other states soon conducted their own sit-ins. Shaw University, a private HBCU in North Carolina, hosted a conference to organize the sit-in movement in April. The Student Non-violent Coordinating Committee (SNCC) grew out of the conference and enabled students across the South to coordinate their activities. SNCC turned its attention to voter registration as proprietors desegregated their facilities. HBCU students and interested others traveled to the deep South and provided voter education classes, transportation to registration and voting locations, and psychological sustenance to disenfranchised African Americans.[6] Activists used local churches, homes, and HBCU campuses to organize their assault on racial domination.

Conditions in Mississippi stalled full-blown direct action in the state. White political and economic terror reigned, and conservative civil rights leaders worried that direct action would lead to violent retaliation and counseled activists to be patient.[7] Militant activists ignored the advice. Medgar Evers, Jackson resident and Mississippi Field Secretary for the National Association for the Advancement of Colored People (NAACP) since 1954, organized an Easter boycott of downtown Jackson stores to protest poor treatment and discrimination in 1960. Local students from Tougaloo College, Campbell College, Jackson State College (a public college), and black high schools canvassed door-to-door to solicit support, but only for a short while and with limited success.[8] The same April, NAACP members on the Gulf Coast organized a wade-in in Biloxi to protest regulations that prevented African Americans from patronizing beaches along the Gulf of Mexico. A white mob chased and assaulted the swimmers as police watched.[9] Intense white scrutiny and reprisals forced Mississippi activists to regroup. Almost an entire year passed before black Mississippians initiated another direct action attack on Mississippi's racial caste system.

In 1961, Jackson became the center of increasing civil rights activity after nine Tougaloo College students staged a sit-in at the whites-only public library in March. The sit-in inaugurated a period of sustained and massive civil disobedience across the state and Jackson in particular. Local NAACP branches and other interested individuals organized and executed a variety of attacks on segregation and discrimination in the city in the next few years. Between 1961 and 1964, activists in Jackson launched another longer lasting and more effective boycott of white stores, conducted sit-ins, pickets, mass marches, and letter writing campaigns, and initiated a school desegregation suit. Police arrested over six hundred people in 1961 and 1962 alone.[10] The assault on Jackson, the urban center and capital of the state, angered white Mississippians. The Citizens' Council, local police, and the Sovereignty Commission jailed, harassed, and killed activists to stem the tide of protest. They also targeted the organizations and institutions in which activists pooled their resources and devised plans of action. Campbell College and Tougaloo College, both of which were located in Jackson, fell under heavy scrutiny.

Mississippi's dismal record on civil rights brought increasing media attention and more civil rights workers in 1964. During the summer months, SNCC spearheaded the Mississippi Summer Project. SNCC hoped to force the state to change its racist policies or coerce federal intervention, highlight the rabid resistance to racial equality, and develop local leadership to sustain the movement.[11] The Project brought hundreds of mostly white volunteers to Mississippi to teach in Freedom Schools and to work in voter registration alongside local activists. After completing a week of training in Oxford, Ohio, in classroom pedagogy, Mississippi history, and nonviolent self-defense, volunteers made the long drive to Mississippi. Their journey often took them through Holly Springs. Some workers remained in Holly Springs and joined other SNCC workers and local activists in a major campaign against segregated facilities and voting rights violations. As one of the only sizable towns in northern Mississippi, Holly Springs and its independent institutions, including Rust College, became invaluable for movement purposes. They also became targets for state intervention.

The Institutional Consequences of Involvement
in the Civil Rights Movement

The Sovereignty Commission and the Board of Trustees of Institutions of Higher Learning policed public HBCU campuses and expected full compliance from their presidents. As an arm of the legislature, on which public HBCUs were economically dependent, college presidents followed the Commission's advice and fired any faculty labeled as an agitator. Tenure did not exist at state-supported HBCUs, nor did the state pretend to value institutional integrity. The Commission also forced the presidents to be agents in its fight against student participation in the movement. Students at Mississippi Vocational College staged a thirty-six-hour walk-out to demand a student government in 1957, the first boycott in an HBCU in Mississippi. The president stalled the issue for four years before allowing the students to form an association. He guaranteed the student government's compliance with college regulations against activism by requiring the presence of two faculty members and the Dean of Students at all meetings.[12] Also in 1957, the Board of Trustees fired the president of Alcorn A&M College after he sided with students boycotting classes to protest pro-segregation editorials written by an Alcorn professor. The Board demanded his immediate resignation, expelled the entire student body, and appointed a new president more amenable to its attitudes on proper student behavior.[13] In 1961, Jackson State College's president dissolved its Student Government Association after accusing it of instigating civil rights activities and "embarrassing" the school when Jackson State students rallied in support of the Tougaloo students arrested at the whites-only library.[14] He also provided the Sovereignty Commission with the names and home address of activist students.[15] Students at public institutions were not dormant, but the nature of state control and the severe consequences leveled by the administration negatively influenced participation in the movement.

Conditions at Mississippi's private HBCUs were different. The high rate of private HBCU student participation in the movement, paired with the fact that college presidents refused to expel or punish activist students for their involvement, infuriated Mississippi racists. Segregationists and their allies railed against what Lieutenant Governor Carroll Gartin called havens for "quacks, quirks, political agitators and possibly some communists."[16] The Sovereignty Commission enlisted the assistance of campus informants and sponsored court injunctions to prevent campus constituents from participating in direct action. The Citizens' Council initiated its own investigations and accused various campus officials of conspiring with communists to overthrow the United States government. Local police regularly visited the campuses and recorded license plate numbers in an effort to gather information and to harass campus constituents and off-campus activists. In extreme cases the legislature itself entertained creative sanctions against the colleges. The state's organized and interconnected network marshaled its forces to intimidate the colleges into compliance with state laws and social codes.

Private status buffered the institutions from direct state intervention since the legislature did not finance the colleges or appoint their boards of trustees. But, institutional vulnerabilities provided the entrée through which the state forced the private colleges to reevaluate their role in the Civil Rights Movement. Campbell, Tougaloo, and Rust were not wealthy institutions. Defending the campuses and their constituents from constant state harassment diverted funds away from college development projects. The state also exploited dissention on each campus. Individual campus constituents maintained different ideas on the path and pace of social reform. Conservatives accused activists of hijacking education for civil rights aims and transforming the colleges into centers for political activity. As white Tougaloo professor John Held stated, "I am in favor of the Negro having every right that he can obtain—but I do not believe it to be the purpose of Tougaloo College to sponsor agitation."[17] Campbell, Tougaloo, and Rust fought back, and private status prevented unilateral Commission success. But, the colleges differed in their ability to negotiate the internal and external pressures threatening to undermine their autonomy.

Of the three institutions, Campbell College was the most vulnerable to state intervention and suffered the most dire consequences. A variety of factors set Campbell College apart. First, it was supported by black religious philanthropy, namely the African Methodist Episcopal (AME) church. It was one of only two black-controlled higher educational institutions in the entire state of Mississippi.[18] The entire Campbell College constituency, from its Board of Trustees, faculty, administrators, staff, and students, was African American. Racial separation was not an anomaly in Mississippi, but black control of a higher educational institution was. Second, AME doctrine supported full racial equality and likened forced segregation with second-class citizenship. White religious philanthropists, including those who created Tougaloo College and Rust College, did not share the same overtly political theological principles though campus constituents often professed radical interpretations of Christian theology. Not all AME members translated church doctrine into direct confrontation with the Southern racial hierarchy, but some did, particularly when the Civil Rights Movement gained momentum.

Beyond its black philanthropic roots, the particular nature of funding also set Campbell apart and made it more vulnerable to Commission aims. The college was uniquely quite poor. The Eighth Episcopal District of the AME church, consisting of Louisiana and Mississippi, supported the institution. The AME church had a nationwide network, but different districts took on the financial responsibilities of particular schools. Campbell, a combined high school and junior college, received little national AME attention as the denomination concentrated its funds and energies on its four-year institutions. Campbell had only a small pool of money on which to rely for support. Lastly, the level of internal dissention on campus regarding the role of Campbell College in the Civil Rights Movement was extreme. Each campus had its own conservatives calling for a return to pure academic education, but disagreements within the Campbell Board of Trustees and between the trustees and the campus administration threatened to disintegrate the institution. The Sovereignty Commission exacerbated the college's problems and pushed Campbell toward ruin.

Tougaloo, on the other hand, was in stronger position to resist Sovereignty Commission efforts. The nature of philanthropic support buffered it. The American Missionary Association (AMA), a group of white religious philanthropists, supported Tougaloo. More importantly, AMA colleges received funding from a nationwide network, not individual districts. AMA headquarters were located in New York, another factor that marked them as different from Campbell and provided an important sense of autonomy since philanthropic agencies with headquarters and donors outside the South were more immune to state pressure. Tougaloo's financial scaffold provided it with more security, but it was far from wealthy. Tougaloo received less money from the AMA than some of the association's other colleges, but it still received more financial assistance than other private colleges in Mississippi. The AMA cared enough about

Tougaloo to work toward costly accreditation requirements before any other philanthropic group did the same for its colleges. In 1948, Tougaloo became the only accredited HBCU in Mississippi, a distinction it kept until the 1960s.[19]

Tougaloo and Campbell were located a mere six miles from each other near the seat of government in Jackson, and students often coordinated civil rights activities and visited each other's campus. What marked Tougaloo as different was the level of campus participation in the Civil Rights Movement. Tougaloo students, faculty, and staff spearheaded some of the most public and most disruptive assaults on Mississippi's racial hierarchy. Tougaloo also had more extensive campus facilities than Campbell College, which made Tougaloo more attractive for off-campus activists seeking a meeting place in Jackson. On-campus events and off-campus demonstrations garnered the college and the movement increasing publicity in national and local media outlets. These factors combined made Tougaloo the Sovereignty Commission's biggest college target. Commission director Erle Johnston Jr., associated his own career advancement with his ability to quash the activism emanating from Tougaloo.[20] Tougaloo was stronger than Campbell, but it was also a bigger threat to Mississippi laws and customs—a fact illustrated by the common racist nickname for the institution, Cancer College. Accordingly, the Sovereignty Commission more aggressively harassed the institution and focused its energies on finding an entrée to exploit. A fortuitous fundraising campaign and a unique charter controversy provided the Commission with the fodder it needed to undermine Tougaloo's role in the movement and make civil rights activism a campus liability.

Rust College was the least influenced by external pressure and was able to protect itself from punitive measures for a variety of reasons. Like Tougaloo, it was funded by white religious philanthropy (Methodist Episcopal Church), maintained a Board of Trustees headquarters outside Mississippi, and was supported by a nationwide financial network. The fact that Rust did not have any peculiar vulnerabilities, like Tougaloo, or extreme financial trouble, like Campbell, frustrated the Sovereignty Commission's agenda. Also, the Commission reserved much of its energy for events in Jackson and at Tougaloo in particular. Sit-ins, demonstrations, and boycotts in the capital embarrassed the state and drew much of the Commission's attention. The Commission monitored the Rust campus, particularly when activist students became more aggressive, but Rust's isolated geographic location made it a secondary target. Even the Mississippi media ignored much of the movement in northern Mississippi as Rust students and their civil rights projects received little noteworthy press.[21] Lastly, the Sovereignty Commission learned from its mistakes in Jackson. Local and national newspapers repeatedly carried pictures of Jackson activists (including some from Tougaloo and Campbell) being attacked by hostile whites and chased by police dogs. The Commission resented the bad publicity, particularly since one of its missions was to soften Mississippi's image and convince the American populace that Mississippi blacks were content with the existing social structure. Commission representatives put their hard lessons to use in Holly Springs and at Rust, but the campus withstood the pressure.

Campbell College[22]

> We think it wise to keep this record of [Negro AME ministers] in case they crop up in future meetings or incidents.[23]

AME ideology on racial equality influenced the campus ethos, but Campbell College and its constituents did not directly confront the existing racial order until the growth of the Civil Rights Movement in the mid-twentieth century. The Sovereignty Commission matched Campbell's increasingly public role in social reform with increasing scrutiny. Investigators monitored church events and, in December 1957, reported that a Bishop admonished members attending a regional conference: "I warn you here and now, in the presence of God and this audience, that if any one of you permit any person, white or black, to advocate segregation in any form, your appointment will be immediately revoked. Further, you will be brought to trial for violation of the honor and traditions of this great denomination."[24] AME publications in the early 1960s articulated an overtly political agenda for AME schools: "The basic concern of the A.M.E. Church in education is training Christian leaders for the struggle of the Negro to secure by his own efforts full rights, privileges and benefits of citizenship and respect for the worth and dignity of human personality without regard to race, creed or nationality—for realization of Christian and democratic ideals of liberty and justice."[25] This aggressive stance put the AME church and its schools in direct conflict with Mississippi's racial hierarchy.

Campbell College, with an enrollment of three hundred in the early 1960s, hosted a few of the civil rights events centered on the economic boycott of white Jackson stores. Chaplain and Dean of Religion, Charles Jones, became heavily involved and invited the NAACP to use the campus for organizing sessions and press conferences by Medgar Evers.[26] The enrollment of almost one hundred black high school students expelled from Burglund High School in McComb, Mississippi, in October 1961, drew the campus deeper into the movement and, in turn, increased Campbell College's visibility in the state. The previous summer, several Burgland students participated in a voter registration drive and sit-ins, and some had been arrested. Fifteen year-old Brenda Travis was sentenced to one year at the Oakley Training School, a school for juvenile delinquents. At a Burgland assembly the following fall, students quizzed the principal about Travis's return. He hedged his answer, and the students initiated an impromptu march through downtown McComb. Police arrested them as they prayed on the steps of City Hall.[27] The principal refused to allow the one hundred sixteen arrested students to re-enroll unless they signed a pledge promising to refrain from participating in any further demonstrations. Many students refused, and Campbell College president Robert Stevens extended offers of enrollment.[28]

The Sovereignty Commission watched in horror as Campbell College constituents joined demonstrations against the state and used the college facilities to plan direct action tactics. President Stevens did not join any demonstrations or participate in the planning of civil disobedience, but he allowed these activities to occur on campus and refused to curtail the involvement of both students and staff. The state of Mississippi considered his offer to enroll expelled Burgland High School students a slap in the face. The Commission, however, reserved some of its harshest criticism for Charles Jones and treated him as a primary cause for concern. Jones made headlines with an attempt (by himself) to integrate the Jackson Trailways Bus Terminal the same day the Interstate Commerce Commission ordered segregated signage to be removed and with his participation in an interracial pray-in at the Jackson Federal Post Office to protest police brutality.[29] Jackson police arrested him and a court convicted him of breach of the peace after both demonstrations. His active involvement in the movement and the support of President Stevens earned both men the dubious distinction of being added to the Sovereignty Commission's "trouble-makers list."[30] As Campbell's role in the movement increased so, too, did Commission efforts to destabilize the institution. In 1960, the Commission sent a list of Campbell's Board of Trustees to local Jackson police to solicit ideas for how to deal with them, and at least one Trustee joined the Commission payroll.[31] But, Campbell's private status insulated it from direct state intervention.

Campbell College officials gave the Commission the opening it could exploit. Conservative AME and Board of Trustees members held gradualist attitudes toward the pace of societal reform and admonished students and staff that a college should focus on academics and not political education. Fearing the campus had spun out of control, four members of the Board of Trustees requested an injunction preventing President Robert Stevens, Dean Charles Jones, and other Campbell College administrators from performing their campus duties in February 1962.[32] The state did not act as a plaintiff, but the ends sought by the plaintiffs certainly buoyed the Commission's cause. The plaintiffs linked their disgust for campus-based civil rights agitation with accusations that Campbell College officials abused its charter, the laws of the state of Mississippi, and financial donations. The Sovereignty Commission kept a record of the court proceedings and watched the situation carefully.[33]

The plaintiffs in the injunction focused part of their argument on Charles Jones. They charged that Jones's election as Dean of Religion was "for the express purpose of preaching to, and disseminating among the students of the college, the radical and unorthodox views held by him, and in order to create dissention among students of the college and to agitate and incite them into a violation of the laws of the State of Mississippi." Jones's aggressive attacks on white supremacy colored the campus atmosphere. He and other activists transformed Campbell from a respected private institution into a hotbed for political activism. The plaintiffs argued: "he invited and encouraged the so-called 'freedom riders' to congregate on the campus of the College, and he undertook to persuade the students of the college to join in the movement, and to violate the laws of the State of Mississippi; and he himself did, in fact, join in said movement and for his willful violation of the laws of the State of Mississippi, he was arrested by the Police of the City of Jackson, and was tried and convicted, and is now out on bond."[34] His actions, according to the plaintiffs, jeopardized the institution.

Campbell's admission of the ousted Burgland High School students aggravated the situation. Plaintiffs complained that the enrollment of the students flouted the laws of Mississippi and unnecessarily politicized the campus. Campbell had been involved in the movement prior to their arrival, but few people outside of Jackson had paid any attention to the college. Their enrollment brought the campus unwanted and negative attention in the white press, a fact that made the plaintiffs very wary. Plaintiffs also attacked the students' right to attend. Their suit argued that the students took the spots of deserving and qualified children of AME church members. President Stevens admitted the high school students "without any regard whatsoever to their educational and scholastic qualifications or good character, and without requiring them to pay the usual enrollment and tuition fees."[35] Complaintants considered these actions a violation of the charter agreement and evidence of bad judgment.

The injunction also illuminated a split in the Board of Trustees. The plaintiffs accused Chairman Frederick Jordan and Dean Jones of mismanaging large sums of money. They complained that the men diverted donations, church assessments, and rent from College-owned property in Mound Bayou for personal gain. Jordan, the suit declared, practiced duplicitous behavior on a regular basis. The plaintiffs offered the example of the purchase and sale of property located near the campus. According to the suit, R. A. Scott, one of the plaintiffs and former president of the College, owned land adjoining the campus. Jordan persuaded individual AME church members that Campbell College should purchase the land for educational purposes and raised the necessary funds. The College bought the land, but Jordan immediately sold it to the state for $2,500. The plaintiffs accused Jordan of keeping the funds for himself rather than depositing the money in the College's accounts. Their final insult came when Jordan, Jones, and President Stevens conspired to solicit funds under the guise of the McComb high school student episode. The accused not only wrongly enrolled the students, they did so "as a publicity 'gimmick' to raise money for their personal gain."[36]

Three weeks after the plaintiffs filed their plea the Chancery Court ordered that the Board of Trustees be reconstituted and demanded that the Council of Bishops remove Jordan as presiding Bishop of the Eighth Episcopal District. But, the Court allowed Charles Jones to continue as Chaplain and Dean of Religion until the trustees election, and it did not object to President Stevens's reinstatement by the new Board if it so desired.[37] Four months later, AME members re-elected fifty percent of the former Board of Trustees and reinstated President Stevens and Dean Jones.[38] The AME effectively reasserted its authority over Campbell and demonstrated the broader AME church's support for the administration. It is unknown if the Court or the Sovereignty Commission expected the trustees to reinstate President Stevens and Dean Jones. It is possible that Commission officials miscalculated the broad base of support for the administrators, and by extension, the Civil Rights Movement. Campbell College regained an important sense of autonomy in its tug-o-war with the Sovereignty Commission.

Campbell College looked very much the same before and after the litigation. The staff remained largely intact, and the Burgland high school students left the college at the end of the academic year. The Campbell College student body remained active in the movement after 1962, and the campus continued to host civil rights events. The difference was that the Eighth Episcopal District of the AME church and Campbell College grew poorer in the process. The court injunction cost the church money, particularly since it pitted campus officials against each other. Campbell College never maintained a large endowment and had been under-funded for years. Neither the Court nor the plaintiffs offered incontrovertible evidence that Trustee Jordan, President Stevens, or Dean Jones mismanaged money, but the validity of the claim was irrelevant as far as the Court was concerned. The financial claims provided a perfect opportunity to exploit institutional weakness. The state stepped in, and this time it sealed the college's fate.

In 1964, the state of Mississippi seized the Campbell College property by right of eminent domain. The campus had deteriorated and gone into debt, and the legislature wrestled control from the Board of Trustees. Legislators never called it an act of retribution, but Campbell's place in the Jackson movement clearly influenced the decision. Campbell College administrators planned to move the campus to Mound Bayou, 174 miles northwest of Jackson, but needed time to do so. They applied to the Board of Trustees of Institutions of Higher Learning, which chartered the creation of any new private or public college, for two separate extensions before vacating the premises. The new presiding Bishop even used the removal of President Stevens as a bargaining chip: more time to build a college in Mound Bayou for Stevens's forced retirement. The Board refused to be swayed, particularly since "the take-over of the property auto-matically will remove Dr. Stevens."[39] The state clearly never sup-ported a rebuilding campaign and did all in its power to prevent it from succeeding. The state purchased the Campbell College prop-erty and deeded it to Jackson State College for its expansion pro-gram under the leadership of Jacob Reddix, Jackson State president and friend of the Sovereignty Commission.[40] A new campus was never constructed due to lack of funds.

The demise of Campbell College provides an extreme example of private HBCU vulnerability to state attempts to quash the Civil Rights Movement. Campbell's role in the movement made it a target for the state, and its financial situation provided an opportunity the state refused to ignore. The nature of its philanthropic support made the campus susceptible to external pressure. Colleges supported by black philanthropy were notoriously under-funded. Tuition, church assess-ments, and donations rarely yielded enough for basic operating costs. Their racial make-up made funding agencies wary, and Northern foundations preferred institutions with, if not a white president, a predominantly white board of trustees.[41] The intense internal dis-sention also facilitated the Commission's efforts. Campbell trustees unwittingly primed the institution for the state's successful interven-tion. Mississippi racists not only halted the college's role in the move-ment, they killed Campbell College.

Tougaloo College

Tougaloo College is finally surrendering to intimidation.[42]

Though enrollment was only five hundred in 1960, Tougaloo College had a national reputation and attracted students from across the country. It maintained high academic standards, had a well-re-spected faculty, and was headed by a strong and independent Board of Trustees located in New York. The state paid little attention to the campus until the 1940s and 1950s when a few campus constituents initiated individual attacks against the racial hierarchy. In 1946, Wil-liam Albert Bender, Tougaloo's African American chaplain, attempted to vote in the Democratic primary but was denied. He later filed a complaint with the state attorney general. Hostile whites burned a cross on the Tougaloo campus in retaliation.[43] In 1958, Tougaloo professor Ernst Borinski, a German Jew, invited Tougaloo students to join his German classes at Millsaps College, a private white institution in Jackson. Borinski taught courses at Millsaps during the summer months, and a Tougaloo student enrolled in his class two weeks after it began. The White Citizens' Council blasted Millsaps in the press, and campus officials moved the class to Tougaloo since Millsaps maintained strict policies on racial segregation.[44] The state monitored these men and other campus constituents who actively challenged the social order but did not consider them much of a threat until the Civil Rights Movement gained momentum and transformed isolated acts of resistance into full-blown civil disobedience. The state and its allies easily contained individual activism but worried about an organized assault on Mississippi laws and customs.

By the early 1960s, the Sovereignty Commission identified Tougaloo as one of its primary targets. The degree of activism on campus was unmatched at colleges across the state. Tougaloo students in the campus NAACP chapter inaugurated the sustained Civil Rights Movement in Mississippi with the sit-in at the Jackson Municipal Library in March 1961, and continued to play a vital role in a variety of other very public attacks on Mississippi's racial hierarchy. Off-campus activists from across the nation identified Tougaloo as a hospitable environment and frequently used campus facilities to plan direct action activities. Key Tougaloo faculty and administrators joined with students to support the Civil Rights Movement in Jackson. Chaplain Ed King and Professor John Salter, two of the most active white staff members on campus, received national media attention for their involvement in certain civil rights projects.[45] President Adam D. Beittel, a white man, supported civil rights efforts, defended the students' right to protest, and was photographed with students, Ed King, and John Salter at a sit-in at the local Woolworth's.[46] By 1964, four white students enrolled at Tougaloo making it the only voluntarily desegregated institution in the entire state. It seemed, at least to the State of Mississippi, the entire Tougaloo campus was involved in the Civil Rights Movement.

The Sovereignty Commission escalated its attacks on the campus as years passed and employed some of the same tactics it used to destabilize Campbell College. In June 1963, the Sovereignty Commission sponsored a court order naming President Beittel, Chaplain King, Professor Salter, student Bette Anne Poole (an African American) along with other individuals, the NAACP, Congress of Racial Equality, Tougaloo trustees, and "their agents, members, employees, attorneys, successors, and all other persons in active concert with them" in a writ of temporary injunction preventing them from demonstrating in any way, shape, or form.[47] The point of the injunction, ending civil rights activism, paralleled the mission of the injunction at Campbell, but it was different in important respects. First, the impetus for the Tougaloo injunction came from an external source, not campus officials. The Campbell injunction revealed a serious ideological split and created an opportunity the Sovereignty Commission happily manipulated. The Commission attempted to create a similar exploitative situation at Tougaloo but failed. Second, the injunction against Tougaloo requested a halt to demonstrations not the termination of employment for individual staff members. The Campbell injunction pitted campus officials against each other and split the campus while the Tougaloo injunction, by the sheer number and variety of campus constituents named in the court order, unified the campus by pitting it against the state. The plaintiffs in neither injunction succeeded in ending campus activism, but they did weaken the institutions by draining scant resources away from other campus projects. At Campbell, the plaintiffs unintentionally weakened the institution beyond financial recovery. The Commission attempted to create dire financial consequences at Tougaloo, but Tougaloo's national financial network was less rocked by the immediate fiscal requirements of defending itself against a court injunction.

Tougaloo withstood the first phase of the tug-o-war, but the state was not easily dissuaded from its task. The Sovereignty Commission tried another tactic and attempted to capitalize on the fact that some Tougaloo constituents resented the college's involvement in the Civil Rights Movement. Dr. John Held, chairman of Tougaloo's Department of Philosophy and Religion, volunteered to become an informant in early April 1964. Held accused Beittel and others of appropriating the college for civil right aims and transforming Tougaloo into a center for political activity. He also had designs on the presidency. While on an invited visit to the Commission's office, Held informed Director Johnston about "the dissension among faculty and students" regarding the policies of President Beittel and Chaplain King, threatened to resign if Beittel was not removed, and offered to identify documents linking Beittel to a communist organization. Johnston, grateful for the assistance, requested a list of students and faculty opposed to and in support of Beittel and King as well as the names of trustees who might be open to Commission concerns. Held and Johnston "worked out a code system for communication and relaying information which would not involve Dr. Held with those at Tougaloo who would be opposed to his contact with the Sovereignty Commission."[48] Days later, "Mr. Zero" [Held?] submitted a list of trustees considered "most vital and influential" (all of whom were white) and those "probably more easily influenced by pressure" (all of whom were African American). The communication also included a list of notable students and a Tougaloo College catalog in which Mr. Zero categorized the faculty.[49]

Meanwhile, Tougaloo's Board of Trustees attempted to broaden the campus financial base. The campus's annual expenses jumped when Tougaloo experienced a rapid increase in student attendance that forced the college to institute a major new facilities campaign in the late 1950s.[50] President Beittel worked hard to solicit funds from individual donors and philanthropic agencies and was in large part successful, but increasing college costs made the task a daunting one. Also, certain financial sources turned away from Tougaloo. The Mississippi branch of the Christian Churches (Disciples of Christ) withdrew its financial support after Tougaloo activists targeted its segregated churches for pray-ins in 1963.[51] Trustees looked to the Ford Foundation's Fund for the Advancement of Education for financial assistance. The Fund supported partnerships between HBCUs and predominantly white northern colleges. Tougaloo and Brown University already shared a friendly relationship, and both institutions entertained a more formal association. In fall 1963, Tougaloo and Brown began the application process for Ford funds.

Tougaloo trustees hinged their financial hopes on the Ford grant and attempted to clear a path for a speedy decision. Tougaloo's public role in the movement became a point of concern. Brown University President Barbaby Keeney warned the Tougaloo trustees that the Ford Foundation was wary of donating the money for the partnership because of the siege situation created by constant state harassment. Brown University shared the same set of concerns. Keeney then targeted Tougaloo's President Beittel, a vocal supporter of the Civil Rights Movement, and urged that the Tougaloo trustees fire him. Keeney believed that Beittel's refusal to curb campus activism was irresponsible and that Beittel's actions unnecessarily politicized the campus and brought it unwanted scrutiny. He warned the trustees that Beittel's firing was imperative to secure Ford funding: "They will not do much, if anything, until they have this assurance."[52] Certain Tougaloo trustees agreed with Keeney's assessment and set about undermining Beittel's presidency. A self-selected group of trustees, the same trustees Mr. Zero identified as most vital and influential, arranged a special meeting with Beittel at Board headquarters in New York in January 1964. They explained to Beittel that the partnership program funded by the Ford Foundation needed consistent leadership for at least ten years, an impossibility for him because he was sixty-five. They then requested his resignation.[53] Their next task was to convince the other trustees, a racially mixed group, that their actions were appropriate and necessary. A few of the trustees expressed anger at the sub-committees' unilateral decision, but they presented a united front in public.[54] Rather than announce the decision immediately, the trustees decided to wait for the official Board meeting in April.

Beittel fought the decision. The Board hired him in 1960, and was fully aware of his liberal leanings since Beittel had been equally involved in civil rights issues while president at Talladega College, a private HBCU in Alabama and Tougaloo's sister-institution under the American Missionary Association.[55] One of his conditions for employment at Tougaloo had been that the Board assure him of job security until age seventy, provided he remained healthy, with the option to continue on a yearly basis after age sixty-five.[56] Beittel found the Board's violation of his contract highly suspicious and accused the trustees of using him as a bargaining tool: "It was indicated that Brown University would not continue our promising cooperative relationship unless I am replaced, and that without Brown University the Ford Foundation will provide no support, and without Ford support other Foundations will not respond, and without foundation support the future of Tougaloo College is very uncertain."[57] The Board resented the implication that an external source prompted their actions, discounted Beittel's claims in a variety of forums, and refused to alter their decision to fire President Beittel.[58]

Meanwhile, the legislature itself employed measures to punish Tougaloo for its role in the Civil Rights Movement. Legislators used materials gathered by the Sovereignty Commission to devise two bills meant to cripple the institution and never pretended otherwise. On 17 February 1964, Lieutenant Governor Carroll Gartin called for an investigation of the College's role in demonstrations and civil rights activities.[59] Other state leaders joined his cause, and three days later, three senators introduced a bill to revoke Tougaloo's ninety-four-year-old charter in the name of "public interest."[60] The argument was twofold. First, Tougaloo's original charter restricted the campus to five hundred thousand dollars worth of assets, a figure Tougaloo passed years earlier with no repercussions. Second, and more to the heart of the matter, Gartin and others accused the College of neglecting its charter all together: "The big question to be decided is whether the school has substituted civil disobedience instruction for the curriculum it was authorized to have under its charter."[61] The legislature also contemplated a bill that allowed discretionary powers to the Commission on College Accreditation.[62] Passage of the bill revoked Tougaloo's reciprocal accreditation from the Southern Association of Colleges and Schools, and the state. The loss of state accreditation prevented education students from receiving state teacher's licenses. The state hoped the loss of accreditation would tarnish Tougaloo's reputation, limit attendance, and force those teachers who received their degrees from Cancer College to leave Mississippi.

Tougaloo mounted an aggressive publicity campaign to call attention to the situation and embarrass Governor Paul Johnson into either vetoing or limiting the influence of each legislative bill. President Beittel, at the same time he was fighting for his own job, aggressively protected Tougaloo from the state's onslaught. He enlisted the assistance of the American Association of University Professors, the United Church of Christ, Tougaloo's sister institutions, the Southern Association of Colleges and Schools, and other institutions and organizations with a vested interest in protecting higher educational autonomy. Tougaloo's allies wrote the legislature and the governor expressing their horror at such a public and offensive disrespect for institutional integrity.[63] Tougaloo's efforts were successful. The bill to revoke Tougaloo's charter died in the Judiciary Committee. The bill separating accreditation passed but held no teeth. The legislature was increasingly disturbed by the bad press created by the situation and did not use the Act against Tougaloo.

The Sovereignty Commission took matters into its own hands in April 1964, months prior to the resolution of the legislative bills. Harassing Tougaloo became a top priority for Director Erle Johnston Jr. With the list of powerful and influential trustees provided by Mr. Zero, Johnston requested a private meeting with a group of Tougaloo trustees to plead his case:

At the meeting it was our purpose to show that the image of Tougaloo as represented by the President, Dr. A. D. Beittel and [Reverend Ed King], had inspired such resentment on the part of state officials and legislators that a show-down clash appeared imminent. We suggested that if Tougaloo had a good man as president and a good man as [chaplain], the institution could be restored to its former status as a respected private college. We also suggested that if such a move could be made by the trustees, the college would have ample time to prove good faith and a change of attitude and possibly avoid punitive action from the Legislature.[64]

Johnston and Shelby Rogers, a Jackson attorney and Commission confidant, flew to the Board of Trustees headquarters in New York. They met with a subcommittee of trustees—the same trustees who, unbeknown to the Commission, had already requested and spearheaded Beittel's forced resignation in January.[65]

The Board of Trustees announced Beittel's retirement at their annual meeting only days after the subcommittee's appointment with the Sovereignty Commission. The timing could not have been worse. The subgroup of powerful trustees delayed the announcement of Beittel's resignation until the April Board meeting to avoid having his resignation associated with Brown University or the Ford Foundation. Meanwhile, the Sovereignty Commission visit became public knowledge and turned into a public relations fiasco. Trustees adamantly denied that Beittel's active support for civil rights contributed to the decision to request his resignation, but the local press and angry campus constituents coupled Beittel's termination with Sovereignty Commission aims. The Commission itself promoted this interpretation: "Our pipeline of information from Tougaloo says the trustees gave as their reason for dismissal of Dr. Beittel that he was 'inefficient.' This will certainly work to our advantage. Had Dr. Beittel been asked to resign because of racial agitation or collaboration with communist front organizations, he could have made a martyr out of himself."[66] The self-congratulation was misplaced. The Commission's visit with the Tougaloo trustees did not prompt the Board's decision, which had been made months earlier, but Tougaloo's involvement in the Civil Rights Movement did. The legislative bills, court injunctions, and constant harassment became costly. The trustees spent time and money needed to improve the college on defending it instead. Tougaloo's role in the Civil Rights Movement became a liability. Trustees made a decision they believed would protect the college and insure its financial future.

The Campbell College situation looked like a cakewalk compared to the battle between the state and Tougaloo. Many of the factors that saved Tougaloo from Campbell's fate became like a double-edged sword. Tougaloo's prestige and private status made it the most important black college in the entire state but also made it the Commission's number one target. Tougaloo's ability to garner national support and media attention prevented the legislature from closing the campus, but the state merely turned to other tactics to rein in the campus. Internal dissention did not reach a level in which the campus disintegrated from the inside out, but it did provide fodder for Commission aims in the guise of informants and conservative trustees. Tougaloo's relative financial security, made possible by a national network and a unique funding opportunity, prevented an immediate fiscal catastrophe. At the same time, the funding opportunity and desire for increased donations made Tougaloo vulnerable and the college's role in the movement a liability. The Commission did not precipitate Beittel's retirement or have an immediate effect on daily campus life and activism, but the immense amount of energy, time, and money spent on destabilizing Tougaloo was not in vain. The Commission and its allies made it costly for Tougaloo to remain in the movement and forced the trustees to take a particular course of action, one they may not have considered without constant harassment by the state of Mississippi.

Rust College[67]

> Holly Springs, in my thinking, is one of the most explosive spots in Mississippi for racial trouble due to the fact that Rust College is located there.[68]

Rust College's geographical location in northern Mississippi made campus facilities particularly important for the movement in that part of the state. In 1962, the campus played a tangential role in James Meredith's enrollment at the University of Mississippi, marking the end of legal segregation in higher education institutions in the state. The Mississippi press reported that Meredith and his legal team drove from Oxford, Mississippi, to Memphis, Tennessee, during his repeated attempts to enroll at the University of Mississippi, but Meredith sometimes spent the night at Rust College instead.[69] Holly Springs was closer to Oxford, and the Rust College campus offered a friendly and secret space to recuperate from the white racist reaction to his enrollment. Two years later, SNCC's Summer Project made the campus invaluable. Student volunteers often traveled through Holly

Springs and spent time at Rust before heading to their respective assignments throughout the state. The campus also became a clearinghouse for Freedom School materials. Books poured in from Northern states and found their way to Rust where students and staff sorted them for distribution.[70]

Rust students also used the campus to launch their own attack on Mississippi's racial caste system. Leslie Burl McLemore, a student at Rust from 1960 to 1964, chose the institution because of its private status, "I wanted to go to a place where I knew I wouldn't have any difficulty with my political activity." He used the shield of the campus to help organize and become the first president of the campus chapter of the NAACP in 1962. He and other students participated in SNCC, the Mississippi Freedom Democratic Party, and various direct action initiatives in Marshall County and other surrounding counties. The Student Government Association, of which McLemore became president, fed the civil rights cause.[71] Students also created a Speaker's Bureau that dispatched its members to local black churches to discuss voting rights issues. Frank Smith, a SNCC organizer sent to Holly Springs to help with voter registration, joined their effort and was impressed by what students had accomplished. According to Smith: "the image of students knocking on doors, the fact of their speaking at churches on Sundays, and the threat of demonstration have served to build respect for them and has challenged the local ministers to no end. They see this and are beginning to work to try to build their images and redeem themselves."[72]

Activist students also spearheaded boycotts against local merchants. In May 1961, Leon Roundtree, a theater owner, received a letter signed by the Rust College student body declaring their intent to boycott the theater if he continued to practice segregation and discrimination against black patrons. Worried about the loss of revenue and the possibility that the boycott would spread to students at Mississippi Industrial College, a private HBCU located across the street from Rust and run by the Colored Methodist Church, Roundtree arranged a meeting with the Student Government Association. He offered to build a colored theater of equal quality, but students rejected his compromise. They demanded, "Permit us to sit where we please, by whom we please, and use the same facilities that everyone else uses."[73] Roundtree refused, and Rust students inaugurated the boycott. The theater keenly felt the economic ramifications, and the boycott spread to other white merchants. In December 1962,

Rust College students boycotted local drugstores. Rather than encouraging patrons to avoid the stores, the boycott called for sit-ins. Students visited each drugstore and made polite inquiries about the possibility of desegregating lunch counters. None of the druggists agreed to desegregate, and one threatened to remove tables and chairs if students attempted to use them. The students held meetings on Rust's campus to discuss the issue and invited each druggist to attend. None accepted the invitation.[74]

As students devised a plan of action so, too, did the Sovereignty Commission. Informed of the events by the druggists, the Commission swung into action. The Commission counseled the Holly Springs police to return the students to campus rather than transport them to jail. The Commission learned valuable lessons from the Jackson police who found pictures of themselves in local and national media brutalizing students with billy clubs and attack dogs. Television cameras hoping to catch Holly Springs police officers abusing students and carrying them to jail would instead find little newsworthy behavior. The Commission advised the police to warn Rust College President Earnest Smith about continued activism and remind him "that good relationships between Holly Springs and the negro colleges had always been maintained in the past."[75] This type of reaction, the Commission believed, would be a "tremendous set-back" and "psychological defeat for Rust College as well as Rust College students."[76] The students, however, were not deterred.

Several Rust College faculty and staff supported the activist students. Most faculty refused to use grades and attendance as a way to deter activism. Leslie Burl McLemore remembered, "No one penalized me because I was not in class, but they made it very clear that they expected me to do my work."[77] Some key faculty members actively supported the movement by loaning vehicles to activist students transporting registrants to the County Courthouse and joining the Regional Council of Negro Leadership, a Mississippi organization that sponsored voter registration drives and economic boycotts and was considered radical by the white establishment.[78] President Smith never participated in any civil rights demonstrations, but he refused to punish campus constituents for their involvement in the movement. When students treated the National Guard convoy escorting James Meredith from Memphis to the University of Mississippi like a celebratory parade, Smith was pressured to rein in the students, particularly after such a public display of disrespect for

Mississippi laws and customs. He refused. He also assisted activist students by calling special faculty meetings to solicit money for bail and demonstrated by example through his membership in the NAACP.[79] Smith's actions angered racist whites, including the mayor of Holly Springs, who asked why President Smith refused to punish activist students the way that President Ed Rankin of Mississippi Industrial College did: "President Rankin made it crystal clear to all students attending M.I. that the institution was a place of learning in which those who would take advantage of it could better qualify themselves for any vocation in life; whereas, Rust College appears to defend those who violated the law."[80] Presidential and faculty support for the movement and student participation in it marked the college as a threat to the state.

Rust College and Holly Springs received less attention than institutions and events in Jackson, but the Sovereignty Commission kept close watch on campus affairs, particularly since "It was the general consensus of everyone that evidently not just one racial agitator was busy agitating out at Rust College, but there were quite a few agitators out there."[81] The Commission began identifying allies as early as the late 1950s, and considered two African American Board of Trustees members potential informants since both publicly opposed the NAACP.[82] Rust's Board of Trustees also included a white Holly Springs bank president, Glen Fant, who maintained close contact with the Commission. In 1961, Fant offered information to the Commission, persuaded fellow trustees to take particular actions, and promised his resignation before he would become a party to "spawning an integration crew at Rust College."[83] Rust students continued to agitate, and Fant resigned his trusteeship when his term expired in 1963.[84] The Commission made little headway in destabilizing the college in part because it focused most of its time and energy on events in Jackson. But, SNCC's 1964 Freedom Summer Project and Rust's geographic importance to it brought the campus under increasing scrutiny.

The Sovereignty Commission, buoyed by its "success" at ousting the leadership at Tougaloo College, set its sites on Rust College and President Earnest Smith in the summer of 1964: "We have put into action a plan for Rust College similar to the plan we used at Tougaloo College.... It is hoped that the case against President Smith will be ready to present to trustees at Rust College within a short time with the recommendation that the president be removed and a new administration return the college to the educational purposes for which it was established."[85] A Commission employee and a member of the Board of Trustees traveled to Holly Springs to reason with Smith and discern what was happening on the campus, but Smith refused to meet with them and ordered them off the campus.[86] Undeterred, the Commission interviewed campus informants who accused Smith of employing a large number of "suspected homosexuals" as faculty, impregnating a young girl, refusing to discipline a white male and black female "caught in the act," and employing a "bunch of white beatniks" to teach summer courses.[87] The Commission gathered the evidence and returned to the Board of Trustees hoping to get Smith fired. Other public officials joined the cause and attempted to undermine Smith's authority. Mayor Sam Coopwood wrote to the Mississippi branch of the Methodist Church and encouraged it to investigate the college and President Smith.[88] Senator George Yarbrough, from Marshall County, pressured the Board of Trustees in New York to take action against Smith.[89] The Commission and its allies attempted to marshal their forces to compel the trustees to take action.

The attempts to oust President Smith failed. He remained president until 1966 when he retired of his own volition. A series of miscalculations frustrated the Commission's efforts. The Commission's assessment of the Board of Trustees was somewhat accurate. Several trustees wanted to insulate Rust from the Civil Rights Movement, and the Board's lukewarm support of civil rights activism frustrated President Smith and contributed to his voluntary departure.[90] But, the Commission miscalculated the level of the Board's antipathy toward the movement. Many of the white Board members from the Mississippi branch of the church were angry about the campus's place in the movement, but the Mississippi Methodist Church donated only a small amount of funds to the college. Rust received most of its financial sustenance from the national church so financial threats from the Mississippi branch carried little weight. The Commission also overestimated the level of dissention between the Board and President Smith. Board members may have tempered their support for the campus-based movement, but they found the Commission's morals charges against Smith distasteful and obvious. The Commission's crass attempts offended the Board, which refused to take any action.

The Commission also misjudged its power over private HBCUs. It did not, by itself, precipitate the president's firing at Tougaloo

College or the demise of Campbell College. Tougaloo's charter and fund-raising crisis and Campbell College's financial situation provided the Commission with a rare opportunity. Rust College's financial situation was not as dire as that at Campbell College, though it was far from wealthy. Nor was Rust in the middle of a charter crisis or a funding campaign like that at Tougaloo College. The Commission considered Rust a threat to the state, but it could not capitalize on fortuitous vulnerabilities. Rust was able to withstand state pressure in part because it received less concerted attention from the Commission, but also because it did not provide the Commission with an entrée to exploit.

Implications

The examination of Campbell College, Tougaloo College, and Rust College during the civil rights era offers implications beyond discrete battles with the Sovereignty Commission. Their experiences offer civil rights scholars evidence of the importance of independent, self-sustaining institutions and the depths of Southern racism. The advent of the Civil Rights Movement severed the uneasy compromise between private HBCUs and the Southern power structure. The state easily dealt with individual campus constituents who confronted the Southern system. Quelling group dissent proved another matter. Government agencies aggressively attacked the institutions and their constituents, an attack made easier by the insecure economic situation of the colleges, internal dissention, and other convenient vulnerabilities. Their private status forced segregationists to invent creative strategies to curtail activism. The state was not the only destabilizing force, but it created conditions under which the colleges struggled to function and were forced to take drastic and costly measures to protect themselves if possible. The experiences of Campbell, Tougaloo, and Rust demonstrate the volatile nature of the era and the lengths to which racists would go to crush the Civil Rights Movement.

Also, the experiences of these three small and isolated institutions illuminate broader themes in the history of higher education. First, the battle between the colleges and the state contributes to the debate over the role of a college in society: should it remain aloof and practice neutrality or should it be pressed into service toward specific social and ideological goals.[91] The state of Mississippi admonished private HBCUs to stay out of the Civil Rights Movement. Activists drafted Campbell College, Tougaloo College, and Rust College to play a role in societal reform despite the state's threats. The institutions became what Aldon Morris describes as movement centers: organizations or institutions that enable a subjugated group to engage in sustained protest by providing communication networks, organized groups, experienced leaders, and an opportunity to pool social capital.[92] Activists used their respective campuses as a protective shield to coordinate an attack on racial domination and eschewed the notion that participation in social reform should wait until after graduation. Student-status protected activists, but the HBCUs themselves became targets. The Sovereignty Commission, legislature, government officials, Board of Trustees of Institutions of Higher Learning, local police, the state legal system, and Citizens' Council marshaled their forces to punish the private colleges and force them to take a more conservative position on the role of a college in society. Private status prevented direct intervention, but the state and its allies were able to make the public role of private colleges a liability.

Second, the experiences of these private HBCUs force a reevaluation of the dichotomy drawn between public and private institutions. The category has proven useful in examinations of higher education, but the experiences of these institutions put a different spin on the question: What is (should be) the relationship between the state and higher education institutions? The Supreme Court addressed the potential danger of the situation in its 1819 *Dartmouth College* decision. The Court found that a privately funded college should not be subjected to legislative whims, public opinion, or the rise and fall of political parties. Education was a public matter, but the faculty and philanthropic interests had the right to act as a private entity.[93] The decision had nothing to do with private black colleges; none existed at the time. But, missionary philanthropists set up private HBCUs with the same assumption: financial and political autonomy from the state and the right to develop curricula, campus policies, and other matters without the fear of state intervention in college affairs. The state violated the autonomy of private colleges after they became involved in the Civil Rights Movement. The campuses were free to encourage group esteem and practice desegregation as long as their campus reality did not directly confront the Southern racial order itself. Private institutions, as Rust's President Smith put it, "were not as free as everyone thought we were."[94]

Third, an examination of private HBCUs in the Civil Rights Movement offers an alternative interpretation of the role of private and public institutions in a democracy. The history of higher education tells us that public institutions democratized higher education. State-supported institutions expanded the educational opportunities for youth previously excluded in a system of private colleges. Under certain conditions, however, private institutions became vital to democratic aims while public institutions could not perform the same role. In the 1960s, when Southern state interests collided with constitutionally protected freedoms, private institutions provided a forum for dissent. Private HBCUs—*because they were private*—were invaluable. Their freedom from state control allowed the colleges latitude not available to public institutions. They paid heavily for their choice and intense external pressures left its mark, but private HBCUs played a pivotal role in the protection of egalitarian aims.

Notes

1. See David Sansing, *Making Haste Slowly: The Troubled History of Higher Education in Mississippi* (Jackson: University Press of Mississippi, 1990), 61–64, 79–80.
2. James D. Anderson, *The Education of Blacks in the South, 1860–1935* (Chapel Hill: University of North Carolina Press, 1988), chapter 7.
3. *Journal of the House of Representatives of the State of Mississippi, 1956,* regular session, 107–108, cited in Yasuhiro Katagiri, *The Mississippi State Sovereignty Commission: Civil Rights and States' Rights* (Jackson: University Press of Mississippi, 2001), 5.
4. *General Laws of the State of Mississippi, 1956,* chapter 365, section 5, 521.
5. "Citizen Council Grant" [1964], Sovereignty Commission Record (hereafter cited as SCR) 99-30-0-46-1-1-1 to 2-1-1, Mississippi Department of Archives and History (hereafter cited MDAH; all Sovereignty Commission Files are located at the MDAH).
6. Clayborne Carson, *In Struggle: SNCC and the Black Awakening of the 1960s* (Cambridge, Mass.: Harvard University Press, 1981).
7. John Dittmer, *Local People: The Struggle for Civil Rights in Mississippi* (Urbana: University of Illinois Press, 1994), 85-86.
8. Ibid., 86–87.
9. J. Michael Butler, "The Mississippi Sovereignty Commission and Beach Integration, 1959–1963: A Cotton-Patch Gestapo?" *Journal of Southern History* 68, no. 1 (February 2002): 107–48.
10. Charles Payne, *I've Got the Light of Freedom: The Organizing Tradition and the Mississippi Freedom Struggle* (Berkeley: University of California Press, 1995), 286.
11. Carson, *In Struggle,* chapter 9.
12. "Negro Students Stage Boycott," *Greenwood Commonwealth,* 22 February 1957; "Negro Student Boycott Settled," *Greenwood Commonwealth,* 23 March 1957; and J. H. White, *Up from a Cotton Patch: J. H. White and the Development of Mississippi Valley State College* (Itta Bena, 1979), 111.

13.   Jerry Proctor, "King Tries to Stop Student Walk-Outs," *State Times,* 8 March 1957; and Board of Trustees of Institutions of Higher Learning, Minutes of Special Meeting, 9 March 1957, MDAH.
14.   "Report Classes Boycotted at Jackson State," *Jackson Daily News,* 7 October 1961, SCR 10-105-0-4-1-1-1; John A. Peoples Jr., *To Survive and Thrive: The Quest for a True University* (Jackson: Town Square Books, 1995), 58.
15.   Jacob Reddix to Albert Jones, 1 April 1961, SCR 10-105-0-2-1-1-1.
16.   "Tougaloo Bill Appears Dead," *Clarion-Ledger,* 14 April 1964, Subject Files Tougaloo College, 1960–1969, MDAH. The statement was made about Tougaloo, specifically, but it fits securely with the government's attitude toward the other private HBCUs in the state.
17.   John Held to [Wesley] Hotchkiss, 2 June 1964, American Missionary Association Archives, Addendum (1869–1991, n.d.), Series A, Subseries Tougaloo Correspondence, Box 110, folder 19, Amistad Research Center, Tulane University, New Orleans, Louisiana (hereafter cited ARC).
18.   The other was Mississippi Industrial College, supported by the Colored Methodist Church.
19.   Clarice Campbell and Oscar Allan Rogers, Jr., *Mississippi: The View from Tougaloo* (Jackson: University Press of Mississippi, 1979).
20.   Erle Johnston to John Salter, 17 August 1981, Tougaloo Office File Register, Brown University-Tougaloo College Cooperative Program, Brown University Archives, Providence, Rhode Island (hereafter cited BUA).
21.   See Leslie Burl McLemore, interview by Joy Ann Williamson, 20 August 2003, Jackson, Mississippi.
22.   All of Campbell College's records were either lost or destroyed. The following information is gathered from other available sources.
23.   "Note," [December] 1957, Sovereignty Commission investigator notes on 88th Session of the West Tennessee and Mississippi Annual Conference of the African Methodist Episcopal Zion Church, SCR 2-5-1-53-54-1-1-1. Charles Jones attended this conference.
24.   Hal DeCell to Governor J. P. Coleman, 16 December 1957, 1, SCR 2-5-2-16-1-1-1.
25.   Sherman L. Greene Jr., "The Urgency for Unification of the A.M.E. Church System of Education," *A.M.E. Church Review* 78, no. 210 (October-December 1961), 28.
26.   Zack J. Van Landingham, "Memo to File 1-23," 2 June 1960, SCR 1-23-0-70-1-1-1.
27.   Hopkins and Downing, "Investigation of Student 'Walk-out' from Burglund Negro High School, McComb, Mississippi; Parade and Demonstrations; Their Arrest, and Hearing in City and Youth Court," 19 October 1961, SCR 1-98-0-25-1-1-1; Payne, *I've Got the Light of Freedom,* 125; and Jacqueline Byrd Martin, interview by Joy Ann Williamson, 27 August 2003, McComb, Mississippi.
28.   Dittmer, *Local People,* 110–11, and Martin, interview.
29.   John Salter, Jr., *Jackson, Mississippi: An American Chronicle of Struggle and Schism* (Malabar, Fla.: Robert E. Krieger Publishing, 1979), 146–147; and John Her[unreadable], "City Declares Segregation Not Enforced in Terminals," *Clarion-Ledger,* 10 April 1962, SCR 2-72-2-36-1-1-1.
30.   Tom Scarbrough to File, 8 May 1961, 2, SCR 2-65-0-42-2-1-1.
31.   Zack Van Landingham to Meady Pierce, 13 April 1960, SCR 2-72-1-56-1-1-1; and Requisition, Sovereignty Commission payment to Percy Greene and T. S. J. Pendleton, 22 January 1962, SCR 97-98-1-317-1-1-1. Percy Greene was the editor of the *Jackson Advocate,* a black newspaper, and was a well-known informant. T. S.

J. Pendleton was a black school principal, minister, and Campbell College Board of Trustees member.

32. *R. A. Scott, et al. v. J. P. Campbell College, et al.,* February 1962, Chancery Court of the First Judicial District of Hinds County, Mississippi, SCR 3-78-0-1-1-1-1 through 19-1-1.

33. A. L. Hopkins to Members of the Sovereignty Commission, 1 May 1962, SCR 7-4-0-77-1-1-1.

34. *Scott v. Campbell College,* 3 (both quotes).

35. Ibid., 3–4.

36. Ibid., 4.

37. *R. A. Scott, et al. v. J. P. Campbell College, et. al., Agreed Decree,* 29 March 1962, SCR 3-78-0-2-1-1-1 through 3-1-1.

38. "Suit Settled at Campbell," *Jackson Daily News,* 28 March 1962, and "Stevens Restored as President of Campbell," *Jackson Daily News,* 2 July 1962, SCR 10-35-1-136-1-1-1.

39. Erle Johnston to File, 13 July 1964, 1, SCR 3-78-0-4-1-1-1.

40. Ibid.

41. Daniel Thompson, *Private Black Colleges at the Crossroads* (Westport, Conn.: Greenwood Press, 1973).

42. Reverend Bernard Law, Reverend Duncan M. Gray Jr., and Rabbi Perry E. Nussbaum to Board of Trustees, 4 May 1964, 2, American Missionary Association Archives, Addendum (1869–1991, n.d.), Series A, Subseries Tougaloo Correspondence, Box 110, folder 18, ARC.

43. United States Senate, 79th Congress, 2d Session, *Hearings Before the Special Committee to Investigate Senatorial Campaign Expenditures, 1946* (Washington, D.C.: Government Printing Office, 1947), 19, 88–90, cited in Dittmer, *Local People,* 3.

44. "Integrated Class at Millsaps College Sent to Tougaloo," *State Times,* 4 July 1958; Gabrielle Simon Edgcomb, "Ernst Borinski: 'Positive Marginality' 'I Decided to Engage in Stigma Management,'" in *From Swastika to Jim Crow: Refugee Scholars at Black Colleges* (Malabar, Fla.: Krieger Publishing, 1993), 124.

45. Ed King joined the Mississippi Freedom Democratic Party, an alternative to the state's Democratic Party that barred black participation, and ran as its vice presidential candidate in a mock election in 1963. John Salter became the North Jackson NAACP Youth Council's adviser and gained national media attention after his picture at the Woolworth's sit-in appeared in the national media in 1963.

46. See Salter, *Jackson, Mississippi,* and Ed King, interview by Joy Ann Williamson, 28 August 2003, Jackson, Mississippi.

47. *Writ of Temporary Injunction,* Chancery Court of the First Judicial District of Hinds County, Mississippi, 6 June 1963, Ed King Papers, Box 8, folder 374, Tougaloo College Archives, Tougaloo, Mississippi (hereafter cited TCA).

48. Erle Johnston to File, 13 April 1964, 1, SCR 3-74-2-17-1-1-1 through 2-1-1.

49. Mr. Zero to Sovereignty Commission, 5 May 1964, 1, SCR 3-74-2-19-1-1-1 through 2-1-1.

50. In 1954, Tougaloo merged with Southern Christian Institute, and the Tougaloo campus absorbed the Institute's student body.

51. "Church Group Cancels Support of Tougaloo," *Jackson Daily News,* 20 September 1963, Box A.D. Beittel Unprocessed, Folder Board of Trustees, Fall 1963, TCA.

52. Barnaby Keeney to Lawrence Durgin, 9 March 1964, 1, Barnaby Keeney Office File Register, Tougaloo College, 1964–65, Miscellaneous Correspondence, BUA.

53. Wesley Hotchkiss to Robert Wilder, 10 April 1964, Barnaby Keeney Office File Register, Tougaloo College, 1964–65, Miscellaneous Correspondence, BUA.

54. Ed King, interview.
55. For a discussion of Beittel's liberalis at Talladega, see Henry N. Drewry and Humphrey Doermann, *Stand and Prosper: Private Black Colleges and Their Students* (Princeton: Princeton University Press, 2001), 148-52.
56. Robert O. Wilder to A. D. Beittel, 20 April 1960, American Missionary Association Archives, Addendum (1869–1991, n.d.), Series A, Subseries Touglaoo Correspondence, Box 110, folder 17, ARC.
57. A. D. Beittel to Barnaby Keeney, 5 April 1964, American Missionary Association Archives, Addendum (1869–1991, n.d.), Series A, Subseries Touglaoo Correspondence, Box 110, folder 18, ARC.
58. Wesley Hotchkiss to Mr. and Mrs. George Owens, 20 April 1964, American Missionary Association Archives, Addendum (1869–1991, n.d.), Series A, Subseries Tougaloo Correspondence, Box 110, folder 18, ARC.
59. "Tougaloo Bill Appears Dead," *Clarion-Ledger,* 14 April 1964.
60. Senate Bill No. 1672, Regular Sess., 1964, Box Tougaloo College History, Folder Accreditation Revocation (State), TCA.
61. "Action on Tougaloo is Due for Delay," *Clarion-Ledger,* 6 March 1964.
62. Senate Bill No. 1794, Regular Sess., 1964, Box Tougaloo College History, Folder Accreditation Revocation (State), TCA.
63. A. D. Beittel to William Fidler (AAUP), 6 June 1964, A. D. Beittel to Hollis Price (President, LeMoyne College), 27 May 1964, and A. D. Beittel to Gordon Sweet (Southern Association of Colleges and Schools), 6 June 1964, Box Tougaloo College History, Folder Accreditation Revocation (State), TCA.
64. Johnston to File, 24 April 1964, 1, SCR 3-74-2-16-1-1-1 through 2-1-1. Ed King's name and title were blacked out in the record, but it is certain that he is the individual to whom the report refers.
65. Wesley Hotchkiss to Robert Wilder, 10 April 1964, Barnaby Keeney Office File Register, Tougaloo College, 1964–65, Miscellaneous Correspondence, BUA.
66. Erle Johnston to Paul Johnson and Carroll Gartin, 5 May 1964, 1, SCR 3-74-2-23-1-1-1.
67. Rust College experienced several different fires that destroyed the college's records. The following information is gathered from other available sources.
68. Tom Scarbrough (Sovereignty Commission investigator), "Marshall County," 19 April 1963, 2, SCR 2-20-1-67-1-1-1 through 2-1-1.
69. McLemore, interview.
70. "No Room for Communists," *South Reporter,* 30 July 1964; and "Book Boom," *Bearcat,* 15 July 1964, Folder *Bearcat* 1964, Rust College Archives, Holly Springs, Mississippi.
71. McLemore, interview, quote p. 8.
72. Frank Smith, "A Second Beginning of the End," 11 May 1963, [n.p.] Voter Education Project Papers, James Lawson Files, cited in Payne, *I've Got the Light of Freedom,* 197.
73. Tom Scarbrough, "Marshall County-Mrs. Clarice Campbell, White Female Teacher at Rust College-Also Rust College-All Negro School," 29 May 1961, 5, SCR 2-20-1-50-1-1-1 through 7-1-1.
74. Tom Scarbrough, "Marshall County," 14 December 1962, SCR 2-20-1-63-2-1-1 through 3-1-1.
75. Ibid., 2–3.
76. Ibid., 3.
77. McLemore, interview.
78. Dittmer, *Local People,* 29–33, and Payne, *I've Got the Light of Freedom,* 31–33.
79. Earnest Smith, telephone interview by Joy Ann Williamson, 13 February 2004.

80. Tom Scarbrough, "Marshall County (Rust College)," 30 June 1964, 5, SCR 2-20-1-78-1-1-1 through 5-1-1.
81. Tom Scarbrough, "Marshall County-Mrs. Clarice Campbell, white female teacher at Rust College-also Rust College-all Negro School," 29 May 1961, 7, SCR 2-20-1-50-1-1-1 through 7-1-1.
82. M. L. Malone to Zack Van Landingham, 9 February 1959, SCR 2-94-0-2-1-1-1; Zack Van Landingham to Director of the State Sovereignty Commission, 6 March 1959, SCR 2-4-10-6-1-1-1; Tom Scarbrough, "Lowndes County," 1 September 1961, SCR 2-94-0-56-1-1-1 through 2-1-1.
83. Tom Scarbrough, "Marshall County-Mrs. Clarice Campbell, white female teacher at Rust College-also Rust College-all Negro School," 29 May 1961, 4, SCR 2-20-1-50-1-1-1 through 7-1-1.
84. Rust College General Catalogue, 1963–1964, Rust College Archives, Holly Springs, Mississippi.
85. Erle Johnston, Jr., to Herman Glazier, 9 June 1964, SCR 2-20-1-77-1-1-1.
86. Smith, interview.
87. Tom Scarbrough, "Marshall County (Rust College)," 30 June 1964, 2 (first quote), 3 (second and third quotes), SCR 2-20-1-78-1-1-1 through 5-1-1.
88. Sam Coopwood to Bishop Marvin Franklin, 29 June 1964, SCR 2-20-1-80-1-1-1.
89. Tom Scarbrough, "Marshall County-Mrs. Clarice Campbell, white female teacher at Rust College-also Rust College-all Negro School," 29 May 1961, SCR 2-20-1-50-1-1-1 through 7-1-1.
90. Smith, interview.
91. Derek Bok discusses this debate in *Beyond the Ivory Tower: Social Responsibilities of the Modern University* (Cambridge, Mass.: Harvard University Press, 1982), though he does not address the dilemma faced by black colleges in the Civil Rights Movement.
92. Aldon Morris, *Origins of the Civil Rights Movement: Black Communities Organizing for Change* (New York: Free Press, 1984), 282.
93. This discussion of the Dartmouth case is taken from Frederick Rudolph, *The American College and University: A History* (Athens: University of Georgia Press, 1990), 207–10.
94. Smith, interview.

Collegiate Living and Cambridge Justice: Regulating the Colonial Harvard Student Community in the Eighteenth Century

John Burton

This article discusses the ways Harvard College and Cambridge, Massachusetts, cooperated in the eighteenth century in order to regulate the student community. The leadership of the two communities was successful in maintaining order through much of the eighteenth-century, but with the outbreak of the American Revolution and the changing social structure of the two communities its aftermath, the ability to enforce student regulation broke down by the end of the century.

Students and townspeople have often come into conflict in America. During the 1960s, student protests spilled over into local communities, increasing tensions between town and gown. Student unrest is not a product of the sixties, however, and has a long history. Students have traditionally engaged in activities that disturbed the peace of their surrounding communities. Kathryn Moore has provided a thorough overview of student regulation for seventeenth-century Harvard. The question remains how did student regulation change as both the college and Cambridge grew in the eighteenth century. This article attempts to understand the role of local authorities in regulating student life at eighteenth-century Harvard. In Cambridge, academic and town leaders cooperated, much like their twentieth-century counterparts, to ensure peace and order, with the result that, prior to the 1760s, student activities did not often lead to student unrest. This harmony was not the result of a separation of town and gown, but grew out of Harvard's integration with the local judicial structures.[1]

New England Puritans believed in consensual order, rule rising naturally from within the community, not imposed from outside it. Town constables, justices of the peace, and county courts were de-

---

History of Higher Education Annual 23 (2004): 83-105.
©2004. ISBN: 0-7658-0839-0

signed to maintain harmony in local communities. Harvard's students had to be similarly regulated, and the college and the town cooperated to ensure peace. The tutors combined with local magistrates and constables to discipline students, investigate offenses, and monitor individual behavior. Harvard's reliance on local authorities mirrored the actions of its English counterpart. Rather than create a separate police force as Oxford did, the University of Cambridge used the local constabulary to monitor its student population. But the English university's powers were more wide-ranging than Harvard's. The Oxford and Cambridge vice-chancellors were authorized not only to call out the local police but to arrest local inhabitants and, under some circumstances, to try them in university courts. Harvard's charter did not grant the college separate legal jurisdiction, nor did the president or fellows have specific rights to judge or punish students. Instead, the Harvard authorities were free to discipline their charges only as long as the students cooperated and remained at the college to be punished.[2]

The need to regulate student life outside the classroom developed from Harvard's decision to embrace a collegiate lifestyle, albeit imperfectly implemented. The college operated in some ways as a separate community, with Cambridge and Middlesex County surrounding but not controlling it. Seventeenth-century Harvard authorities chose collegiate living less from a need to govern and control unruly students than from a desire to create a collegial community. Particularly in the seventeenth century, Cambridge authorities, like any Puritan leaders, were prepared to enforce order and to discipline any of their citizens. The more important benefit the leadership may have sought from collegiate living was the development of personal connections between the students as part of a self-defined intellectual community.[3]

Disciplining students had been a common occurrence at Harvard since its founding. Written regulations described an ideal society; in fact, students regularly broke the rules and had to be corrected. Although Harvard drew upon a much narrower set of punishments than did the local judiciary, college authorities emulated the magistrates by stressing verbal persuasion, not physical force, to maintain peace and only flirted briefly with corporal punishment in the seventeenth-century. For more serious infractions or for intransigent students, the college had either to rely on local authorities or expel the scholars. Moreover, the town magistrates and local minister were usually also members of Harvard's governing bodies, creating an interlocking group of community leaders to ensure the peace. Most problems in the seventeenth century involved young male towns-men disturbing the peace of the college, not rowdy students disrupt-ing the town. When complaints did occur from the town, Harvard responded quickly to punish the offenders. The college also con-firmed that the town watch had "at all times . . . full powr of inspeccon into the manners and orders of all persons related to the Coll, whether wth in or wth out the precints of said Coll . . . any usage, or custome to the contrary not withstanding," but the Corporation did restrain the watch from laying "violent hands on any of the students" in the Yard. Thus Harvard defined the town watch's authority over schol-ars broadly when they were in the town but more narrowly within the college precincts. Although the watch was allowed to enter the Yard, if students were seized within college bounds, town authori-ties could secure them only until the president and fellows were no-tified.[4]

By the early eighteenth century, Cambridge youth were no longer posing a significant nuisance to collegiate life. Instead, Harvard au-thorities focused primarily on the regulation of their own young men. After abandoning whipping and flogging in the seventeenth cen-tury, the college officials could still handle a wide variety of infrac-tions without recourse to the local officers or courts. By 1734, the regulations had further expanded to enumerate punishments for ly-ing, stealing, and breaking open "any Chamber, Study, Cellers, Ches[t,] Desk or any place under lock & key." Students were not to keep distilled liquor on campus or entertain strangers (non-college members) in their rooms. They could be fined for being absent from prayers in the college hall, public worship in the Cambridge meet-inghouse, or the divinity professor's lectures. Missing the Sunday church service was the most serious of these offenses; the fine was three shillings.[5]

At the same time, the students were beginning to resist the author-ity of the faculty. Their resistance brought into question the relative jurisdictions of both the college and the county counts. Not only were professors added to the faculty in the eighteenth century, but the tutors, who lived with the students and were responsible for much of their instruction, were older, remained at the college longer, and were more comfortable with exercising their powers. In 1718, one of the tutors, Nicholas Sever, charged one of the masters students,

Ebenezer Pierpont, with "contemning, reproaching and Insulting the Governmt of the College." Pierpont had been the Roxbury schoolmaster for several years while waiting to apply for his second degree, during which time complaints had come to the attention of the fellows of the Harvard that the students from the Roxbury school were ill prepared for college. When Harvard rejected two of Pierpont's students in 1717, one of the students' fathers accused Sever of rejecting his son for personal reasons. Pierpont complained that the Harvard fellows were a set of "Rogues, Dougs & tygars." The Corporation, in turn, denied Pierpont his masters degree. To forestall Pierpont's appeal to the Overseers, Harvard President John Leverett reported the case to them himself, and the Overseers concurred with the college's actions stating, "Well, there is an End of it, and no more to be sd." Pierpont, unsatisfied, took his case to court.[6]

The college authorities were reluctant to accept judicial oversight. When Leverett received a summons from Pierpont for the Corporation to appear before the governor, he petitioned the executive to refer the case back to the Overseers, arguing that if the matter were carried into the courts, it "wilbe hurtfull to the rights and Privileges of the College, and tends to weaken the Governmt therof." But Pierpont had some powerful allies, including Cotton Mather, who still resented the choice of Leverett over himself as Harvard president. At the Overseers' meetings, Mather made a strong appeal to Governor Samuel Shute on behalf of Pierpont. The Overseers held two meetings, the governor presiding, to persuade the two to settle their differences. Because Pierpont's defense was so weak and poorly presented, the Overseers urged him to sign an apology. Above all, the Harvard authorities wanted to get the case out of the local courts and included in the agreement a clause that Pierpont would promise to stop "any further prsecutions in the Law against Mr. Sever." Sever agreed to sign, but Pierpont refused. The case went forward in the Middlesex County court, which denied Pierpont satisfaction, noting that the matter had "already had an hearing according to the Charter of Harvard College and Laws & Customs there of before the Corporation and Overseers of the sd college." The county court preferred to respect the rights and privileges of the college and was unwilling to press its advantage in the situation.[7]

The Pierpont-Sever case did not close the door to civil suits involving the college and its personnel. In 1733, Leonard Vassall sued tutor Daniel Rogers for striking Vassall's son, a student at Harvard.

Young William Vassall had passed his tutor while walking on the streets in Cambridge; Rogers had doffed his hat but Vassall had kept his hat on his head. Rogers, in accord with college custom, retaliated by boxing Vassall's ear. Vassall sued Rogers, arguing the tutor's authority did not extend beyond the college. Ultimately, the Supreme Court found for Rogers, leaving intact Harvard's right to regulate students within both the college and the town.[8]

In 1734, the year after the Vassall-Rogers case, the Corporation voted that "no Scholar (or his Parent, or Guardian in his behalf) Shall exhibit to any Other Authority, than that of the College, a complaint Against any of the Governours or resident members thereof, for any injury cognizable by the Authority of the College, before he has sought for redress to the President and Tutors." If the student and his family could not get relief from the Corporation, they were to appeal to the Overseers. Any scholar who went directly to the courts "shall forthwith be expelled." Although Harvard had used the county court in the past for its own interest, it was now doing all it could to maintain its judicial independence when the court might be used against it. These requirements did not allow students to flout local authority, however. Harvard's regulations of 1734 required scholars to show "due respect & honou[r] in speech and behaviour" not only to the president and fellows but also to the "Magistrates . . . and Elders" of the town.[9]

Court cases in the seventeenth century had closed the door to collegiate oversight of townsmen. To prevent undesirable contact between scholars and Cambridge residents in the eighteenth century, Harvard had to focus on the scholars. For example, in 1735, William Woodhouse, a barber, kept showing up at the college and promoting improper behavior among the students. The college labeled Woodhouse as "a person of a dissolute life" but could not take direct action against him. Although Woodhouse was the chief problem, the cautions and potential punishments were directed at the scholars. Woodhouse was "strictly forbidden coming to the College," but the scholars were also "publickly charged upon their peril not to keep his company, nor receive him into their chambers upon any pretence wtsever." Woodhouse must not have heeded the college's warning, because five years later, the students were once again reminded not to "Entertain or associate, with, Either Wm Woodhouse of this town, or Titus, a Molattoe slave of the late Revd. Presdt Wadsworth's." The two potential trespassers' names were posted in the buttery as a daily reminder to the students to shun them.[10]

Just as Harvard expected students to respect the Cambridge authorities, officials would not tolerate unruly behavior either on campus or in the town. In 1749, for example, the college punished two students for "a Disturbance to certain Persons met for a Private Worship At the house of Mr Wm. Morse." Harvard was willing to discipline students for infractions within Cambridge and responded to complaints from townsmen about the behavior of scholars.[11]

To better control its students, Harvard tried to co-opt some of the power of local authorities by having the tutors or other college officers appointed justices of the peace. Harvard personnel could then hear cases and punish offenders not only as officers of the college but also as officers of the local court. Leverett had been a justice of the peace but had resigned his office on becoming president. Henry Flynt was commissioned a justice of the peace for Cambridge while a Harvard tutor and had the "full power of any Justice in Cambridge for the advantage and better government of the Colledg." But Flynt hesitated to use these powers. When Josiah Parker, a tavern keeper in Cambridge, was accused in 1722 of "abusing [one of the students] by blows etc," Leverett asked Flynt to hear the case. In spite of the tutor's clear right to do so, he refused to conduct a trial alone, explaining, "I was a Stranger to such things and might take wrong stepps." Flynt also felt his duties at the college prevented his giving proper attention to the law because he "was not Engaged in a particular Study and could not attend to aquaint myself as I should." Leverett, who was probably prepared to give all the guidance that was needed, retorted, "You know how to Judge of a matter that is before you." He suggested further that if Flynt "did not now begin," he would "never do anything," and that "these things were as plain as could be desired." But the president had no luck persuading Flynt to exercise his judicial authority, and the college had to continue to rely on the Cambridge magistrates to discipline the townsmen and keep peace in the larger community. In spite of his unwillingness to exercise the powers of his office, Flynt continued to be appointed a justice of the peace as late as 1737.[12]

Thus, in cases extending beyond the college, Harvard called on the magistrates for assistance. One such case occurred in 1751. One evening, tutor Jonathan Mayhew was "disturbed by the rowlling of a Logg twice down the Stairs leading to his Chamb. from above." Mayhew got out of bed to investigate and, in the dark, was "pushed down from the Top of the Stairs by a Stranger, whm he found standing on them." Mayhew asked for the help of another tutor, Belcher Hancock. The tutors then called on Samuel Danforth, the Cambridge magistrate, to investigate because "of a Stranger's being found to be concerned with this Insult." Danforth came to the college and accompanied the tutors to the room of Joseph Gerrish, one of the suspected students. There they found Stephen Miller of Milton and Ebenezer Miller of Braintree, brothers of another student, John Miller. Danforth led the examination of the students and two "strangers." The malefactors blamed "One Browne of Providence" for rolling the log down the stairs and pushing tutor Mayhew after it. After questioning by the two tutors, however, John Miller confessed that Mr. Brown was fictional. In fact, it was Benjamin Gerrish, Joseph's brother, "who did what they had charg'd upon this Browne," and the others finally agreed with Miller in front of Danforth and the two tutors. Although Danforth had been called to investigate, the case was then turned over to the college authorities; Miller was degraded eighteen places in his class and Gerrish was expelled. Gerrish's more severe punishment was due to his "giving false Testimony upon Oath, before one of his Majesties Justices of the Peace." Although the college did not want the local authorities appearing on campus unrequested, when the Harvard officers called upon them, the tutors expected the students to pay appropriate respect. Gerrish missed his commencement in 1752, but he made a public confession the following year, was restored to his rank, and received his degree. The "strangers" apparently went unpunished. In spite of Danforth's presence during the investigation, the case was not recorded in the Middlesex County court.[13]

Although the aims of the magistrates and the college authorities were the same, Harvard made a clear distinction between punishments imposed by the town and punishments imposed by the college. For the most part, students did not come before the local authorities, but from time to time exceptions did occur. In 1758, James Lovell, a resident graduate studying for his master's degree, was living in the college but taking his meals with Jonathan Hastings, a Cambridge tanner, who lived at the north end of the commons. Hastings's daughter Susanna died giving birth to an illegitimate child, and she may have named Lovell as the father. Although Lovell at first denied paternity, the next year he confessed in the Cambridge church to fornication. The college was not satisfied with this confession, and the faculty ordered Lovell to make another one "publicly in the [college] Chapel." The Puritan reliance on public confession satisfied both groups. Not only was Lovell restored to his privileges at the college but he was also admitted to full communion at the Cambridge church the next year. By the 1760s, Harvard had gained a *de facto* autonomy, even if the local courts had *de jure* authority. Although the college resisted local judicial oversight, its officials urged local authorities to restore order in the town when the peace of the college was threatened, punished students for local complaints, and required scholars to have proper respect for local magistrates. This balance between autonomy and peaceful cooperation became difficult to preserve in the decade preceding the Revolution.[14]

By the late 1750s, Harvard was once again in the midst of a housing shortage. The Corporation noted in 1759, "There are now so large a number of students belonging to the College, that a very considerable part of them, are oblig'd to live out of the College in the town." About seventy students were taking lodgings in Cambridge in 1759; sixty-four would do so in 1760. The Corporation again petitioned the General Court for "some inlargement of the College buildings." By the 1760s, most of each freshmen class had to start their college careers in town lodgings, moving into college housing their second or third year. Harvard at the same time was relaxing its requirement that all students dine in the college. Students living in the college were required to eat in commons, but students living in town were now allowed to dine with householders "upon the invitation of any housekeeper in the town to dine or sup gratis."[15] Corporation Records, Harvard University Archives, 2:123, 130, 139; Overseers Records, Harvard University Archives, 2:70; Faculty Records, Harvard University Archives, 2:116, 5:139.

Not only was the college housing more of its students in town, but the regulations also began allowing scholars to leave Cambridge on occasion. In 1763, the Corporation decided that students could leave town for one day without permission of the tutors and that seniors could leave for two days so long as they did not miss any of their lectures. Not everyone approved of this new leniency. The visiting committee of the Overseers complained in 1765 that students living in town should be "prevented [from] breakfasting in the town's people's houses" and asked that the Corporation provide those students with breakfast in the college hall. Likewise, when the Overseers approved the college's new calendar in 1766, they asked that students not be allowed to leave Cambridge except during official college breaks. It was supposed to be the professors' responsibility (since they lived in Cambridge) to oversee the students living in the town, but the Overseers reported that professors Wigglesworth and Sewall were not visiting the chambers of the town dwellers. Wigglesworth was partially excused for his oversight, as his "bodily infirmities" prevented him from doing so, but close oversight of students living in private homes was probably unreasonable. The Corporation did not respond to the Overseer's criticisms.[16]

Although Harvard began to relax some of its regulations, the changes did not occur fast enough to suit the students. In 1761, the college eased restrictions on students' entertainments, allowing the scholars to "entertain one another & strangers with punch." The Corporation explained that punch "as it is now usually made is no intoxicating liquor." Whether punch as the students made it was not intoxicating was another matter. Overall, students were socializing more, and the number of infractions for drinking and card playing rose. The infractions in 1761 were not unusual. For example, several students stole "boards and tools" from the Cambridge church construction site, but after a complaint from the housewright building the church, the youths confessed and made full restitution. By the end of the decade, however, student unrest and disorders had reached unprecedented proportions.[17]

This relaxation in student regulation came at an unfortunate time. Although the tutorship at Harvard College had been a strong and stable position at Harvard through much of the eighteenth century, the average tenure for tutors dropped from more than eleven years in the 1740s and 1750s to less than four years in the 1760s. The shorter length of service left both less experienced tutors in charge of the students and increased the turnover of faculty. Moreover the tutorship underwent a curricular transformation. Up until the 1760s, each tutor taught the entire curriculum to a given class, making the connections between a tutor and his students quite strong and lasting over four years of college. In 1767, the tutors began to teach specific subjects, reducing the connection between tutors and a specific class and so probably weakening faculty oversight. Coincidentally, the length of service for Cambridge selectmen also dropped after the 1760s from an average of more than seven years in mid-century to less than five years in the 1760s and 1770s. Both the college and the town went through several decades of weakened leadership around the years of the American Revolution.[18]

In response to this student unrest and weakened faculty oversight, Harvard tried to strengthen collegiate living. During the second half of the eighteenth century, the college built several new buildings to accommodate its students. The General Court appropriated £2500 in 1762 for one new dormitory, Hollis Hall. Most students were living on campus, but some still lived in town. The construction of new housing failed to accomplish Harvard's goals. Ultimately, after a century of struggling with strict enforcement of a collegiate lifestyle that was more an ideal than a reality, the college shifted its focus. By the end of the century Harvard was paying more attention to the types of homes in which students were living than to getting all scholars on campus. The college now turned to local family homes as a positive alternative to other types of housing, particularly private boarding houses and taverns. The faculty ordered that "no student be permitted to occupy a room in any house in the town of Cambridge where a family does not reside, nor in any building where Sprituous liquors are retailed or a tavern is kept." Students were also barred from dining in these establishments. Although Harvard remained primarily residential, the administration became reconciled to some students living in the town.[19]

Pre-Revolutionary Student Disorders

Harvard students in the 1760s were older than their predecessors had been a generation before, entering college at about age seventeen rather than around age fourteen or fifteen. They chafed under administrative paternalism and felt their lives too closely regulated because they could not leave Cambridge without permission and had to eat in commons. Moreover, after decades of strong presidential rule, leadership weakened when President Holyoke's health deteriorated before his death. The tutors, now less experienced, were unprepared for the vacuum in executive leadership, and discipline suffered. One student reported that there "was much deviltry carried on in College" during this period. In 1766, students complained to the senior tutor about the quality of the butter served in commons. The tutor rejected the complaints. When the same rancid butter appeared at table the next morning, the students walked out of commons and breakfasted in town. The faculty was able to restrict this first protest to a single incident. As was Harvard's preference, the Cambridge authorities were not called for assistance. Instead, Holyoke and the faculty drew up a written confession of guilt to be signed by each of the participants if they wanted to remain at college.[20]

The faculty could not handle the next set of protests so easily. In spite of a liberalizing of the regulations in 1767, a rebellion broke out again in 1768. This time the spark was recitations. Until 1768, unprepared students had been able to avoid recitations by answering "nollo," or "I don't want to." Beginning in March 1768, the Corporation decreed that only seniors could refuse to recite. The scholars stonewalled the new regulation by refusing *en masse* to participate. Some then vandalized their tutors' rooms. When it was reported that tutor Joseph Williard had shut up a freshman, Thurston Whiting, in the tutor's room all day without food in a vain effort to tell who was behind the disorders, the college went up in a storm. Sixty or seventy students attacked Williard's room, breaking his windows.[21]

The faculty panicked when it appeared that the demonstration could not be contained within the college bounds, and someone called for the Middlesex County sheriff. When the students heard rumors that the county militia was approaching the Yard, they armed themselves and set off to meet the soldiers at the commons. Confrontation was averted when one of the students, Stephen Peabody, learned that the guard had been sent to protect college property, not to arrest the students. The protest fell apart after Whiting recanted his accusations against Williard, explaining that he had not been held against his will. Harvard did not have to seek further assistance from Middlesex or Cambridge authorities. Instead, it handled the matter itself as it had for the past century: the scholars publicly confessed and were reintegrated into the Harvard community.[22]

Two years later, student disorders spread out of the Yard, across the commons and into Cambridge. In March 1770, five Harvard students were charged in Middlesex County court with breaking into the home of John Nutting and assaulting and threatening to kill the occupant, Samuel Butterfield. The reasons for the attack are unknown. The event's chief historian, Theodore Chase, believes that Nutting was not the intended victim. Moreover, although the events occurred two weeks after the Boston Massacre, no specific political cause can be identified. Chase suggests that the event was an outgrowth of personal animosities between scholars and townsmen. Butterfield was about the same age as the college students, and some personal antagonism may have existed between him and them. All of the students involved in the incident had histories of disciplinary problems. John Frye, a master's candidate and probably one of the leaders, had already been admonished by the faculty for disturbances within the college that had also affected "many Inhabitants of the Town." On March 21, Frye had been especially busy violating the college regulations. In addition to breaking into Nutting's house, he had entertained "women of ill Fame" in his room at Harvard.[23]

As if they were not in enough trouble already, on May 9, Frye and two other students assaulted Captain William Angier, a tanner, in order to persuade him not give evidence in the forthcoming trial. Angier subsequently testified to the college authorities that he had seen Frye, Winthrop Sergeant, and Thomas Saunders entertaining prostitutes in March. He stated that the three students did "assult, ill-treat, and threaten the said Capt Angier, in such a manner, that he apprehend himself in danger from them." They also "threatened his wife." Such treatment of town residents by students was unparalleled. The college officials were particularly concerned that the scholars' actions would make it more difficult for the faculty to procure the testimony of town residents in the future. In the upshot, the Corporation "rusticated" all three students, sending them to study with rural pastors. [24]

Had the case ended there, it would have been only an example of extreme student violence, highlighting town-gown tensions but not suggesting any changes in the balance of power between the college and the local judiciary. But the same day, violence broke out when students tried to stop local authorities from arresting the three culprits. Although the town's actions may seem justified today, they were unprecedented in 1770. No Harvard student had ever been arrested by local authorities in the eighteenth century, nor had any been punished except by college officials since Goodman Healey had been hired to whip students under President Hoar in the 1670s. The students rescued their fellows, but the accused were later apprehended and required to give bond to appear the second Tuesday in May at the Middlesex County courthouse. Though the case was subsequently dropped, the offenders protested the college's punishment later in May by walking out of the college chapel.[25]

The county then brought in a second indictment of disrupting the peace against four of the students who had tried to stop the earlier arrest. The court described the defendants as "infants above the age of fourteen years and all students now residing at Harvard College in Cambridge." They were accused of participating, along with "fifty other evil minded & disorderly Persons," as "Rioters, Routers, and Disturbers of the Peace." The jury found all four guilty. The students then appealed to the Superior Court, but the outbreak of the Revolution intervened. Although the case was dismissed in 1776, it was unique in the colonial era as the only occasion when students were called into the Middlesex County court. A possible precedent had been set: students were not immune from prosecution in the local courts. Moreover, punishment by the college authorities did not necessarily preempt action by local officials.[26]

Student disorders persisted in the post-Revolutionary period, but civil authorities did not prosecute any scholars, Harvard handling most complaints directly. When Harvard officials received a complaint from Edward Richardson of Watertown that Daniel Murry, a student, was "abusing, in language" Richardson's wife and son, Murry was quickly degraded in order to "deter . . . all the Members of this society . . . from maletreating any person in the vicinity of Harvard College." Further student infractions took place, but punishment was left to college authorities. Wine was stolen from a Cambridge resident; the college privies were set on fire, endangering homes in the town; and a student was found to be keeping "at his own expense" a "lewd Woman" in a local house. In the 1780s, the faculty began keeping a set of "student disorder papers," outlining each offense. Most of the violations affected only the college, but the loud noise and disturbances often drifted into the town as well. At first, Harvard tried to expand its own authority into the town in order to rein in the students. The college saw the taverns as the main culprit and believed that if their regulation was transferred to Harvard, peace would return to the community.[27]

Harvard Students and Cambridge Taverns

Puritans were not teetotalers and taverns were an accepted part of life, but students were barred from frequenting them throughout the colonial period. As early as President Dunster's time, Harvard had protested tavern keepers "harbouring students unseasonably," and Dunster made an agreement with local tavern owners to keep student purchases to a minimum. Scholars were only to purchase bread and beer from local ordinaries when supplies at the college were inadequate. Although students occasionally were chastised for frequenting ale houses in the early eighteenth century, it was not until mid-century that Harvard began to express concern. Taverns had become a focus of debate in New England life. In 1738, the *Boston Evening Post* defended taverns as "very Necessary and Beneficial" for the "Entertainment of Strangers and Travellers" but criticized them as haunts of town residents. In Cambridge, the total number of establishments had increased significantly. In 1650, the town had one authorized tavern, by the 1670s, three, in 1700, seven, and by 1750, eleven. This figure amounted to one tavern for every 135 inhabitants, approaching Boston's ratio of one for every 100.[28]

At first, Harvard turned to the town authorities for assistance with the problem of student patronage of taverns. In 1751, the Corporation asked the "Justices and Selectmen of the town of Cambridge, that they would use their interest that neither the retailers nor innholders of said town, do sell to any of the students of Harvard College being undergraduates any rum or spirits whatsoever." In 1763, the Overseers expressed different fears about the students frequenting taverns. In their annual visitation of the college, the Overseers instructed the Corporation "to project some method for preventing Innholders & Retailers from Supplying the Undergraduates with Wine & Spirituous Liquors upon Trust or Credit." They recommended that the General Court pass a law requiring the Middlesex County Court of General Sessions (which approved licenses for the Cambridge taverns) to cancel the licenses of establishments that fell under the disapproval of the college authorities. The Overseers were as much worried about the students' pocketbooks as about their sobriety.[29]

Harvard reacted to these concerns by reissuing regulations that required students to refrain from frequenting local taverns, and the Corporation "earnestly requested of his Majesty's Justices of the Peace of the County of Middlesex, on whom the keepers of the public houses and Retailers . . . have dependence for their licenses, that they would be pleased to enforce the observation of this law . . . within three miles of the college." Because students were adept at leaving Cambridge to find entertainment, Harvard also asked the Charlestown selectmen to "exert themselves effectively to suppress all Practices within their Township so immoral in their Nature & of such dangerous Tendency." More directly, they asked the Charlestown authorities to take action against the Ship Tavern, "a

House of bad fame" that employed one or more "lewd" women. By 1767, Harvard no longer had only liquor and prostitutes to worry about. The concerns of River City, Iowa, had reached eighteenth-century Cambridge: a pool table had been installed in one of the taverns! The Harvard faculty protested to the selectmen that "we are inform'd that a Billiard Table hath lately been set up in Cambridge not far from the College viz. at the house of Capt. Samuel Gookin, by a Person who is not an Inhabitant of this Town." The Corporation asked that the selectmen "take such steps as they in their Wisdom may judge necessary to prevent, the dangerous Effects wch may Naturally be expected from gaming Houses." There is no record of the town taking any action against Gookin. Harvard continued to complain to the town authorities about taverns throughout the 1760s, and the town tried to rein in abuses. For example, the selectmen voted in 1773 "that they earnestly Entreat all such who shall have approbation or Recommendation to sell strong drink, that they would not allow young men . . . to have Strong Drink or intertain them." Although townsmen occasionally complained to the college of the drunken activities of the students, they were more interested in the profit the taverns brought to the community.[30]

The Corporation also asked the selectmen to help enforce its regulations against dancing. In 1766, the Corporation protested that "a dancing school hath lately been open'd in Cambridge & diverse scholars of this house have attended it, without leave from the Governmt of the College." The Corporation asked the selectmen to close the school, as "the continuance of sd school will be of bad consequences to this society." The selectmen were not convinced of the dangers and took no action. Dancing continued. Elizabeth Cranch reported on visiting Harvard in 1771 that "all such as Learn to dance are so taken up with it, that they can't be students."[31]

After the Revolution, Harvard authorities threatened direct action against both taverns and dancing. In 1783, the Corporation directed the president to "write the Select Men of the town of Cambridge, requesting them not to permit any of the students of the College to have use of the Town Hall for a Ball." These dances may have been part of larger community problem. The selectmen were concerned about outsiders coming to Cambridge for "entertainment," and they appointed a committee, including James Winthrop, the Harvard librarian, to devise ways of restricting the events. Neither the selectmen nor the Harvard authorities were able to stop dancing and other student entertainments. John Quincy Adams reported attending horse races, dances, militia meetings, and teas in Cambridge during his student years in the late 1780s.[32]

Harvard authorities took more direct action against taverns. The Corporation distributed copies of the college laws respecting student drinking to the Cambridge establishments and asked the innkeepers to help enforce the college regulations, or else Harvard would oppose the renewal of their licenses. February and March 1789 were particularly trying months. Drunken students regularly returned to the college in a "noisy and tumultuous manner." To the tavern keepers' credit, in at least one instance the scholars found the Cambridge taverns closed to them and had to ride "two or three miles to a public house from whence they did not return 'till about four o'clock the next morning." Harvard decided more forceful action was necessary and asked the legislature to transfer the right to license taverns from the county to the college. In their petition, the Overseers inquired

> whether it be not needful to the welfare of the university that the Governors of it, or some of them, should have some control over the appointment of Innholders within a given distance from the College and that application should be made for the appointment of a Magistrate or Magistrates from among the immediate Governors of the college to prevent or suppress the disorderly conduct of the those do not belong to it.

At this possible expansion of college authority, the Cambridge selectmen sat up, took notice, and petitioned that Harvard's request "might not be granted, & that they [the selectmen] might be allowed an hearing." The legislature received both sets of petitions and chose a course of inaction. Harvard did not receive expanded licensing or judicial powers, and the life of the college continued to be plagued by liquor and loose women. Maintaining order in the community, even during Harvard-sponsored events, required the cooperation of both the town and college authorities.[33]

Commencement and Cambridge Disorders

Commencement was one of the most important of these occasions. Graduating seniors celebrated with their families and friends, and many alumni returned to the college. The crowds attracted merchants and peddlers, so that the whole event had the trappings of a county fair. Morison estimates that by the late seventeenth century, several hundred visitors came to Cambridge at commencement, and "hucksters and cheap-jacks came too, in order to cater to the crowd in its lighter moments." Beginning in 1687, the commencement ceremony moved from the college hall, which had become too small to house the crowd, to the Cambridge meetinghouse. Dinner was served in the hall to the graduates, and parties continued in their lodgings into the evening.[34] As early as 1681, Harvard recognized that it needed assistance in patrolling the college and policing visitors because the student revelries were getting out of hand. There was too much drinking, and too many strangers were coming in and out of the college. In response, the Overseers appointed Samuel Andrew, a resident master, "to execute the office of Proctor for the comencmnt week." His new assignment was to keep intermixing between the scholars and uninvited visitors at a minimum by ensuring that no one lingered in the college during the commencement service and that all "strangers" left by nine o'clock on commencement evening. The proctor then closed the college to all except the students, reminding visitors that "the usual recourse of any to the colledge . . . excepting scholars is displeasing to the hon. & Revd Overseers."[35]

The college was successful at self-regulation into the eighteenth century, but by the 1720s, Harvard authorities were finding the crowds, festivities, and noise of commencement more than they could handle. They therefore instituted "private" ceremonies restricted to graduates and their families, in which public events were kept to a minimum, hoping to discourage visitors from coming to Cambridge. To keep the crowds down, the college no longer held commencement on a fixed date (traditionally the first Wednesday in July). Instead, it announced the date of the ceremony in the Boston newspapers only a couple of weeks in advance of the event, hoping the peddlers and non-academic visitors would be unable to attend at short notice. At the same time, the Corporation tried to restrict the student's private parties by limiting the list of beverages and provisions the students could offer their guests, with strong punch specifically forbidden.[36]

These efforts failed to reduce the problems at commencement. In 1732, the Overseers instructed the Corporation "to consult wth the Justices of the peace that Live in Cambridge about the Time of Commencement particularly on the Commencement day & the Night following." President Wadsworth described a meeting between the Corporation and two of the local officials "about proper means to prevent disorders at Comencement." The justices suggested that the college ask the undersheriff, a constable, and four or five assistants to attend commencement, estimating that "furnish'd with a Warrant from the Justices, [they] would be a sufficient number to watch and walk as there should be occasion toward evening on Commencement day, and the night following." The college would pay the men's salaries of ten shillings apiece and twenty shillings for the "captain" of the guard. In 1736, with new provisions for security, Harvard returned to holding commencement on the first Wednesday of July.[37]

Throughout the rest of the century, Harvard paid the local constabulary to secure the streets of Cambridge during commencement. At first, the guards' responsibilities were to patrol the town while Harvard's faculty maintained order within the college. Because disorders continued on commencement night, in 1737 the guards were charged with preventing "the disorders both in the town & college." The guards were usually Cambridge townsmen headed by the local constable. Over time, their number increased from the constable and four assistants in the 1730s to ten assistants in the 1780s. To end the festivities, the guard was charged in 1766 "not only to strike the Booths on Commencement evening" but to direct visitors to remove their belongings and be out of town by the next morning.[38]

Harvard further restricted students' activities on the evening of commencement. Punch was allowed in 1759, but larger "entertainments" were not permitted. In spite of these precautions, a riot broke out after commencement in 1761, and four students had to be rusticated. Drinking, entertainments, and dancing were all feared by the college authorities, who restricted graduates' receptions to students and family members. Some students and their parents circumvented the college regulations by holding parties in town, but these affairs were subsequently banned, except when hosted by students whose parents lived in Cambridge. Given that the scholars had already graduated, the only penalty the Corporation could inflict was withholding the graduates' master's degrees, a severe punishment that was usually overturned a year or two later.[39]

After the Revolution, Harvard began to ask that the local magistrates remain in town through the day following commencement "to preserve peace and good orders." The town also began to show increased concern about the students' parties. In 1786, the selectmen formed a committee "to devise by-laws to prevent these entertainments." The guard was increased to twelve in the 1790s, with at least two magistrates in attendance. Over the course of the eighteenth century, commencement had been transformed from a

Harvard-regulated activity to a community-wide event. It fell to local authorities to preserve the town's peace. Balls also became an
accepted part of student life, by the 1790s, Harvard allowed students to use rooms at the college for these events.[40]

* * *

In the aftermath of the American Revolution, cooperation between
Harvard and Cambridge to maintain order in the community began
to break down. Visiting the United States in 1788, J. B. Brissot de
Warville reported that "Boston has the glory of having given the
first college or university to the new world." As an afterthought,
he mentioned that the college was actually located "four miles
from Boston in a place called Cambridge." Brissot de Warville's
view of Harvard as Boston's college was a sign of a larger transformation in town-gown relations. In the new republic, Harvard
was increasingly tied to the metropolis of Boston and less its own
town. Faculty members were connected to a Beacon Hill elite and
students were mostly sons of Boston merchants and traveled regularly to the city for parties and shopping. At the same time, Cambridge was becoming a working-class suburb with interests increasingly divergent from that of the college. People visiting Harvard
during this period should be excused for not realizing they had left
Boston.[41]

By the late eighteenth and early nineteenth century, a sense of
gentility and refinement extended to Harvardians—both faculty and
students. In the 1770s, John Winthrop, professor of natural history,
chronicled his adoption of the custom of taking tea in the afternoon
and entertaining dining companions in the evening. Most of his guests
were either faculty members or provincial politicians; he had little
interaction with other Cambridge elites, and the Harvard faculty withdrew from town life. The social life of students also changed. Drinking and card playing became popular entertainments. The increase
in tavern attendance in the eighteenth century did not solidify town-
gown relations, but put Harvard at odds with Cambridge. The economic benefits of the taverns outweighed the town's desire for or-
derliness and control. Harvard's attempt to usurp the power of local
courts to license taverns was defeated, but not without forcing overt
confrontation between town and college authorities.[42]

Because Harvard was unable to regulate the community, it worked
instead to reduce student interaction with townsmen. This battle be-

came all the more important as Cambridge went through a social transformation of its own. In the final decades of the eighteenth century, the town began to grow quickly. The new neighborhoods to the east and north were mostly working-class communities with few ties to the college or to the central settlement. Many of the new inhabitants were Baptist or Roman Catholic, rather than Congregationalist, Unitarian, or Episcopalian like the students. Harvard responded to the newcomers by sequestering the students. Although they were allowed to worship in the churches in Old Cambridge, they were barred from those in east Cambridge. Students were urged to mix with faculty members and a few socially prominent townsmen rather than with the new town dwellers. The best symbol of this new attitude toward the community was the orientation of Holsworthy Hall, a dormitory built in 1811. For the first time, Harvard built a building that did not face or give direct access to the Cambridge common. Holsworthy turned its back on the town and opened into the Yard. Later in the century, Harvard raised the height of the wall surrounding the campus and added iron gates to keep out townsmen.[43]

By 1800, Harvard College could not effectively isolate its students from the temptations of the surrounding community. Although the college resisted town oversight in the eighteenth century, it had to rely on local police to maintain order in unusual circumstances, particularly at commencement. Moreover, students came to Harvard expecting to participate in local entertainments—dances, balls, and other social events. Although scholars continued to be punished for infractions, they regularly went to taverns, played cards, and brought liquor into their rooms. College attendance was no longer merely a scholarly endeavor; it was also a social experience. The separation of oversight between the college and the town and these new social temptations increased frictions. But the case of Harvard's regulation of student life demonstrates the importance of studying college life, not in isolation, but within a larger community context. Students were not only subject to collegiate oversight but also that of local authorities. Similarly, infractions could occur both within the college and outside it. If the academic and town leadership could cooperate, student life could be successfully regulated, and town-gown tensions minimized. Colleges were community institutions, and the regulation of student life involved the entire community.

Notes

1. Kathryn McDaniel Moore, "The Dilemma of Corporal Punishment at Harvard College," *History of Education Quarterly* 14 (fall 1974): 335–39.
2. David Hackett Fischer, *Albion's Seed: Four British Folkways in America* (New York: Oxford University Press, 1989), 189; Jurgen Herbst, *From Crisis to Crisis: American College Government, 1636–1819* (Cambridge, Mass.: Harvard University Press, 1981), 5–8; Harvard Charter of 1650, in *American Higher Education: A Documentary History*, eds. Richard Hofstadter and Wilson Smith, vol. 1 (Chicago: University of Chicago Press, 1961), 10–12.
3. Corporation Records, Harvard University Archives, vol. 2, p. 139; Clifford Shipton, *Sibley's Harvard Graduates: Biographical Sketches of those Who Attended Harvard College* (Boston: Massachusetts Historical Society, 1873–1975), vol. 4, p. 381, vol. 7, p. 517. The Massachusetts leadership's own experience at the University of Cambridge highlighted the importance of interpersonal contact during collegiate education to the creation of a Puritan intellectual elite. See Francis Bremer, *Congregational Communion: Clerical Friendship in the Anglo-American Puritan Community, 1610–1692* (Boston: Northeastern University Press, 1994), 17.
4. Moore, "Corporal Punishment," 335–39; *Harvard Records*, Colonial Society of Massachusetts, *Collections* 15 (1925): 44–45, 205; Samuel Eliot Morison, *Harvard in the Seventeenth Century*, vol. 1 (Cambridge, Mass.: Harvard University Press, 1936), 24.
5. *Harvard Records*, Colonial Society of Massachusetts, *Collections* 15 (1925): 142–44; 16 (1925): 593.
6. *Harvard Records*, Colonial Society of Massachusetts, *Collections* 16 (1925): 441; 49 (1975): 285–87; Shipton, *Harvard Graduates*, vol. 6 (1942), 99.
7. *Harvard Records*, Colonial Society of Massachusetts, *Collections* 16 (1925): 441–42; Overseers Records, Harvard University Archives, 1:13–14; John Leverett, Diary, Harvard University Archives, 172, 178; Shipton, *Harvard Graduates*, vol. 6 (1942), 100.
8. *Harvard Records*, Colonial Society of Massachusetts, *Collections* 16 (1925): 610–15; Overseer Records, Harvard University Archives, 1:133–34; Shipton, *Harvard Graduates*, 350.
9. *Harvard Records*, Colonial Society of Massachusetts, *Collections* 15: 137, 145.
10. Faculty Records, Harvard University Archives, 1:82.
11. Ibid., 1:228.
12. Henry Flynt, Diary, Typescript, Harvard University Archives, 403–4. In 1737, President Holyoke was also appointed justice of the peace for Middlesex County. Neither Flynt nor Holyoke appears to have actually heard cases; see *Boston Evening Post*, 14 November 1737.
13. Faculty Records, Harvard College Archives, 1:347–55. Shipton provides a brief account of the incident in Shipton, *Harvard Graduates*, vol. 13, 231–32, 271–72.
14. Faculty Records, Harvard University Archives, 2:100; Shipton, *Harvard Graduates*, vol. 14, 31.
15. Corporation Records, Harvard University Archives, 2:123, 130, 139; Overseers Records, Harvard University Archives, 2:70; Faculty Records, Harvard University Archives, 2:116, 5:139.
16. Corporation Records, Harvard University Archives, 2:167–8, 253; Overseers Record, Harvard University Archives, 2:173, 3:9.
17. Corporation Records, Harvard University Archives, 2:143; Faculty Records, Harvard University Archives, 2:142. This section of the chapter benefits from two previous studies of Harvard disorders by Shelden Cohen and Theodore Chase. I have fo-

cused on the town and county involvement in the student disturbances. For greater detail on the student disturbances, see Cohen, "The Turkish Tyranny," *New England Quarterly* 47 (December 1974): 564–83, and Chase, "Harvard Student Disorders in 1770," *New England Quarterly* 61 (March 1988): 25–54.

18. John Burton, "Harvard Tutors: The Beginning of an Academic Profession," *History of Higher Education Annual* 16 (1996): 5–20; John Burton, "Puritan Town and Gown: Harvard College and Cambridge, Massachusetts, 1636-1800" (Ph.D. diss., College of William and Mary, 1996), 18, 42.

19. Faculty Records, Harvard University Archives, 2:355; Bainbridge Bunting and Robert Nylander, *Survey of Architectural History in Cambridge, Report Four: Old Cambridge* (Cambridge, Mass.: Cambridge Historical Commission, 1973), 150-54. By the mid-eighteenth century, rooming off campus was more than just a residential option. Edmund Trowbridge, a Cambridge lawyer, offered not only rooms but also optional legal study for those students choosing to live with him. Trowbridge usually had only one or two students in residence, but from the 1730s to 1770s, at least a dozen scholars combined their studies at the college with Trowbridge's legal tutelage. See Shipton, *Harvard Graduates*, vol. 8, 510.

20. Cohen, "Turkish Tyranny," 564–66.

21. Ibid., 567–70.

22. Ibid., 571–74.

23. Faculty Records, Harvard University Archives, 3:153–54; Court of General Sessions of the Peace, Middlesex County, Record Book, 1748–1777, Microfilm, Massachusetts Archives, 495–98; Theodore Chase, "Harvard Student Disorders," 30-34. Winthrop Sergeant, another of the students, was not content with his infractions of March. In May, he "fired pistols charged with ball in the town of Cambridge in such a manner as to endanger the lives and Property of the Inhabitants." Surprisingly, the town did not bring formal actions.

24. Faculty Records, Harvard University Archives, 3:153–54; Chase, "Harvard Student Disorders," 37–38. Chase does not include much discussion of the Corporation meeting of May 1770.

25. Chase, "Harvard Student Disorders," 39–41.

26. Court of General Sessions of the Peace, Middlesex County, Record Book, 1748–1777, Microfilm, Massachusetts Archives, 495–98; Chase, "Harvard Student Disorders," 43–45. For an evaluation of the effect of the American Revolution on student life at Harvard, see Sheldon S. Cohen, "Harvard College on the Eve of the American Revolution," Colonial Society of Massachusetts, *Publications* 59 (1982): 187–90.

27. Faculty Records, Harvard University Archives, 3:185, 193–95, 4: 185-88; Student Disorder Papers, Harvard University Archives. In 1790, a Harvard student called in the Cambridge constable when an altercation broke out among some of the scholars. The malefactors were brought before James Winthrop, Cambridge justice of the peace, but Winthrop dismissed the case "as too trivial to require the cognizance of a court of law." See Dennie-Vose Correspondence, Massachusetts Historical Society, 7-27 May 1790.

28. Morison, *Seventeenth Century*, vol. 1, 93; *Boston Evening Post*, 16 June 1738; Pulsifer Transcript, Massachusetts Archives, 3:216, 4:150; Middlesex Court of Sessions, Record Book, 1686–1746, Massachusetts Archives, 86, 212; Record Book, 1748–1777, 112; David W. Conroy, *In Public Houses: Drink and the Revolution of Authority in Colonial Massachusetts* (Chapel Hill: University of North Carolina Press for the Institute of Early American History and Culture, 1995), 9.

29. Corporation Records, Harvard University Archives, 2:12–13; Overseers Records, Harvard University Archives, 2: 140, 187.

30. Overseers Records, Harvard University Archives, 2:200; Corporation Records, Harvard University Archives, 2:208; Faculty Records, Harvard University Archives, 3:51, 229; Selectmen Records, 1769-83, Microfilm, Early Massachusetts Records Series.
31. Corporation Records, Harvard University Archives, 2:260; John Adams, *The Works of John Adams, Second President of the United States*, ed. Charles Francis Adams (Boston: Little, Brown and Company, 1850), vol. 2, p. 289.
32. Faculty Records, Harvard University Archives, 5:131; Town Records B, 26 June 1786, Microfilm, Early Massachusetts Records Series; John Quincy Adams, *Diary*, ed. D. Gray Allin et al. (Cambridge, Mass.: Belknap Press of Harvard University Press, 1981), vol. 2, pp. 10, 109, 120, 139, 142, 161.
33. Corporation Records, Harvard University Archives, 3:274; Faculty Records, Harvard University Records, 6:16–17, 22–24; Cambridge Selectmen's Records, 1788–1804, Microfilm, Early Massachusetts Records Series, 10 June 1789; Overseers Records, Harvard University Archives, 4:22–24. Copies of the petitions can be found in the Belknap Papers 161.B.13c, 161.B.14c, Massachusetts Historical Society.
34. Morison, *Seventeenth Century*, vol. 2, pp. 465-67.
35. *Harvard Records*, Colonial Society of Massachusetts, *Collections* 15 (1925): 242.
36. Ibid., 16 (1925): 549–50, 583; Shipton, *Harvard Graduates*, vol. 8, p. 110.
37. Overseers Records, Harvard University Archives, 1:116; *Harvard Records*, Colonial Society of Massachusetts, *Collections* 16 (1925): 648, 33:487.
38. Faculty Records, Harvard University Archives, 1:94, 2:250, 4:240-42.
39. Corporation Records, Harvard University Archives, 2:120, 127-28, 329; Faculty Records, Harvard University Archives, 2:141–42; Overseers Records, Harvard University Archives, 3:19.
40. Corporation Records, Harvard University Archives, 3:233, 265, 285, 307; Faculty Records, Harvard University Archives, 6:81, 312; Letters of Curtis Chamberland to Francis Cabot Lowell, 5 February 1793, 2 April 1793, Francis Cabot Lowell Papers, Massachusetts Historical Society.
41. J. P. Brissot de Warville, "The Air of Cambridge is Pure," *The Harvard Book: Selections from Three Centuries*, rev. ed., William Bentick Smith, ed. (Cambridge, Mass.: Harvard University Press, 1982), 441. For the changes at Harvard, see Ronald Story, *Harvard and the Boston Upper Class: The Forging of an Aristocracy, 1800–1870* (Middletown, Conn.: Wesleyan University Press, 1980), chapters 3, 4, and 6.
42. Shipton, *Harvard Graduates*, vol. 9, p. 247; John Winthrop, Diaries, Harvard University Archives.
43. Henry Binford, *The First Suburbs: Residential Communities on the Boston Periphery* (Chicago: University of Chicago Press, 1985), 18–44. Until the 1810s, views of Harvard inevitably were from the vantage point of the commons, showing the college open to the community. By the 1820s, views of the interior of the Yard were as common; see Hamilton Vaughan Bail, *Views of Harvard: A Pictorial Record to 1860* (Cambridge, Mass.: Harvard University Press, 1949), pl. 36–41. Similar changes occurred at Yale, which also built walls around the campus and reoriented the buildings inward. See Juliette Guilbert, "Something That Loves a Wall: The Yale University Campus, 1850–1920," *New England Quarterly* 68 (June 1995): 247–77.

Envisioning an Urban University: President David Henry and the Chicago Circle Campus of the University of Illinois, 1955-1975

Fred W. Beuttler

In the decades after World War II, numerous states expanded universities to handle the wave of students. The Chicago Circle campus of the University of Illinois opened in 1965, but its particular mission was unclear. U of I president David Henry was a leading national spokesman for the new urban universities, but his vision of an "urban mission" for Circle clashed with the political realities of campus expansion and especially with faculty aspirations for comprehensive research. This early controversy over mission has shaped the further history of the university, helping it over a period of retrenchment and laying the foundations for UIC's development as a significant model of American higher education, the comprehensive urban research university.

"Just as universities make great cities, so a great city makes a great university," proclaimed Mayor Richard J. Daley, in October 1963, during the groundbreaking ceremony for the new Chicago Circle Campus of the University of Illinois. Daley had worked for over twenty-five years to bring a major public university to Chicago, a dream that finally saw its fulfillment when Circle Campus opened in February 1965. But what was to be the relation of the new university to the city? While there was some talk nationally in the mid-1960s of an "urban land grant" on the model of the Morrill Act of 1862, there was no clear consensus as to what this type of institution should look like, or even whether it was a good model.[1]

In 1955, the same year Richard J. Daley became mayor of Chicago, the University of Illinois Board of Trustees selected David Dodds Henry, a former president of Wayne University and then chief

History of Higher Education Annual 23 (2004): 107-141.
©2004. ISBN: 0-7658-0839-0

academic administrator of New York University, as president of the University of Illinois. The Board gave Henry an explicit mandate to establish a permanent campus for the university in the Chicago metropolitan area. While the issue of the site for the campus was hotly contested, with the trustees preferring a suburban site and Mayor Daley insisting upon a downtown location,[2] the main area of concern was over its so-called "urban mission." In an unpublished memoir, Henry commented that there was "too little understanding of the urban mission," and that many faculty "had no notion of the meaning of the charge to the Circle campus."[3] Conflict over the priority given to research also dogged relations between the Urbana campus and Chicago, with persistent and lingering impressions by Chicago faculty that Urbana, and Henry in particular, had little desire to see the Chicago Campus fulfill a significant research and service role for the urban community.

What was this "charge" to the new Circle Campus? Henry referred to Circle's "urban mission," but what was it, and how was it to be accomplished? Was its urban mission to be defined by the students it served, or by its research on the urban environment? Should its courses and research have a specific focus upon the city and its problems, seeing the city as a laboratory? Or should the campus concentrate on service, confining itself to a more limited role, which would not unduly compete with the state's flagship university in Urbana? These questions created significant controversy in 1960s and still are areas of current confusion.

These questions recur in the history of higher education, but perhaps more sharply in the case of Illinois. In the three decades after the end of World War II, higher education was transformed by both the G. I. Bill and the massive increase in enrollment of the babyboom generation. In many states, such as California, New York, Pennsylvania, and Wisconsin, educational coordination became paramount in order to manage the wave of students.[4] The increasing dominance of urban regions also forced a reorientation in higher educational thinking, as universities began to be located, by plan or demand, in highly concentrated urban areas. The University of Illinois' expansion into Chicago was by no means unique, but because of the specifics of Illinois and Chicago, it is more than just an illustrative case study. Illinois was comparatively late in setting up structures of higher education governance, and its regional politics even further limited the time available to manage the growth of higher education. Because of this, the common questions of the meaning and purpose of higher education became especially acute at Circle Campus.

David Henry's vision of an urban university dramatically shaped the historical development of the University of Illinois at Chicago.[5] He was not a minor character, but one of the major academic statesmen of his generation. To understand his vision may help illuminate the larger history of the rise of urban higher education. Henry's conception of a distinctive urban mission of the university underwent a process of development from his early years as president through the construction, staffing, and programming of the Circle Campus, but they generally centered around two concepts: access and service. As his later reflections suggest, he was not able to persuade the University of Illinois, Chicago Circle (UICC) faculty, which continued to push for the Chicago Campus to become a comprehensive research university.

Many new urban universities were created or dramatically expanded in the 1950s and 1960s, and there are many parallels in their histories. A number were quite ambitious, sharing with the Circle Campus faculty the desire to build first rank research universities. Most of the new urban universities, however, developed into at best only second tier institutions. Circle Campus in the 1960s and 1970s was typical of this pattern. But the university that developed after that was not, for in less than twenty-five years it achieved the coveted status of a Carnegie Research I institution. Now, almost forty years after its birth, it boasts of over $200 million in funded research, with a budget of over a billion dollars. Only part of this was due to the merger of the Circle Campus with the University of Illinois Medical Center, which created the University of Illinois (UIC) at Chicago in 1982. Rather than attempt to write a brief history of the rise of UIC here, a task that properly requires a book length study, this article will focus on the distinctive mission of Circle Campus through a close examination of the vision of the university president who ruled over its creation. David Henry was the most important president of the University of Illinois from 1920 to 1980, and it was Henry who oversaw Illinois' growth into a major graduate research university, with a student body of over fifty thousand on three campuses. Henry's vision for an urban campus was significant historically, for the idea evolved in the midst of difficult circumstances.

The growth of Circle Campus into a research university was due in large part to the early controversy over its distinctive mission. Most universities accept their mission willingly, without undergoing an enormous amount of controversy. Circle was different. In its founding years two visions competed with each other, and in that struggle the intellectual groundwork was laid for its later development into a research university. In this sense, a close examination of David Henry's vision, and how this changed during the historical development of Circle Campus, holds a key to understanding the particular place and mission of urban universities in late-twentieth-century America. Looking at UICC's history from 1955 to 1975, UICC struggled over whether it was to be primarily an urban university emphasizing access and service, David Henry's vision, or whether its destiny was to be a comprehensive research university. It seems that what it was working towards institutionally in this period was a reconciliation of these two visions, to develop a new model in American higher education, the comprehensive urban research university.

The Preparation of an Administrator:
David Henry's Early Career

David Dodds Henry was one of the major academic administrators of the middle-twentieth century. While not as widely known as his contemporaries Robert Maynard Hutchins of the University of Chicago or Clark Kerr of the University of California, he was a leader in a wide variety of fields. Over the course of his career he was chief academic officer and president of Wayne University, provost of New York University, and the longest serving president of the University of Illinois, from 1955 to 1971. In addition, he was a nationally recognized educational leader, one of the few who served as president or chairman of six national organizations: the Association of Urban Universities, the American Council of Education, the National Association of State Universities and Land-Grant Colleges, the National Commission on Accrediting, the Association of American Universities, and the Carnegie Foundation for the Advancement of Teaching. In addition, he served on several national study groups, including the Carnegie Commission on Educational Television, the President's Committee on Education Beyond the High School, the Carnegie Commission on Higher Education, and the national Board on Graduate Education. He was even chairman for a term of the United Negro College Fund.

Personally, Henry was a rather humorless individual, stubborn and obstinate at times, but he was a hard-working administrator who avoided controversy and seldom tolerated dissent. He was relatively unimaginative, with few original ideas, for he was a reformer and a manager. He knew he was not "brilliant," but he made up for it as "work was my recreation as well as my stress."[6] In examining David Henry, the task is, as one historian put it, to face "the dramatic problem of portraying a bore without allowing the bore to bore us."[7] This is not necessarily a slight at Henry, who realized this about himself. In his first memoirs, he admitted,

> I have not regarded myself as having the personal qualities that are of special interest to other people. Certainly, I am not "charismatic" in any way. I have been submerged in my work so completely that I have often felt that I have no personality or personal interest to others apart from career. While the career has had many dramatic moments, including some crises for me and for my work, they have been isolated incidents in a rather colorless progression of duties and responsibilities, albeit heavy and important ones.[8]

He admitted one exception, however. He approached his vision of education out of a sense of "missionary zeal" for, as he put it. "I started my academic life in the outreach department at Penn State, and it was that early experience, with the Wayne emphasis, that led to my deep and abiding commitment to extending educational opportunity. Indeed, this became the central motiff [sic] in my whole career, a crusade, a cause."[9]

Henry was born in October 1905 in Western Pennsylvania, about 25 miles from Pittsburgh. His paternal grandfather, surnamed Heinrich, was a coal miner who had emigrated from Germany in the 1880s. He settled in the west Pennsylvania coal country, where he worked in the mines until retiring around 1915. Henry's father was a machinist for the railroads, until he brought the family to Chicago around 1913 to attend the Moody Bible Institute. His father was unschooled, at least not beyond eighth grade, but felt called to religious service. He was a rather strict fundamentalist and ambitious for the ministry. In Chicago, the Henrys lived in a number of one-room apartments, around Chicago and Wells streets, "within walking distance" of Chicago's Navy Pier.[10] An only child, young David would occasionally accompany his father on street missions. After Moody Bible Institute, his father was called to a succession of small Baptist churches in Colorado and Pennsylvania. As David Henry remembers, his father "had a violent temper, easily aroused," and relations between them were quite strained. His parents later divorced.[11]

As a child Henry was a loner, not active in sports and with few friends, although he did join the "Lone Scouts of America," an organization that brought the values of the Boy Scouts to rural children. His chief childhood activity, in addition to household chores, was reading. The family returned to the Pittsburgh area in time for David to attend Schenley High School, several blocks from the University of Pittsburgh and Carnegie Tech. Henry thrived at Schenley, a new school which emphasized college preparation, and excelled in social and academic activities, becoming president of the Classical Club, president of the senior class, valedictorian at commencement, and the recipient of the Civic Honor Award. He moved away from the strict fundamentalism of his father, becoming president of the "Hi-Y" club at the YMCA and assistant superintendent of the Y's Sunday School.

From Schenley, he attended The Pennsylvania State University, excelling in liberal arts and finishing 5th or 6th in his graduating class of 500. To support himself, he got a typing job copying letters in the president's office. His extracurricular activities were in preparation for his later work, involving varsity debate, editor of the yearbook, editor of a new literary magazine, and finally president of the senior class. The *New York Times* took notice of him, calling the young Henry "the busiest college student in America." Upon graduation in 1926, he was awarded a fellowship for graduate study, so he continued at Penn State, earning his M.A. in English in 1927 and his Ph.D. in 1931, writing a biography of the poet William Vaughn Moody for his dissertation.

In 1927, he was hired full time in the Department of Engineering Extension, where he was to prepare liberal arts courses and organize classes throughout the state. This experience oriented him to the needs of commuting and adult students. From the extension department, he moved into an instructorship in English, later joining the faculty of Battle Creek College, where he finished his dissertation. Battle Creek had been founded by Dr. John Harvey Kellogg to train professionals for his Battle Creek Sanitarium. Henry was rapidly given administrative assignments, becoming Dean of Men after his first year, and later the director of the School of Liberal Arts. Henry later considered this a key "turning point" in his life, as he discovered his talent for administration.[12]

With the Depression, Battle Creek College experienced serious financial difficulties, which soon led to its closure. Battle Creek's president had foreseen the looming disaster, so he ran as a Democrat for State Superintendent of Public Instruction for Michigan, and won. Henry accompanied him to Lansing, where he became Assistant Superintendent for Higher Education in 1933. Henry threw himself into the work, helping to win Michigan's first substantial appropriation for the public schools, organizing the Michigan Council on Higher Education, and even administering the New Deal WPA program in adult education.

When the Republicans took back the superintendent's office in 1935, Henry accepted a position as assistant to the executive vice president at Wayne, which was then under the control of the Detroit Public School system. He was to remain at Wayne for seventeen years, as it grew from Junior College, to City College, to Colleges of the City of Detroit, and to Wayne University. It was Henry who laid the groundwork for its later development into Wayne State University.[13]

In 1939, upon the retirement of the executive vice president, Henry was appointed to the position, which made him *de facto* head of the university. Detroit's Board of Education was the board of trustees for the university, which caused some serious difficulty over authority as the superintendent of schools was also president of the university. This structural flaw was soon corrected, however, as the board separated the office of superintendent from the university president in 1945, naming Henry to that role. One of Henry's major goals in this period was to push the board to yield jurisdiction to the State if Michigan would take financial responsibility, a move that was not fully completed when Henry left Wayne, but well on its way at that time. Wayne was one of the first to move from municipal university to state university, a move initially opposed by most of the other municipal universities in the country, but which they eventually followed.[14]

Henry and the university were embroiled in some controversy, which seemed to foreshadow his future at Illinois. Wayne's location made it vulnerable during the Detroit race riots of 1943, and a change of location was seriously contemplated. Henry seemed to prefer a suburban site for the university, but inability to secure significant funding forced an incremental expansion of the campus. In addition to race, there was the threat of domestic subversion, and like other states around the country in the late 1940s and early 1950s, Michigan created its own investigative commission to expose communists. In the spring of 1949, David Henry vetoed a lecture by Herbert Phillips, a communist philosopher recently dismissed from the University of Washington. Defending his action, Henry, who two years earlier had claimed that "the University has no right to differentiate among American citizens on the basis of political belief," this time insisted that "it is now clear that the Communist is to be regarded not as an ordinary citizen . . . but as an enemy of our national welfare . . . I cannot believe that the university is under any obligation in the name of education, to give him an audience."[15]

By 1952, Henry felt that he had accomplished all he was going to accomplish at Wayne. He had administered the university for thirteen years, from age 34 to 47. He felt himself somewhat worn out physically, after a seven-day a week, day and night schedule, and he was admittedly rather thin-skinned, taking any criticism towards the university personally. A state referendum on educational funding had just been turned down. In addition, a teachers union with a chapter at the university had just formed, which was increasingly taking an adversarial stance towards the administration. It was time to leave.

David Henry left Wayne after a fond farewell ceremony, which included a gift of a personal car. He accepted a position as chief academic officer at New York University (NYU), under Henry Heald, who had recently been head of the Illinois Institute of Technology, and who later would run the Ford Foundation. The shift from a public to a private institution was not great, David Henry later recalled, as the missions of NYU and Wayne had much in common: "Both were urban, emphasizing service to commuting students. Both had comprehensive professional programs. Both had severe financial problems." Henry settled into his new position, but after only a couple of years allowed his name to be circulated for possible presidencies. He was approached by the University of Illinois' trustees, who offered Henry the position.

Henry had some misgivings about accepting Illinois' presidency. After the war Illinois had as its president George Stoddard, a dynamic leader who sought to awaken what he called the "sleeping giant" in Urbana. An internationalist active in UNESCO, he sought to move Illinois up into prominence, but soon fell afoul of a rather politicized trustee board.[16] At midnight on a Friday night in July 1953, a rump board summarily fired Stoddard and his provost, Coleman Griffith, ostensibly over Stoddard's handling of a scandal in the medical school, but in reality over long-standing political differences. In his place the trustees appointed an internal caretaker as interim, and began searching for a new president. The public and faculty were outraged over the midnight firing, and few candidates would consider taking over a university with such a board, so the search dragged on. Interestingly, Stoddard ended up at NYU, where he and Henry consulted frequently about the situation at Illinois.[17] After a change in the presidency of Illinois' trustee board, Henry decided to accept the position.

Bringing Public Higher Education to Chicago

After the passage of the G.I. Bill, the University of Illinois had agreed to admit all qualified Illinois veterans, but quickly found that it simply could not meet the demand at the Urbana campus. In 1946, it created two temporary campuses for the incoming students. These branches offered only the first two years of instruction, although they were not junior colleges, for admission requirements and courses were the same as at Urbana. One branch was in western Illinois, at Galesburg, where the University occupied part of the wartime Mayo Hospital complex. About three thousand students enrolled, many of them disabled veterans recuperating at the hospital. The university administration closed it after three years, when the Urbana campus could absorb the transfer students. The second campus was the "Chicago Undergraduate Division," housed in warehouse space on Chicago's Navy Pier. When the Navy Pier campus opened in October 1946, there was no public university in the entire Chicago area, only two small teachers colleges, although there were of course a number of private universities. Student demand was heavy for this U of I branch campus, with around four thousand students attending each semester, and this demand continued after the initial wave of veterans. Within a few years student and community pressure forced the trustees to keep the campus open, as a first step towards a permanent degree granting institution.[18]

One of the key individuals behind this community pressure was Richard J. Daley. As a first-term legislator in 1936 he had introduced a resolution calling for a public university in Chicago. In 1945, he introduced four bills into the state senate, to direct the University of Illinois to establish a branch in Chicago, *"to provide liberal and practical education customarily offered at the college or university level."*[19] These bills were referred to the senate education committee, then under the control of senators favorable to Urbana's interests, who subsequently tabled it, where it died on adjournment. In 1951, Daley's allies in the state house were able to introduce another bill, with similar language. It was amended by Urbana Republicans to limit the branch campus to only offer a "full undergraduate education," and in this form passed that same year.

This was the mandate from the state, and it is significant that it took political pressure from a powerful Chicago politician to secure passage in the state legislature, which forced a very reluctant university to build a branch in Chicago. The political context here is important. The president of the U of I at that time was George Stoddard, who generally opposed expanding the Navy Pier branch, believing that it was premature and would dilute the state's resources for the flagship campus in Urbana. This opinion was widely shared among the Urbana faculty. Stoddard's firing in the summer of 1953 had delayed planning for the Chicago campus; making the situation increasingly urgent by the time David Henry assumed the presidency.

One of the main reasons for the sense of urgency was the rising tide of enrollments that demographers and university planners predicted in the mid-1960s. In addition, the larger percentage of college-age students attending college raised the potential tide to enormous proportions, possibly doubling or even tripling college populations within ten years. One practical difficulty, however, was that Illinois at that time was operating under two handicaps—first, there was no central coordinating body for state higher educational planning, so each university had to make its case individually before the legislature; and second, the state was operating under biennial budgets, which meant that if appropriations for expansion were not sufficient in a given biennium cycle, it would delay planning by two full years. In addition, the state was strongly segmented politically, with the nation's second largest city heavily Democratic, its growing suburbs almost exclusively Republican, and the rural downstate countries mixed between the Republican northern and central counties, and the far south, which was southern Democratic. These political alliances would shape the expansion of higher education into urban Chicago.

Upon taking office as president of the University of Illinois in 1955, David Henry knew the university trustees' "highest priority among new developments" was progress "toward the realization of plans for a permanent undergraduate degree granting division" in

Chicago. From the very beginning of his administration then, David Henry concentrated on fulfilling this mandate for a permanent campus. University plans, however, raised serious debate within Chicago and downstate, as private universities in Chicago questioned the need for a new institution, and downstate legislators were "uneasy about the open-endedness" of the Chicago campus. Because of this, Henry devised a strategy "to advocate limiting the immediate commitment to a permanent home for the current program, as longer-range polices and issues were debated."[20] In the fall of 1955, Henry began delivering public addresses before varied audiences, pushing for a new campus and implying longer-range goals for the campus, but without listing any controversial specifics. At the student convocation on the Navy Pier campus on 20 October 1955, Henry outlined some of his concerns, seeing the development of a permanent urban campus as essential. "The urban student body of America is a very large and important one. The commuting students represent half the college population. The growth of the urban universities has made a major impact upon the equalization of educational opportunity and will continue to do so."[21]

In January of 1956, speaking before U of I alumni in Chicago, Henry called for a permanent Chicago "undergraduate center." Continuing the strategy of putting need before program specifics, Henry stressed issues of demand, equity and expense, arguing for a "regional distribution of educational service." "The University undergraduate center in Chicago located where its students live, meets the logic of demand, the equity of need, the expedience of minimum expense in serving the greatest number." Henry stressed the urgency of the task ahead: "We must make immediate progress in providing permanent facilities for the present program, even while the question of expansion of that program is under review."[22]

The following fall was the tenth anniversary of the Navy Pier campus, supposedly only a temporary institution. Convocation on 18 October 1956, was a celebration of the accomplishments of the campus and its faculty, as Henry praised the fact that over 37,000 students had attended the Chicago Undergraduate Division since its inception. Henry projected a permanent campus in 1963, seven years in the future, to the restrained applause of students, parents, and faculty. He announced that the University trustees had recommended a suburban site for the permanent campus site, in forest preserve land called "Miller Meadows," about twelve miles from Chicago's

Loop. "The University has made its recommendation in the best interests of the students who will use the campus, with a view to economy, accessibility, and the future growth of the community," but Henry did not elaborate, for as he put it, the "question is a highly technical one."[23] Henry placed the Chicago branch within the context of the larger University's needs. The U of I was growing by approximately one thousand students per year, necessitating new staff, faculty wage increases, new support for expanding academic programs in nuclear physics, computers, agriculture and medical research, student housing at Urbana (which had the lowest percentage of student housing in the Big Ten), and limitations on program facilities. While a priority, Henry made it clear that the Chicago campus was only one of many, in an age of overall university expansion.

Henry's discussion of the potential site for the new Chicago branch campus was significant, however, as he was generally supporting the proposed suburban location. Traditionally, the flagship Urbana campus had drawn students primarily from northern and central rural counties and from Chicago's suburbs, both wealthier and heavily Republican, while the students and faculty at the Navy Pier branch were in large part urban, ethnic, and Democratic. Most were first generation college students. This not-so-subtle political divide would shape the future of a new urban campus, both in its location and in its mission. While obviously aware of this division, Henry's main concern was in first rallying support for a new campus, one in which he had to raise financing for campus construction, while avoiding alienating potential supporters by making the new campus's mission too ambitious. As this was a common problem among many states as they expanded into urban higher education in the 1960s, it is useful to examine closely Henry's thinking as it evolved.

Henry's "Urban University" Ideal, 1958–1960

By the late 1950s, David Dodds Henry had emerged as one of the key national spokesman for the new "urban university." In a series of addresses at various urban universities around the country, such as at Wichita, Wayne University, Akron, as well as before the Association of Urban Universities (AUU), David Henry developed his understanding of the mission of an urban university. In late 1958, he collected his speeches together for an extended introduction to a proposed publication by the AUU on urban higher education, although it was never published. These texts provide an essential source for understanding Henry's thinking before the development of the program at U of I's Chicago campus. Here he stressed two main themes, access and service.

In Henry's view, as higher education developed in the twentieth century, there was a move away from pastoral settings due to the "economic impossibility of taking all students to rural areas." Strangely, though, he avoided addressing the Jeffersonian tradition, which had made educators suspicious of cities and urban life. Still, urban universities were to "emphasize functional education" and "vocational service," to "relate itself to the life of the community." Henry sought to articulate a distinct philosophy for the urban university, but he had a better idea of what it was not, rather than what its positive role could be:

> The urban university in the generic sense is still not widely recognized as a distinct type among the colleges and universities, nor are its mission and its character understood by the general public. It is much more than a poor man's college, proud as one may be of that designation; much more than an educational service station for the part-time student, vital as is that function; much more than a second-choice institution for those who would prefer to go somewhere else but cannot.

What he saw as primary was its service responsibility to its community. The urban university had "a special obligation to respond to the immediate educational needs of the community in which it is set"; consistent with appropriate university standards. Within those bounds, "it plans its offerings with direct reference to these needs; and that within the limits of its resources it is hospitable to all local requests for those intellectual services which a university may legitimately render."[24]

He placed special emphasis upon increasing access and opportunity to what a later generation would call the "non-traditional student." In an address at Wayne in 1954, reaffirmed years later in Illinois, Henry called for programs for "the adult searching for avocational and recreational satisfactions or self-improvement." He also expanded the concept of university research for the urban university, "to include application of research to any and all efforts that make for improvement in living, or add to our prosperity." Seeing little utility in the dividing line between basic and applied research, something that was increasingly becoming an important rhetorical device to defend the designation of "university" to an urban campus, Henry considered "any effort arbitrarily to exclude the university from applied research" as "an unnecessary, harmful limitation on free inquiry and comprehensive graduate training."[25] Yet in practice, and as any university researcher knows, this has the effect of collapsing basic research into applied training.

Community service then became central to Henry's conception of the urban university: "Thus, the urban university has come to be defined not only as one located in an urban center, serving the young people of the urban community, but as one which in many ways seeks to relate itself to its community. In thus interacting with its community, the urban university has deepened the dimension of direct community service from higher education." This was a common refrain:

> In the concept of a free and prosperous America, the university must be wholly in the service of the community—a service complete by the definition of those served and complete in the scope and variety of offerings." That community orientation would make the urban university as "an influence for community harmony," at the "core of community integration," a potential "neutral ground where partisans on all other issues may join in a common effort for furthering the public interest. The university has political immunity and commands social understanding and respect.

It was to focus on social research, staff consultation, hospitality to community organizations, and problem-solving. The urban university then could be "an instrument for the harmonization of the various elements in the general social structure."[26]

What Henry envisioned by 1960 was what he called the "community-centered urban university," which would emphasize two things: applied research, often of a contract nature with industry and government; and an openness to adult and continuing education students, which would include large numbers of part-time evening students in an "urban evening college."[27]

The Founding Years of the University of Illinois, Chicago Circle

This was Henry's vision for an ideal urban campus, but this vision was to undergo serious modifications over the next few years, as it clashed with the specifics of Chicago and Illinois politics. Henry's initial strategy for university expansion in Chicago was to concentrate on the physical construction of the campus, before the school's academic program was fully developed, as site selection, acquisition, campus planning, development, and construction were more dependent upon outside funding and the State's biennial budgeting structure than the academic program. Concerns involving the physical plant drove campus planning, as did the selection by Henry of Norman Parker to head the new campus. Parker, an engineer and head of Urbana's mechanical engineering department, had prepared some of the initial campus program planning documents in the late 1950s, but this was focused primarily on departmental space needs and location, rather than on academic programs.

In order to get the funding necessary for the construction of the Chicago Campus, it was essential to pass a large bond issue. The first bond issue had failed in 1958 and only narrowly passed in 1960. Even though the majority of funding went for universities throughout the state, only Cook County and the two downstate counties near St. Louis voted for the bond issue; downstate voters were generally opposed. Without the elective power of Mayor Daley's Democratic organization, the bond issue clearly would have failed. The city-downstate split in Illinois' political culture was to limit the expansion of the Circle Campus, and provided a restrictive context for its further development. In addition to downstate opposition to university expansion in Chicago, there was also hostility on the part of the region's private colleges. In order to get support in Springfield for the bond issue, David Henry and U of I needed to make a number of quiet commitments to the Chicago area private colleges, especially DePaul, Loyola, Roosevelt, and the Illinois Institute of Technology, that would limit the Chicago campus' growth. "We were narrowly prescribed as to what we could do," Norman Parker recalled later. "We were told to stay out of graduate work, we couldn't have a night program and we couldn't even offer evening courses without at least a year's notice." This "gentleman's agreement" also limited Circle Campus' expansion into dormitories and professional programs, such as law and business administration. Evening courses were not offered at Circle until over a decade later, and it was almost twenty years before a full night program was begun in limited disciplines. These two issues: downstate political opposition and the "gentlemen's agreement" with Chicago's private colleges, served to narrow Henry's original vision of UICC's "urban mission."[28]

The demand for a new campus was clear by the mid-1960s, as the Chicago Circle Campus soon became the fastest growing campus in the nation. Classes began at the new Circle Campus in February 1965, and the student body rapidly grew from around 5,000 at Navy Pier in fall 1964, to almost 8,500 in winter 1965–66, to 17,500 by winter 1970–71, Henry's last year as president. This was an increase of over 340 percent in six short years.

After the opening of Circle Campus, David Henry continued to sell his vision of an "urban university," but with a more limited scope due to the restrictions on a night school and professional programs. He was optimistic in speaking with the university's Citizen's Committee on 13 May 1966, in Chicago: "The Urban University in an urban America will be at the center of American thrust in days ahead," with its emphasis upon "issues of urban living," urban government, arts, and culture. His optimism, however, was tempered by a note of uncertainty: "Non-urban scholars will also have their contributions but the potential of the urban-located and community oriented campus remains to be fully defined."[29]

That December the campus was awarded a prize by the "Chicago Builder's Congress," where Henry took the opportunity to emphasize the direct and indirect economic impact of the university on the city. "Only recently have economists begun to treat education as economic capital, not just human capital and assess the measuring devices." He boasted of the $10 million annual payroll, plus the almost $100 million in building costs. About the only thing Henry did not boast in was the amount of concrete used in its construction, although that was probably why the builder's association awarded the prize. While clearly a sales-pitch, this was how Henry sold the Circle Campus to its urban environment. Of greatest importance was its "indirect economic benefits," for with the commuter campus, students lived, worked, and spent money in Chicago, with graduates often remaining in the city to work. Henry pointed to the campus's potential to attract business and industry, along with the availability of faculty expertise. "Someday," Henry hoped, "we may be able to put all of this into a formula."[30]

Intellectual Infrastructure:
Towards a Comprehensive University?

While Henry and Parker were concentrating on building the physical infrastructure, other administrators were creating the intellectual infrastructure of the new campus. University Provost Lyle Lanier, a psychologist and a member of the "Southern Agrarians,"[31] seemed to have wanted to create a research university in Chicago with an emphasis upon urban affairs, but still focused upon basic research.[32] In that aim, he was assisted by another psychologist, Glenn Terrell, who was dean of liberal arts at Chicago Circle, later becoming "dean of faculties," the school's chief academic officer. In 1967, he left to assume the presidency of Washington State University. While at Circle, Terrell concentrated on building up a strong, research-minded faculty, by hiring aggressive department heads, major scholars, and promising younger faculty. The watchword was to create a "UCLA in Chicago," a comprehensive research school which would rival Urbana. What this meant was a rapid expansion, not just to undergraduate education, but especially into graduate study, including the Ph.D., as quickly as possible.

However, Henry's vision of the Circle Campus was as an "urban university," defined by access and service, expanding educational opportunity for undergraduates and providing service to the city. Many of the new department heads, however, saw this as a limiting role that would relegate the new university to second class status, rather than as a potential equal to Urbana, Northwestern, and even, someday, the University of Chicago. Growing rapidly, with little direction from Circle chancellor Norman Parker, ambitious department heads were pretty much left to their own initiative to create new graduate programs. Most aggressive were the departments of philosophy, history, chemistry, and mathematics, which developed doctoral programs within two years of the move to the Circle Campus. Other departments under less aggressive leadership only slowly tried to catch up. An internal division quickly developed in the Circle Campus, between those faculty who emphasized teaching and who often had been retained from the Navy Pier campus, and the new research oriented faculty.[33] The latter soon came to feel that Henry was consciously restricting the growth at Circle Campus by trying to limit its role to that of an urban service school for undergraduates.

Internal dissension over the direction of the Circle Campus reached a crisis point in 1966, a little over a year after the campus had opened. In April, David Henry and Provost Lyle Lanier met with about forty-five of the key department heads and deans at the Circle Campus, trying to explain university organization and governance. Speaking from hand-written notes, Henry explained that the "objective for Chicago Circle administration has been maximum operational autonomy within university-wide structure." He was careful to explain the focus of the central administration, emphasizing that the "central administration is NOT an Urbana administration," and that department heads should make that clear to their faculty. Henry asked for "understanding and patience." A further concern was that "internal administrative unity" was "essential for progress," for external elements in the state were "quick to take advantage . . . to create uncertainty and lack of confidence." Competition for graduate work, new buildings, and new programs in the state and at the Board of Higher Education level was fierce, and "taking internal gripes and criticisms" to students, press, and legislature, "plays into the hand of those who would hold back the U of I." In his notes he had crossed out, but still thought, "some damage already done."[34]

The research-oriented faculty were not persuaded, for they doubted David Henry's and the larger University of Illinois' commitment to graduate study in Chicago. "There is evidence that the administration of the University, while now making public acknowledgment of the necessity for graduate study at Chicago Circle, is as a matter of fact impeding its development by means of its internal policies." In a publicly released memo, the research-oriented faculty listed numerous arguments, such as the need for graduate training in numerous fields as an entry for employment, and the lack of graduate training in anything but private universities in Chicago. One major argument was over faculty recruitment, for outstanding faculty "cannot be induced to join the university unless they have available the possibility of teaching at the graduate level and the means for pursuing their scholarly interests and research." They were skeptical of Henry's vision of a high-quality university devoted only to undergraduate instruction, pointing out as well that federal money was available for infrastructure construction, but only contingent on graduate instruction. This was especially true in the natural sciences and engineering.[35]

The faculty charged that the operating budget for Circle Campus was adequate to only maintain the campus, not rapidly to develop graduate programs. Especially damning, in their view, was the lack of serious funding for the library and inadequacies of laboratory space and equipment.

If the delays in construction materialize, Chicago Circle will be without a minimum graduate library, without research laboratories, and without major graduate programs in essential areas, until the fall of 1971. This five-year delay would not only damage our graduate programs extensively, but would also hurt the quality of our undergraduate instruction. It is inconceivable that Chicago Circle could assemble and retain a high quality faculty for the instruction of our undergraduates if library, laboratories and graduate programs are not at hand. The damage inflicted on this institution would extend far beyond the five year period under discussion. It is not unreasonable to state that, with this delay, the Chicago area would be deprived of a first-rate full university for another generation.[36]

By 1966, it was the perception of many faculty at Circle that Henry and his administration were "insensitive" to the needs of the Chicago campus. Within two years of its opening, the Circle Campus had seen some of its major faculty, with national reputations in their fields, resigning for other, more promising universities. Dean Glenn Terrell left in 1967, which further eroded the research emphasis on the Chicago campus. Faculty agitation for advanced graduate instruction was not completed, however, when a more serious challenge developed, although this time not between the Urbana campus and Chicago Circle, but rather at the State level.

Excursus: The Wayne State Centennial, 1968

In the midst of the increasing controversy in Chicago and in downstate Illinois, David Dodds Henry accepted Wayne State's invitation to keynote their centennial celebration on June 18, 1968. Henry spoke on the program theme, "The Urban University and Urban Society," and his address provides an important snapshot of his thinking in the midst of the Circle Campus controversy. Henry had been a national spokesman for urban university education for over fifteen years by that point, but his experience at Circle had chastened him. His own faculty was undermining his vision of access and service. Returning to Wayne gave him an opportunity to reflect on these experiences, but more significantly, they gave him a platform to respond to his most persistent critics, the research faculty at UICC. This speech should be interpreted as a rhetorical defense of his own work in Chicago, raising up Wayne as a successful model of an urban university, against the research faculty's vision of Circle Campus.[37]

David Henry was, of course, deeply honored to be chosen as centennial speaker, as he had spent almost half his professional life at Wayne University. He pointed to the rapid growth of the institution, with praise to the builders of the institution: "Let those under 30 remember that they were not the first idealists; that they were not the first missionaries of social service; that they were not the first to dream of improvements in our social structure." Educational opportunity was one of the chief purposes of the university, and Henry singled out for special praise Wayne's "urban commitment:" "Wayne was ahead of its time in its urban commitment," a position "not academically fashionable" in the 1930s and 1940s. Wayne's leaders "conceived of this institution as being uniquely related to this metropolitan community in the supply of graduates, in the applications of research and in extramural research to the community at large. We were told in those day that these objectives constituted a parochial approach to higher education, that the University's high academic goals would be blunted, that the search for relevance to the City would make the University educationally irrelevant," or, in perhaps a better phrase, though crossed off in his draft, "an educational service station rather than an educational powerhouse." Henry was pleased to call the critics wrong, for Wayne was able to attract capable faculty "into the laboratory which every great city constitutes," and its reputation has increased as the "problems of the cities are now seen as primary problems of the Nation."[38]

In that contentious summer, midway between the riots after Martin Luther King's assassination in April and the Democratic Convention in Chicago in August, Henry pointed to the nationwide expectation of "university contributions to the solution of urban problems." He noticed some limitations on that mission, first in "the epidemic of student convulsions on our campuses" especially when race was involved: "If public confidence in the university system can be weakened, all institutions will be irreparably damaged." Like many defenders of the university that summer, Henry reemphasized "reason, intellectual analysis, and rational debate" as the framework for university policy and governance. He defended institutional neutrality, seeing a second serious threat to the urban university in "the insistence of those who would alter its corporate character from one of neutrality in community conflict to one of social activism." Henry feared the loss of relative autonomy if universities as institutions were perceived as agencies of social transformation.[39]

The third great threat to urban higher education, he believed, was "the policy drift that transmutes institutional service into retailing of training at a low level of educational achievement. In my view, the concept of the 'urban grant' university as a parallel to the land-grant university of the 19th century is a false analogy." In a new note, he stressed the need to concentrate resources and focus on maintaining quality: "In servicing society, the highest utility [of universities] is in their distinctive functions, and if they become unduly enmeshed as agencies of social welfare, these functions will be eroded. We must be on our guard, therefore, against the inadvertent kind of mayhem which attenuates core purposes in a vast disarray of welfare services."[40]

Finally, with an interesting comparison, he drew explicit parallels between Wayne State and Chicago Circle, for each derived "its strength from its character as a people's university," with broad concern for public welfare, "unrestricted by elitism of any kind." He emphasized again the service function of the urban university: "Education for relevance must remain a constant in the changing public university." Both Chicago and Wayne, as "people's universities," emphasized the key functions of the university: "discovery of new knowledge, its useful application, the preparation of specialists and the broad education of all who seek it." There were many in Illinois, however, who would seek to use Henry's rhetorical vision of Circle to restrict its development, an irony that would be lost on Circle's research faculty and Henry, but one that was to be extremely significant for UICC's future. [41]

State Battles: The Attempted Dismembering of the University of Illinois

David Henry struck a new note at Wayne State with his emphasis upon the concentration of resources and the maintenance of quality, for there were serious threats to limit the University of Illinois' growth. Illinois in the mid-to-late 1960s was in the midst of serious turmoil over the governance of higher education. Before World War II, the University of Illinois was the only comprehensive public university in the state; the other institutions of higher education were basically normal schools or community colleges. U of I's Board of Trustees were state constitutional officers, elected on staggered six-year terms, like senators. After WWII, the normal schools throughout the state began expanding, leading to increased calls for state appropriations. Southern Illinois University, under a dynamic president and supported by a powerful state legislator, grew exponentially, gaining southern Illinois as its territory and seeking to supplant the University of Illinois' extension service in that part of the state.[42] University expansion was basically seen by legislators and the public as yet another interest, with legislators competing against each other to see who could bring state education money home to their districts. By the late 1950s, the situation called for coordination, if not state control, so a study commission was formed which recommended the creation of a central state Board of Higher Education (IBHE).

The IBHE was created in 1961, after the funding had been secured and planning was underway for Circle Campus. The IBHE was given a mandate to coordinate the further growth of higher education in the state and to create a series of master plans to manage its expansion.

The most important executive director of the IBHE in the 1960s was Lyman Glenny, who had been involved in the creation of the California system. Glenny definitely did not want to see Illinois develop a centralized system like that in California. Instead, he proposed what came to be known as the "systems of systems" approach, where university expansion would be governed under five different boards of trustees, with the IBHE to act as a coordinating and budgetary agency. Each "system" would govern a different "type" of university, such as the "multi-campus comprehensive land-grant" institution, the U of I; an "emerging multi-campus comprehensive university," such as the Southern Illinois University (SIU); the "liberal arts colleges"; and the regional normal schools. The fifth governing board would control the expanding community colleges.[43] Glenny and the IBHE informally adopted the "system of systems" approach in 1965, over the protests of David Henry and the University of Illinois, who saw the "systems of systems" as limiting U of I's ability to expand. The IBHE was also to manage the relations between the public universities and the private colleges and universities within the state, and the privates had representation on the IBHE. The rapid expansion of the student population in the late 1960s pushed the IBHE to propose, in addition to Circle Campus and SIU's branch in Edwardsville, near St. Louis, the creation of at first four, then two "senior colleges," which would provide the last two years of undergraduate education along with selected master's degree programs.[44]

In this context, David Henry had hoped for an increased role for the University of Illinois, to manage and in large part control the expansion of other universities in the state. But now, instead of having direct access to the legislature as he did before the creation of the IBHE, Henry had to go through this coordinating institution. The IBHE philosophy was based on regional balance and managed competition between schools, and thus was structurally, and with Glenny, personally, opposed to an increased role for Urbana. As the Circle Campus was being built, Henry sought to continue a two-year branch at Navy Pier, but this proposal was rejected, to the amusement of many at the IBHE. As the IBHE planned for two "senior colleges" in 1966–67, Henry sought to gain control over a proposed campus in the state capital in Springfield. At one private meeting, Henry pleaded with the chair of the IBHE's committee on governance, Jim Worthy: "Goddamn it Jim, we can have the new school open and running this fall, not sometime a couple of years from now. We've got curricula. We've got faculty. We've got the resources. All we have to do is rent a few store fronts and we'll have a new university." Yet this was exactly what the IBHE did not want; instead, they wanted innovative and tailored curricula, and that was felt could only be done outside Urbana's control.[45] Henry lost on his bid to increase the dominance of Urbana, and he watched as its relative share of the state budget diminished, as resources went to build up other institutions around the state.

The victory of Republican Richard Ogilvie in the 1968 governor's race dramatically changed the context of Henry's plans for the University of Illinois in general, and specifically the Circle Campus. Henry's limited vision of UICC's urban mission back-fired when the new governor appointed the former vice-chancellor at UICC, James Holderman, as executive director of the Illinois Board of Higher Education. The highly ambitious son of a prominent downstate Republican politician, Holderman had received his doctorate in political science, moving rapidly from the Urbana faculty to various administrative posts at Circle Campus, and finally vice chancellor in charge of administration. Barely thirty years old, Holderman had attempted to force out UICC's chancellor Norman Parker, but failing that, he jumped at the chance to head the IBHE. Assuming the executive director's position in July 1969, Holderman immediately sought to reorganize governance within the state university system, hoping eventually to dismember the University of Illinois by establishing Circle Campus as a freestanding institution.

Circle Campus had long had difficulties with autonomy from Urbana. All major hiring decisions, plus numerous minor administrative matters, had to be cleared with the Urbana administration. Earlier, in 1964, UICC head Norman Parker had complained of his limited, subsidiary role, but the only thing that had really changed since then was his title. One extremely telling example of Parker's limited authority was during the worst snowstorm in Chicago's history, in January 1967. Chancellor Parker had to get permission from President Henry before he could close the campus during the peak of the emergency, and that only after great difficulty and long delay.[46] In addition, there were severe restrictions placed on faculty involvement with City of Chicago departments, which seriously weakened the flexibility of faculty to develop working relationships. Most faculty and staff at UICC and at the IBHE realized that Circle needed increased autonomy.

Holderman used this desire for autonomy to build up pressure for a freestanding campus. Frequently declaring "the days of educational empire building in Illinois are over," Holderman attacked the expansion of graduate education. "During the 1960s," Holderman argued, "an extremely high demand for PhDs was created by the space program, plentiful foundation and defense funds for basic research . . . and ambitious industrial research programs. Unfortunately, much of the demand has now evaporated, but our massive national capacity for producing graduate degrees remains."[47] Holderman seized on the idea of "urban mission" as a means to break Circle Campus off from the University. He specifically targeted graduate programs, arguing that they unnecessarily duplicated private-university programs and competed with Urbana. He defined Circle Campus's "urban mission" like David Henry had earlier, as one of opportunity and service rather than graduate research. Under Holderman's administration of the IBHE, graduate programs at Circle Campus began to be turned down, and he moved to restrict ones that were already approved.

David Henry found himself increasingly on the defensive by 1970, as his earlier vision of "urban mission" was now being used to pressure for the dismemberment of the University of Illinois. Henry argued in stormy public hearings for the necessity of maintaining the link between Circle Campus and Urbana, for only then could it become a research institution. The establishment of the "senior colleges" was also a threat, for these further diluted increasingly limited state educational dollars. As the concept of "urban mission" became increasingly restrictive under Holderman and the IBHE, Henry sought to argue that the UICC was to become a research university, like Urbana, rather than like the more limited senior colleges: "Any change of campus governance at this critical point in [Circle Campus's] development would set the timetable for the development of the institution back many years, and would permanently deprive Chicago of a comprehensive state-supported educational institution if accompanied by the apparent change in mission contemplated for the Chicago Circle Campus under all three of the governance proposals." All three plans would all have made Circle a stand-alone institution and limited it to an urban mission of service and access.[48]

According to Henry, the university's long-range educational mission for the Circle Campus was "that the nation's second-largest metropolitan area should have a public university of the first rank—offering graduate, research, and public-service programs commensurate in scope and diversity with the varied needs of the area's people and with the magnitude of the problems of its physical environment."[49] It was not to be "a mere replica" of Urbana, for it would have "greater emphasis . . . upon professional education and applied research related to the problems of urban society," but it must remain "an integral part" of the University, "dedicated to the basic educational values of the land-grant movement, and determined to find creative expression for them in the complex and turbulent urban environment of the 1970s." Chicago needed a campus with "a level of quality in its unique spectrum of educational functions that would be essentially equivalent in general" to the main campus in Urbana. In addition to the need for a "broad spectrum of educational opportunity" that Circle Campus provided, Henry argued that "Only a public university *of the kind* conceived for the University of Illinois at Chicago Circle . . . would enable an urban society to make the kinds of investment in its human resources that are necessary to its viability and to its capability for self-improvement." To further emphasize the integral link between campuses, Henry pointed to the wide variety of advanced intercampus programs, for example, with the Medical Center campus in bioengineering, public health, and psychopharmacology, along with several joint plans with Urbana, such as in social work and survey research. The most significant reason, however, was the availability of federal and private funds for advanced graduate and research programs. If the Chicago campus was separated, "it is a virtual certainty that several hundred million dollars would be lost to the State and to the Chicago metropolitan region during the critical remainder of this century," for without the link to the University of Illinois, it "would be unable to attract the kinds and level of resources that will be available only to a major public university of top rank." Henry strongly defended the multi-campus system, for it is "the University's general thesis that all three of its campuses share common goals, even though each has a distinctive mission within the University system," for they "comprise a unified educational whole greater than the mere aggregation of its parts."

There are numerous ironies here as Henry sought to prevent the dismemberment of the University of Illinois. While in the earlier period, he had sought to limit Circle Campus to an urban service school, a "people's university" on the model of Wayne State, now, when powerful forces sought to create a fully autonomous campus that would emphasize urban service, Henry switched to defending Circle's research mission, in some ways conceding the point of the research faculty. Henry's vision of an urban university was modified in the face of the reality of competing political pressures.

Interestingly, the Chicago Circle faculty now strongly backed Henry and his rhetorical support for research at the UICC. As a colleague of Holderman's at the IBHE put it, "We felt very strongly Circle ought to be severed from Urbana so it could fulfill its unique urban mission. To our astonishment, we ran into extraordinarily loud and angry resistance from the faculty at Circle."[50] Indeed, one of Henry's most vocal opponents in 1966, chemistry department head Bill Sager, now was one of the chief defenders of the linkage between Urbana and Circle Campus. Holderman's strategy had backfired, for the strong research minded faculty at Circle, which had earlier clashed with Henry over his vision of a restrictive "urban mission," now publicly supported Henry and the ties of Circle to the Urbana Campus.

Retreat, Retrenchment, and Retirement

David Henry, with strong vocal support from the UICC faculty, was able to prevent the dismemberment of the University of Illinois, but another blow to his plans came soon afterwards. Governor Ogilvie, in his third budget that took effect on July 1, 1971, returned the proposed budgets for the public universities, saying that they were "outlandish." "We must take a hard look at our commitment to higher education in Illinois," Ogilvie declared in his budget message on 3 March 1971. "It is essential that we begin asking whether this system which has doubled its expenditures in the past four years has produced corresponding results. In the face of widespread student dissatisfaction and public impatience with the quality of higher education, it is essential that we ask why the system has failed to satisfy the very people it exists to serve."[51] Ogilvie's budget kept higher education equal to fiscal 1970, but redistributed the share, increasing support to private institutions and community colleges. The University of Illinois budget was reduced by $7 million, as was SIU's, but "state aid to private institutions (mostly medical) increased by $10 million, state support for community colleges rose by $7 million, as did student aid." As one later interpreter put it, "Although these developments were detrimental to the University of Illinois's ability to maintain its stature as a research university, they were far more damaging to the developing state universities with immature programs and less tradition," such as Chicago Circle.[52]

By this point, David Henry was sixty-five and ready to retire. He had served as president of the University of Illinois for seventeen years, longer than any other president to that point, and he realized that it was time to step down. In his last commencement address as President of the University, delivered in both Urbana and Chicago, in June 1971, one can sense the mood of foreboding and crisis: "American higher education is in a state of flux matched by few periods in its centuries-old history. The turbulent reassessment of traditional values and procedures so characteristic of the current generation of youth continues to affect the University as a whole and society in general." Henry saw that one of the key failures of universities was their inability to gain the understanding of the public that it was a special purpose community—with a specific purpose different from the larger society. Because of this, there was a broad loss of confidence in higher education, leading to a looming "financial crisis of major proportions," leaving universities "the prospect of receiving what is left over, after other public service needs are fulfilled."[53] Overall, the mood was of decline.

This dark outlook for the future of higher education continued, as Henry passed into his role as educational statesman. He served on Clark Kerr's Carnegie Commission on Higher Education, and later wrote a gloomy history of higher education, *Challenges Past, Challenges Future: An Analysis of Higher Education Since 1930.*[54] His thesis was that the 1970s were a far more serious crisis for higher education than the height of the Great Depression of the 1930s. He spent much of the decade organizing his papers and drafting a long, defensive memoir. A decade later, in the early 1990s, he drafted yet another memoir, privately published and dedicated to his grandchildren, entitled *Recollections in Tranquility.*[55] This second memoir emphasized the Wayne years, and had very little on Illinois. If it is true, as Garrison Keillor suggests, that, "no innocent man buys a gun, and no happy man writes his memoirs,"[56] it is significant that David Henry wrote two memoirs before he died.

Towards a New Model: The Urban Research University

The professional depression Henry felt in the mid-1970s was reflected at Chicago Circle as it approached its tenth anniversary. Enrollment had climbed over 300 percent since 1965, from 5,400 to over 18,000, where it roughly stabilized. Still, it lacked a sense of a distinctive identity. The chancellor at Circle, Norman Parker, stepped down when David Henry did, and Parker was replaced by physicist Warren Cheston. Cheston sought to move Circle towards open admissions, looking towards the model of the City College of New York, which had adopted that policy in 1969. Unwittingly, Cheston used the same rhetoric of "urban mission" that had proved so divisive before, and which predictably led to a faculty revolt almost immediately. Faculty opposition, budget pressures, plus personal scandal, plagued Cheston's tenure, and he soon announced his resignation.

In early June 1975, the *Chicago Sun-Times* published an extensive five-part report on the campus, entitled "UICC's 'Urban Mission?'" The first article was entitled: "Circle: university in name only?" under a heading "A 10-year identity crisis." The reporters found the university "still mired in confusion over what it means to be an urban university." While some of the problem was due to the "strife-worn, lame-duck chancellor" at Circle, more significant was its lack of central purpose or plan. Rather than a unified institution, it was "more a collection of medieval-like fiefdoms—the departments or colleges—led by feudal lords perpetually at war with each other and with the crown prince—the administration."[57]

The reporters reiterated the central problem with the university: "For 10 years, Circle has been unable to determine clearly what it should be about—its 'mission.' . . . Should it become a comprehensive, traditional university like UCLA, Michigan or Urbana? Or ought it be a unique, urban-oriented institution tailored to the particular needs of city students and metropolitan issues?" The reporters did not mention it, but perhaps Circle Campus was becoming an urban university after all, as it reflected the malaise of the city of which it was a part.[58]

David Henry continued his fight against the Circle faculty in his memoirs, where he strongly criticized the seeming failure of the UICC faculty to embrace an "urban mission." They had "too little understanding of the urban mission. Many of the faculty came from non-urban institutions and had no notion of the meaning of the charge to the Circle Campus. Worse, some had little enthusiasm for it." They modeled their efforts on traditional research universities, rather than embracing the "urban mission." But if the new faculty failed to understand this "urban mission," it was because Henry did not understand the significance of the attachment of the Chicago Circle Campus to the University of Illinois. Central to the mandate of the University of Illinois was graduate research, but Henry was critical of the speed by which aggressive faculty pushed for graduate research in Chicago. He insisted that his administration was "committed to the development of graduate work in due course, but felt that the first obligation was to fulfill the pledge made to the people of Illinois . . . completion of the undergraduate program, physically and educationally, would have priority."[59]

Yet given the nationwide dynamic of higher education in the mid 1960s, it was probably not possible to build a strong university without a serious commitment to advanced graduate training. The rapid expansion of the 1960s was followed by severe cut backs in the 1970s throughout the nation. Loss of public confidence was part of it, but external factors also limited funds available for higher education. Practically speaking, the University of Illinois had only about six years to create a university in Chicago of any type, and whatever was created, that was all that it had for the next two decades at least. Henry's vision of an "urban university" was based upon service and access, a limited role, and if this had been fully implemented, Circle Campus would have remained a limited institution. His vision clashed with many of the new faculty, who sought to create a "Harvard on Halsted"[60] or a new UCLA, which would have challenged Urbana. But given the competitive and democratic environment in Illinois, this was not realistic either, for the private schools successfully limited the Circle Campus at its founding with a "gentlemen's agreement," and the other colleges and universities in the state, both public and private, were able to distribute funding and resources throughout Illinois, balancing institutions rather than concentrating on a few peaks of excellence. Henry's idea of an urban university was a limited one—research, but limited to applied, rather than the basic research of a comprehensive research university. Yet the research faculty's position was also limited in its vision—in not seeing the significance of its location, and the possibilities of both the strategic situation and the University's position in a restricted and competitive environment. The research-minded faculty were right in pushing for rapid growth in graduate programs, for that was the way to develop a strong, nationally known faculty, and also to win the federal funding that was contingent upon graduate instruction, but they were not able to see the larger context of higher education in Illinois. Only when graduate research at Circle Campus was threatened by the IBHE's attempt to explicitly mandate a restrictive "urban mission," were David Henry and the research-oriented faculty able to make common cause. But by then it was too late for any major expansion, and thus Circle Campus was barely able to maintain its position.

Each of these visions for the University of Illinois at Chicago Circle was unrealistic, as it did not take into account the needs of Chicago and the dynamic of the advancement of knowledge. What was needed was to see the campus as a new model for a university, as a comprehensive urban research university. This would not be merely an analogy of the nineteenth-century land-grant model, but rather one which emphasized basic fundamental research in urban, regional, and national issues. Perhaps one smaller-scale example is the University of Chicago's first department of sociology in the early twentieth century, which, by focusing on local and regional issues, built one of the strongest research traditions in sociology, helping to make it an internationally known university. What was not seen in the 1960s, either by David Henry, the Circle research faculty, or even the IBHE, was that the University of Illinois at Chicago Circle was in the process of developing a new model of higher education, of the comprehensive urban research university.

Epilogue: Becoming a Research University

The story of the Circle's "urban mission" does not end in the 1970s, of course. Circle Campus struggled throughout the decade, limping along with limited finances and an undergraduate student body recruited through open admissions. As a commuter campus, it was known by many in the Chicago area as a school of last resort: "If you couldn't get in anyplace else, you could always go to Circle." In most disciplines, however, the strong, research-oriented faculty that had been hired during the period of expansion between 1965 and 1970 did not disappear, but continued to be productive scholars. Among fellow academics, Circle was known as a campus where its faculty were better than its students, a mediocre undergraduate campus with good graduate programs.

By the late 1970s, Circle's administration and faculty began to incrementally improve the campus, with a slow but steady increase in admission standards, the development of an evening program, and an expansion of graduate degrees. While these improved Circle, what really transformed the campus was the vision of a new University of Illinois President, Stanley O. Ikenberry, who took over U of I in 1979. Ikenberry had come from Penn State, and saw the university's potential. It was Ikenberry who transformed the Circle Campus into a research university.

Circle Campus had been built in the 1960s on Chicago's near west side, a little over a mile east of the University of Illinois' Medical Center campus. The Medical Center had had a long and distinguished tradition, with some of its academic units dating back to the mid-nineteenth century. After World War II, the Medical Center had expanded, adding colleges of nursing and allied health professions to its professional colleges of dentistry, medicine, and pharmacy, and developing strong graduate programs in the life sciences. Under David Henry's administration, there was virtually no contact between the Medical Center and the new Circle Campus. Each reported directly to Henry as president in Urbana, and virtually the only time Circle and Medical Center faculty and administrators came together was at Urbana.

When, in the late 1970s, Henry's successor as president, John Corbally, suggested publicly that perhaps the Medical Center should merge with Circle, Henry warned him against it. Corbally let it drop, and soon retired from the university. His suggestion was a shrewd one, however, for it allowed his successor significant flexibility. Ikenberry, as a new president, could safely explore the possibilities. If the merger idea failed, he could always blame his predecessor; if it succeeded, it would be his accomplishment. There was significant opposition from some at Circle Campus, and the College of Medicine was almost unanimously hostile to the idea. Ikenberry debated whether merging the campuses was the right decision.

Ikenberry realized that it was essential to consult with David Henry. Henry was still at Urbana as an elder statesman, where he served as an emeritus professor while writing his memoirs. Henry considered a possible merger as a disaster, saying that it was against Circle's urban mission, which was to be an undergraduate division of the university, without any graduate or research programs. Henry also believed that it would ultimately be a threat and rival to the flagship campus. After meeting with Henry, Ikenberry knew what he needed to do. "For me, that confirmed that I was doing exactly the right thing," Ikenberry later recalled.[61]

On his first day as president, Stanley Ikenberry walked through the neighborhood from the Medical Center to Circle Campus, symbolically linking the two and signaling that the merger would be his major policy goal. After three years and in the face of significant opposition, he succeeded in consolidating the two campuses, creating the University of Illinois at Chicago in 1982. That made the new campus the largest, most comprehensive research university in the Chicago area.

Ikenberry rejected the remedial "urban mission" idea for the new campus. "My view of the urban mission was that it ought to be our urban mission to become the very strongest university that we could possibly become in the inner city of Chicago."[62] Working with the faculty, Ikenberry continued the gradual rise in admissions standards, and he even created an Honors College at the Chicago campus. In 1987, the Carnegie Foundation published its new rankings, and it acknowledged the fact that UIC had become a Research I university, based on its funded research and production of doctoral degrees. In the mid-1990s, UIC developed its "Great Cities Commitment," as a major interdisciplinary research effort directed at urban issues, not only in Chicago, but also for urban areas worldwide. Through special funding, the Great Cities program implements hundreds of teaching, research, and service programs, ranging from urban transportation studies to neighborhood planning to public health initiatives. With a goal of "civic engagement," the Great Cities initiative has developed numerous partnerships with community and government agencies.

Within thirty years of its opening, UIC emerged as one of four major research universities in Illinois. The conflict over visions of its relation to the city had been resolved. While there was a strong institutional memory of David Henry's vision of an "urban mission," the campus had embraced the ideal of academic excellence, graduate education, and basic research. In becoming the University of Illinois at Chicago, the campus reconciled the two visions, possibly developing a new model in American higher education, the comprehensive urban research university. Only time will tell if this is indeed a distinct model for the future of higher education.

Notes

1. The origins of an "urban grant" idea has been traced to Paul Ysvilaker of the Ford Foundation, who first proposed a system of urban-grant universities at the annual meeting of the Association of Urban Universities in 1958. Maurice R. Berube, *The Urban University in America* (Westport, Conn.: Greenwood Press, 1978), 125. See J. Martin Klotsche, *The Urban University: And the Future of Our Cities* (New York: Harper and Row, 1966). Klotsche was chancellor of University of Wisconsin at Milwaukee. See also Clark Kerr's speech before the New York City College's Phi Beta Kappa chapter, "The US today needs 67 Urban Grant Universities to stand beside its 67 land Grant Universities," *New York Times*, 22 October 1967. It was printed by City College in a pamphlet, entitled "The Urban-Grant University: A Model for the Future" (New York: City College, 1968).

2. See George Rosen, *Decision-Making Chicago Style: The Genesis of a University of Illinois Campus* (Urbana: University of Illinois Press, 1980), and Adam Cohen and Elizabeth Taylor, *American Pharaoh: Mayor Richard J. Daley: His Battle For Chicago and the Nation* (Boston: Little, Brown, 2000).

3. David Henry, *Career Highlights and Some Sidelights,* Memoir, June 1983, p. 256. University Archives, President's Papers, David D. Henry Papers, 2/12/20, Box 25 (hereafter cited as DDH Papers). David Henry's papers are located in the University Archives, Urbana, Illinois. Henry had all his speeches as Illinois' president bound in orange bindings, with a concluding memoir, written between 1976 and 1984, bound separately. He later wrote a second memoir that was also privately published.

4. For a general history, see Roger L. Geiger, *Research and Relevant Knowledge: American Research Universities since World War II* (New Brunswick, N.J.: Transaction Publisher, 2004 [1993]).

5. The University of Illinois at Chicago (UIC) was officially formed in 1982, with the merger of Circle Campus with the University of Illinois Medical Center.

6. David Henry, *Recollections in Tranquility,* memoir, privately published in Florida (1993), p. 30. A copy is in the DDH Papers, Box 29. Other copies exist at Wayne State and The Pennsylvania State University.

7. Daniel Boorstin, "Universities in the Republic of Letters: A Review of Laurence Veysey's, 'The Emergence of the American University,'" *Perspectives in American History* 1 (1967): 371.

8. David Henry, *Career Highlights,* iii.

9. Ibid., 93.

10. An interesting irony, as Navy Pier would be the site of the temporary Chicago undergraduate campus of the University of Illinois, from 1946 to 1965.

11. Henry, *Recollections*, 12.

12. Ibid., 42.

13. Leslie L. Hanawalt, *A Place of Light: The History of Wayne State University. A Centennial Publication* (Detroit: Wayne State University Press, 1968).

14. See Henry, *Recollections,* 60.

15. Quoted in Ellen Schrecker, *No Ivory Tower: McCarthyism and the Universities* (New York: Oxford University Press, 1986), 91–92.

16. Winton Solberg, "Academic McCarythism and Keynesian Economics: The Bowen Controversy at the University of Illinois," *History of Political Economy* 29, no. 1 (1997): 55–81.

17. George D. Stoddard, *The Pursuit of Education: An Autobiography* (New York: Vantage Press, 1981).

18. There was suspicion in Chicago that the Urbana administration did not particularly favor a permanent branch in Chicago. The previous president, George Stoddard, had publicly dismissed calls for a full undergraduate campus, and the legislature had to force the trustees to do it, passing a bill to that affect in 1951. It took fourteen years for that campus to be opened.
19. Illinois State Senate, 64th General Assembly, Senate Bill No. 388 (1945).
20. David Henry, "A Call for Action," 1955, DDH Papers.
21. David Henry, "Convocation at Navy Pier," 20 October 1955, p. 3, DDH Papers.
22. David Henry, "Statement on 'Chicago Undergraduate Center,'" at alumni meeting, LaSalle Hotel, Chicago, 19 January 1956, DDH Papers, "A Call to Action," pp. 4, 6.
23. David Henry, "Navy Pier Convocation Speech," 18 October 1956, p. 5, DDH Papers.
24. David Henry, "Collection of Speeches for AUU," 1958, p. 9, DDH Papers.
25. Ibid., 14.
26. Ibid., 20–21.
27. Ibid., 18.
28. *Chicago Sun-Times*, 1 June 1975, p. 46.
29. Remarks before Citizen's Committee, 13 May 1966, Chicago Circle File, DDH papers, 2/12/20, Box 27.
30. David Henry, "Award of 'Chicago Builder's Congress,'" 1 December 1966, pp. 5, 9, Chicago Circle File, DDH Papers, 2/12/20, Box 27.
31. See Lyle Lanier, "A Critique of the Philosophy of Progress," in *I'll Take My Stand: The South and the Agrarian Tradition*, Twelve Southerners (New York: Harper, 1930).
32. There is some significant controversy over Lanier's role in Circle's development. As University Provost, Lanier had control of university academic affairs and Circle's expanding academic program, but he also worked very closely with Henry. What appears to be the case is that Lanier sought to increase the quality of Circle by encouraging the hiring of research faculty, while at the same time limiting their ambitions to expand into doctoral level programs that would unduly compete with the flagship campus in Urbana. This was an unsustainable position, although most of the Circle research faculty's anger was directed at Henry, rather than Lanier.
33. See Milton Rakove, "Research vs. Teaching: Our Circle Campus Opportunity," *Chicago Sun-Times*, 16 May 1965, sec. 2, p. 3.
34. David Henry, DDH Papers, 2/12/20, Box 3, and Adm. Org – Chicago Circle.
35. "Memo by Research Oriented Faculty," April 1966, Office of the UIC Historian Files, UIC.
36. Ibid.
37. David Henry, "The Urban University and Urban Society," address at the Wayne State University Centennial, 28 June 1968, p. 11, DDH Papers, 2/12/20, Box 12, manuscript 308.
38. Ibid.
39. Ibid.
40. Ibid.
41. Ibid.
42. Speaker of the Illinois House Paul Powell held the University of Illinois budget hostage until they acquiesced to Powell's desire to create a separate board of trustees for Southern Illinois University. See Robert E. Hartley, *Paul Powell of Illinois: A Lifelong Democrat* (Carbondale: Southern Illinois University Press, 1999), 50.
43. See Illinois Board of Higher Education, *A Master Plan for Higher Education in Illinois* (Springfield, Ill.: 1964).

44.   Carol Everly Floyd, "Centralization and Decentralization of State Decision Making for Public Universities: Illinois, 1960–1990," *History of Higher Education Annual* 12 (1992): 101–18.

45.   James Worthy memoir, privately published, chapter 11, p.14, Office of the UIC Historian files, UIC.

46.   Ibid., 28.

47.   Taylor Pensoneau, *Governor Richard Ogilvie: In the Interest of the State* (Carbondale: Southern Illinois University Press, 1997), 173–75.

48.   "University's Official Response to Board of Higher Education Study on Governance," *Faculty Letter From the Office of the President, University of Illinois*, no. 206, 6 November 1970, p. 8.

49.   *Provisional Development Plan*, p. 34, quoted in Ibid., at 10.

50.   *Chicago Sun-Times*, 2 June 1975, p. 26.

51.   Pensoneau, *Governor Richard Ogilvie*, 183–84.

52.   Roger Geiger, *Research and Relevant Knowledge*, 265.

53.   David Henry, "A Crucial Confrontation in a Turbulent Time," Commencement address, 19, 20 June 1971, p. 10. in *Interpreting the Public University and the Land-Grant College Tradition, 1955–1971*, ed. David D. Henry (December 1976), 796, DDH Papers.

54.   David D. Henry, *Challenges Past, Challenges Future: An Analysis of Higher Education Since 1930*, The Carnegie Council Series (San Francisco: Jossey-Bass Publishers, 1975).

55.   David Henry, *Recollections in Tranquility* (1993).

56.   Garrison Keillor, *Lake Wobegon Days* (New York: Viking, 1990).

57.   *Chicago Sun-Times*, 1 June 1975, p. 5.

58.   See, for example, Janet Abu-Lughod, *New York, Chicago, Los Angeles: America's Global Cities*, (Minneapolis: University of Minnesota Press, 1999), especially her chapter on Chicago from the 1970s to the 1990s, entitled, "Postapocalypse Chicago."

59.   David Henry, *Career Highlights*, 257.

60.   The main street through the Circle Campus was called Halsted.

61.   Stanley O. Ikenberry, interview by Fred Beuttler, Office of the UIC Historian, 9 November 2000, p. 13.

62.   Ibid., 16.

Review Essay

From Donnish Dominion to Economic Engine: Explaining the Late 20th-Century Revolution in English Higher Education

John F. Halsey and W. Bruce Leslie

Throughout most of the twentieth century discussions of higher education in Britain were, like higher education itself, confined to a small group of people. Universities were presumed to be outside the experience of most Britons. The small-scale, intimate Oxbridge college provided the model. Higher education enjoyed considerable autonomy, even when public funding provided most of the resources, but without a strong connection to the wider society it lacked a public constituency. Since the Robbins Report of 1963, higher education has been a matter for a wider public debate, a debate sharply politicized by Mrs. Thatcher's budget cuts of 1981. This essay reviews three scholarly monographs and a government White Paper that shed light on Britain's rapid transition from an elite to a mass system of higher education, one whose tidal waves have even lapped at the once impregnable defenses of Oxbridge. The narrow, pre-1963 debate limited the sector's place in the affections of the British public, forcing the Major and Blair governments to justify their arguments for expansion on narrowly instrumental grounds.

Harold Silver, *Higher Education and Opinion Making in Twentieth-century England* (London: Woburn Press, 2003).

Joseph A. Soares, *The Decline of Privilege: The Modernization of Oxford University* (Stanford, California: Stanford University Press, 1999).

Ted Tapper and David Palfreyman, *Oxford and the Decline of the Collegiate Tradition* (London: Woburn Press, 2000).

Department for Education and Skills, *The Future of Higher Education* (Stationery Office, 2003).

History of Higher Education Annual 23 (2004): 143-165.
©2004. ISBN: 0-7658-0839-0

Throughout the year 2003, higher education regularly made headlines in English newspapers. From January, when Tony Blair's government issued its White Paper on higher education (*The Future of Higher Education*), until the parliamentary vote a year later, debates, editorials, and even street demonstrations sought to sway public opinion. When the vote finally came in January 2004, Blair barely overcame an unprecedented revolt in his Labour Party. This fierce and very public debate over higher education jars with the enduring image of sophisticated Oxbridge "dons" blissfully secluded from outside pressures. Higher education in Britain seems to have changed beyond recognition, and done so very quickly. As late as 1990 when Margaret Thatcher was ousted as prime minister, the UK had the least accessible higher education among developed countries. Little more than a decade later it arguably led the world in the proportion of its young people attaining degrees. David Lodge's marvelous novels contrasting the slow-paced, inefficient "University of Rummidge" with California's high-energy "Euphoria University" are still funny but, like Monty Python skits denigrating Australian wine, now seem to come from a different age.

Not only did the world of English higher education appear to be insulated from external demands, but its inhabitants took it for granted that few could benefit from being included, and few would have any interest in universities apart from those who had shared their experience inside Oxbridge, or institutions modeled on Oxbridge. And higher education in other countries, even the United States, was seen as a far away world which had little if anything to teach them.

The separation from economic considerations allowed academics to direct their own activities in what A. H. Halsey called "donnish dominion," and the small scale enabled them to give students individual attention. But this ultimately had a price, since the vast majority of people had no connection with universities, and critics saw them as an obstacle to social mobility rather than its means. When higher education needed political support, it had few friends apart from those in high places and at High Tables.

Has "massification" changed everything? These four works explicate various aspects of the revolution in English higher education and express the uncertainty that pervades its practitioners. The first provides the historical context for the changes, two write from the seemingly indomitable Oxbridge, and the last, the Blair government's White Paper, exemplifies many of the changes.

The Cozy World of English Universities, 1900–1970

As Harold Silver's *Higher Education and Opinion Making in Twentieth-century England* demonstrates, for most of the twentieth century, higher education in England was an enterprise that attracted little public interest and whose direction was decided by small coherent reference groups. For the first seven decades the opinions that shaped academia were rarely "public," and the debates he discusses attracted little outside attention.

It was not always so. In 1867, John Stuart Mill gave his famous inaugural address as the Rector of the University of St. Andrews, in which he argued that it was not the purpose of a university to give students professional training, but instead to expose them to the "light of general culture." Mill's lecture was immediately published in a widely circulated "People's Edition." But, for much of the following century discussions in England about the nature and value of higher education took place within a narrow social milieu whose members did not address the people. Indeed, they did not seem to recognize the idea of a "general culture." Universities were set apart.

Discussions in the early twentieth century centered on the cautious expansion of the civic universities founded in the nineteenth century, mainly in the industrial cities of the Midlands and the North. This caution was already entrenched; in 1888 the Victoria University had been created as one federal university rather than three separate ones (in Manchester, Leeds and Liverpool) because of "a certain timidity, a fear lest an increase in the number of degree-giving bodies should reduce the value of degrees" (Silver, p. 15). What went on in the university was necessarily a minority taste. Too many students would spoil the consommé. This contrasts dramatically with the United States, where no matter what one's religion, race, ethnic group, sex, or state, there was almost sure to be an institution connected to an aspect of one's identity.

In Britain, exclusiveness rather than inclusiveness ruled, and the role of higher education in social reproduction was rarely questioned. Much of the recruitment into elite positions came from the universities, and access to university education was disproportionately skewed towards the sons (and much later the daughters) of people at the top. It is hardly possible to overstate the lack of connection between the universities and the general population. In a society that was, in George Orwell's phrase, "the most class-ridden under the sun," this was no surprise.[1] The social separation between social classes was reflected in the segmented education system.

Not all the writers Silver discusses wrote within this elitist paradigm. In 1920, Lord Haldane advocated that universities become much more involved with the broader society; he was a great champion of adult education. For reasons both of social justice and national economic interest, Haldane believed it was wrong to exclude so many young people from university. Those advocating the creation of new institutions in places such as Hull argued that a university could be a driving force in the life of the community. But for most English writers about higher education, Oxbridge remained the ideal type.

Silver provides an intriguing example in the work of "Bruce Truscot" (the pseudonym of E. Allison Peers, professor of Spanish at Liverpool University). Truscot's book *Red Brick* (1943),[2] argued forcefully for reforming the twelve civic universities into residential institutions that would expand the system along preexisting values. Central to these values was a shared domestic life; students who lived in university residences had a quality of university experience that was denied to those who lived at home or in "digs." His book had wider appeal than most of the writers Silver discusses, but again the Oxbridge college provided the norm.

Indeed, the debates seemed to be an extended dialogue with Cardinal Newman. Silver convincingly (but surprisingly given the secularity of modern England) shows that religion played a prominent role. For instance, Walter Moberly's very influential *The Crisis in the University* (1949)[3] was inspired by a conference convened by the Student Christian Movement and the Christian Frontier Council.

The world Silver describes had the advantage of permitting coherent discussions of the purpose of higher education, mostly about cautious evolution within agreed boundaries. But whether they were advocating change, like Adolf Lowe,[4] or stressing cultural continuity with the past, like F. R. Leavis,[5] most writers addressed themselves to insiders.

This continued to be true even after the watershed year of 1946 when, for the first time, government provided more than half the funding for higher education. Since they took it for granted that few people could appreciate university education, opinion-makers, and those they sought to influence, belonged to a small social group. The debate was carried on in the rarified atmosphere of the correspondence columns of *The Times*, or the *Universities Quarterly*. Michael Oakeshott even argued in the 1950s that it was unfortunate to ask what a university was for, since it was "not a machine for producing a particular result; it is a manner of human activity" (Silver, p. 136). Peter Finch helpfully explained that to ask what the purpose of a university was, or should be, was to commit a category mistake, "since universities belong to a category which does not logically permit the predication of a purpose" (Silver, p. 136).

To a remarkable extent, governments accepted this. The University Grants Committee acted as the bridge between the state and the universities, but allowed relatively little traffic to cross. The mere fact that the state was providing most of the funding the academics spent did not mean that it had any place in telling them how to spend it.

Universities were divorced from the experience of the vast majority of people who, it was assumed, had no engagement in the life of the mind. For them higher education resembled the House of Lords, a venerable institution which added luster to the fabric of the society in some mysterious way, but did not appear to touch their lives at all.

Although it has had a lasting impact, this elitism could not last. When higher education needed greater resources, it could not draw on popular affections. Most people had little idea what use it was. And when it was attacked, English academia had few allies.

From Donnish Dominion to Academic Accountability

The famous Robbins Report of 1963 may be taken as the transition to the new world of English higher education. Its central principle was that every student with the ability and desire to participate in higher education should be able to do so. That entailed expansion. But still the Oxbridge collegiate model remained the policymakers' gold standard. Making existing universities much bigger would deviate too far from the collegiate ideal. The immediate result of Robbins was a new generation of institutions that were mostly built in non-industrial cities. Indeed they even sounded like a Shakespearian dramatis personae: York, Essex, Sussex, Lancaster.

Nevertheless, Robbins changed English higher education profoundly. From then on every government would have a policy on higher education. The direction of thinking is illustrated by the changing names of the government department responsible for educational policy: from Department of Education, via Department for Education and Employment, to Department for Education and Skills. Higher education expenditure would have to jockey for position with competing public spending priorities. Universities were expected to contribute to economic growth, and, later, to be part of the attack on social exclusion. Internally, the growth in the role of university administrators spelled the end of "donnish dominion." And the expensive tradition of unhurried personal contact between tutor and student would increasingly be under threat.

All this coincided with profound changes in British society in the 1960s. The postwar years of economic growth came to an end, and for several decades the story of the British economy would be one of decline by comparison with other industrial capitalist societies in Europe and North America. From the last days of the Macmillan government onwards, the language was of the need for economic innovation and modernization, and for financial self-discipline and value for money.

The social structure had also changed. Observers still saw the English as people who were separated into social classes, and who immediately classified one another on the basis of the way they spoke, but there was a new fluidity to the class system. The idea of a limited "pool of ability" was rejected, and social deference was in terminal decline.

Robbins's argument for expansion was based both on economic efficiency—the need to stop wasting part of the population's potential—and social justice—no one with the academic qualifications should be excluded. Those, like Kingsley Amis, who shouted "More Means Worse," were fighting a losing battle.

The Labour victory in 1964 gave added impetus to expansion, upgrading technical colleges into "polytechnics," a full-fledged part of higher education, though on the second rung of a "binary" system. Leaving the polytechnics under the auspices of local government emphasized their lack of autonomy and their links with the local community.

The "stagflation" of the 1970s influenced policymaking profoundly. The 1972 White Paper made it explicit that the future of the sector would reflect demographic changes and the state of the economy. Higher education was a significant item of government expenditure, and when the government needed to make economies, higher education would not be spared. Most expansion would take place in the polytechnics, which had lower unit costs. There were fewer references by governments to the intrinsic value of education, than to "value for money." Policy documents, both Conservative and Labour, began to speak of "contraction and closure, amalgamation, cost effectiveness, efficiency, selectivity, concentration, standards, quality—all acting as proxy for the parent vocabulary of (greater) accountability" (Silver, p. 212).

But it was the Thatcher government that administered the shock therapy in the 1980s. Media images of protesting students and smug radical dons played into Thatcherite analysis of English economic underperformance. In July 1981, the government announced cuts in the recurrent grant amounting to 17 percent over the next three years. This went further than simple budgetary belt-tightening. The University Grants Committee (UGC) had already become significantly more involved in university management, even specifying institutional targets for student numbers in arts and science subjects. By 1985, when the government's plans for the development of higher education into the 1990s were published, it was clear both that the key consideration for higher education policy was economic, and that the state's role would be central.

All three books describe how those drastic cuts and demands for accountability left an indelible impression on English academia. The government threatened closures and ended tenure. The UGC was replaced by the less friendly Higher Education Funding Council for England. Then, in the early 1990s, John Major's government removed the growth cap. Its goal of doubling access to one-third of young people was quickly met and Tony Blair then upped the ante to one-half. Enrollments of women and mature students especially surged. But more accountability than funding accompanied this leap into mass higher education. Spending per student plummeted, and the need to manage the changes meant inevitably that key decisions were no longer taken within departments. The academics struggled with their loss of autonomy under the new managerialism. The locus of direction setting had clearly shifted from the educational visionaries described by Silver to the bureaucrats of central government and central administration. And the goals of higher education were to be consonant with the governments' political needs.

In a few short years, British higher education had been transformed. The growth from an age participation index in single figures in the 1960s, to 17 percent in 1987, 32 percent by 1995, and in 2003 43 percent, had effects across the board. Unit costs were reduced, with a worsening of staff-student ratios, and corresponding "productivity gains" of twenty-five percent since 1990. Universities grew larger, partly through mergers. They developed marketing strategies to compete for bright students and productive faculty.

The Robbins Report said relatively little about what universities were for. What was significant about Robbins, Silver argues, is that it represented a change in the way the debate about higher education was conducted in England. No longer were professional academics talking largely to one another; now there was greater public interest in universities, and what was more, the pace and the agenda were being set "by governments, committees, official reports and those who spoke on their behalf" (Silver, p. 165).

The terms of this public interest were narrowly instrumental. Cultural exposure, citizenship, well-roundedness, and ethics played little role. To be sure, these authors warn us not to exaggerate the shift towards materialism. Tapper and Palfreyman maintain that labor markets and generating intellectual capital have always driven higher education and Silver points out that economics has always provided the context. But the extent to which expectations of higher education have been limited to economics is striking, especially in a trans-Atlantic context.

The image that higher education was above economic concerns made it vulnerable to the charge that it was failing to respond to the modern world and indeed was part of the problem rather than the solution. Most people had accepted that universities were not for them, and so higher education was, as the saying goes, of academic interest only. The idea that higher education should address the position of marginal groups in society, which is taken for granted in any discussion of public colleges and universities in the United States, was rarely advanced. Those advocating a greater public investment in higher education could draw on no available understandings of its role other than the instrumental argument for an expanded number of graduates.

Having disdained the majority of the population for so long, the universities had few allies to defend themselves from successive governments' economic expectations. For those who have seen England as a bastion of academic values and liberal education, the shift toward instrumentalism is shocking.

Will There Always be an Oxbridge?

What about Oxbridge? Oxbridge remains the lodestone that turns all compasses in English higher education. Even after a decade's headlong rush into mass higher education, Oxford and Cambridge continue to attract a lion's share of scholarly attention, including two books reviewed here. Tapper and Palfreyman admit that they write from the stance of those "who have been both seduced and infuriated by the magic of Oxbridge" (p. xi).

The changes that characterized post-World War II higher education in England can be seen writ small in Oxford. Soares describes a prewar Oxford, which included a good many of the elements in the image portrayed in *Brideshead Revisited*—it was an elitist, leisurely institution with a humanistic bias. Women, scientists, and those conducting research were marginal. The colleges were largely autonomous, and the University's central management had a minimal role. After the war Oxford changed. By the early 1960s, 40 percent of faculty were in science and technology, although most were still socially marginal as few were members of a college. In 1964, all faculty were brought into the college system. Tapper and Palfreyman show that this profoundly affected the relationship between the colleges and the University. Science teaching was incorporated as far as possible into the framework of the college tutorial system, but inevitably much of the organization of science teaching had to be undertaken centrally. Both because of the scale of new scientific knowledge, and because it needed to be taught systematically and sequentially, University lecture courses had to be developed. The role of the University increased, at the expense of collegial donnish dominion.

Soares' account of Oxford's modernization includes a fascinating discussion of something that gained importance in Britain under the Labour governments from 1997: social inclusiveness. In 2000, the Chancellor of the Exchequer Gordon Brown made Oxford's rejection of a state school applicant (who was admitted by Harvard soon afterwards) a cause célèbre. How inclusive is modern Oxford? Drawing on Daniel Greenstein's analysis of the social origins of Oxford students between 1900 and 1967, Soares makes the dramatic claim that the modal Oxford student now has a "modest" social background. This is a difficult case to make.

What is certainly true is that after World War II the university introduced a number of meritocratic reforms, including the elimination of the paradoxically named "commoners." These men were no more "common" than the Public Schools they had attended were public; they were usually from wealthy families; they had weak academic credentials and little work was expected of them. Their places were taken by hard-working students of demonstrable ability. But this shift towards meritocracy is not the same as a greater social inclusiveness. The reforms encouraged the private sector of secondary education in Britain to focus on academic achievement in order to maintain its links with Oxbridge. Even fifty years later, almost half of Oxford students came from private secondary schools, compared with just over 20 percent for British universities as a whole.

Modern Oxbridge is, as Soares shows, socially more wide-ranging than it used to be. Greenstein's analysis shows that the percentage of "new men" at Oxford, undergraduates whose fathers were "manual workers, clerks, small shopkeepers," and "boys with fathers in industry" increased from 16 percent before the First World War to 38.4 percent after WWII (p. 101). But these categories are imprecise. There are, for example, widely different kinds of jobs "in industry." Some of these "new men" were newer than others. And Soares' interchangeable use of terms such as "working class" (p. 2), "blue collar"(p. 2), "the lower classes" (p. 36), and "white- and blue-collar working class" (p. 101) compounds this difficulty. Certainly there are fewer toffs. By the 1960s "fewer than half as many sons of lords attended Oxbridge as had done before the war"(p. 103). Although the social origins of its students are more modest than they once were, Oxford is still much posher than most British universities. At the end of the century, figures from the Higher Education Statistics Agency showed that while just over half (52 percent) of the UK students admitted to higher education came from the top two social classes, the figure for Oxford was 79 percent.

The persistence of this social profile made Oxbridge vulnerable to three successive hostile governments, which were determined to make universities more entrepreneurial and open. As Joseph Soares vividly describes, Oxbridge's mystique came back to haunt it. The hostilities were opened by one of Oxford's own—Margaret Thatcher. As a scientist and a woman, she had been outside the charmed circle of Oxford collegiate life in the 1950s. She was amenable to the idea that Oxbridge's pretensions bore much of the blame for England's economic woes.

The leisurely, individualized teaching style, indeed the whole collegiate system, is under pressure according to Tapper and Palfreyman. The tutorial system may be the jewel in Oxbridge's crown, but it is increasingly difficult to reconcile with the need to produce high-level research. As unit resources fall, Oxbridge can no longer assume support for whatever direction it charts. But it can resist government pressure better than the other 100+ universities. Only Oxford and Cambridge have endowments that would place them among the top 100 in the United States.

However, as that wealth is very unevenly distributed between the colleges, only the wealthy few can contemplate foregoing some of their government funding in exchange for greater autonomy. Tapper and Palfreyman foresee a very uncertain future, with several possible results for the collegiate tradition. They are betting that the colleges will differentiate more dramatically between richer ones focusing on research and the rest on teaching. In their most likely scenario, teaching and research become separate career paths and the collegiate tradition is marginalized.

The challenge for those who enjoy the "pleasing social context" of the Oxbridge college (to quote one of Tapper and Palfreyman's interviewees) is to avoid being perceived as smugly irrelevant. If Oxbridge does become increasingly disconnected from the rest of the sector, not everyone will regret it. Silver recounts that as long ago as 1960 Lord Hailsham, whose grandfather had played such a central role in developing the Regent Street Polytechnic in central London, told a conference that Oxbridge's very excellence had a baleful influence on the rest of the sector, by making it harder for institutions to respond to local need.

Instrumentalism Triumphant—The Blair White Paper

The Labour Government's proposals for higher education, as detailed in its very controversial White Paper, *The Future of Higher Education*, and amplified in the legislation narrowly approved in January 2004, are based on three central ideas, all of which echo concerns of the past. Higher education in Britain needs to expand in order to make Britain economically competitive, universities are underfunded, and too few young people from poorer families are attracted into higher education. The expansion of the sector is designed to achieve Tony Blair's often-repeated target of an age participation ratio of 50 percent. The measure that incited fierce public debate and attracted headlines allows universities to increase their tuition fees from £1125 a year to £3000. This looks like a strange way to seek to attract under-represented groups into higher education, but the innovation is that all loan payments will be deferred until a graduate's income reaches £15,000.

The idea of differential pricing for domestic students is quite new to British universities (derided as "marketization" by opponents), and so it is hazardous to predict how it will work, but the overwhelming majority of universities say that they plan to charge the full amount. Prestigious universities will not want to charge less for fear of looking cut-price. And some of those serving the least advantaged students intend to charge the full amount in order to maximize their aid to poorer students.

Clearly, these proposals mean even greater regulation by government. For instance, the price of increasing fees will be greater transparency in admissions. Thus, universities that charge more will have to demonstrate that they aggressively recruit students from underrepresented parts of society.

The White Paper's other proposals attracted less public debate, but are a historical shift in the structure of higher education. To compete internationally, research funding will be directed at a small number (guesses range from four to twenty) of research-intensive universities. Most universities will become "non-research-intensive," dropping their doctoral programs and assuming a role similar to American comprehensive and liberal arts colleges. And in order to reach Tony Blair's goal of 50 percent participation, the White Paper redefines higher education by proposing two-year "foundation courses." These job-related programs will be offered either by existing universities or by further-education colleges and resemble the curricula offered in American community colleges. The proposed structure is strikingly similar to the American pattern of research-intensive universities, four-year colleges, and community colleges. Indeed the White Paper specifically draws attention to the fact that relatively few American colleges and universities award doctorates, and offers the California State University system's twenty-three campuses as examples of successful teaching-centered universities.

Since 1992, the United Kingdom has had a "one size fits all" system. The influential Research Assessment Exercise results in league tables that rank on the same scale all "universities" (about

115, each with doctoral granting rights) ranging from poorly funded former institutes of higher education to Oxbridge. The White Paper returns to differentiation, but instead of the pre-1992 "binary" divide, there is to be an American-style "trinary" system.

For historians, the White Paper raises the question of whether the post-WWII European social democratic model of free, or nearly free higher education can survive mass higher education. The White Paper explicitly accepts a more American model that demands higher contributions from students and more entrepreneurial activity by universities. It justifies these changes partially on the grounds that higher education is a private as well as a public good and to fend off the threat that rich American research universities will lure the best UK researchers. The White Paper is also a historic marker for what it does not say. It promotes higher education almost solely on economic grounds. The ideals, enunciated by Newman and Mill in the nineteenth century, that shaped the debates Silver describes in the first six decades of the twentieth century, are absent. The idea of contributing to the civic mission or cultural development barely receives lip-service. And Oxbridge is valued not for the collegiate system and humanistic learning, but for world-class research. Immediate economic payoff in what is seen as a threatening world is a nonnegotiable demand.

Conclusion

These books enable us to locate the origins of changes that shocked academia when they hit with ferocity in the 1980s. The White Paper culminates trends that, with hindsight, can be traced back to the Robbins Report.

Interestingly, none pays much attention to the dramatic difference between Thatcher's policies and those of her successors, one Conservative and one Labour. Whereas Thatcher sought to limit enrollments, John Major threw open the doors. The result was two different sets of financial pressures, the first resulting from the economic doldrums of the 1970s and Thatcher's cuts in the 1980s, and the second from slowly increasing government funding in the 1990s overtaken by skyrocketing enrollments.

The three books give us penetrating insights into the world of Oxbridge, and at times the Redbricks, where the dramatic increase in governmental involvement and the resulting accountability that has penetrated the donnish world are the main concerns. Changes in

Oxbridge governance loom larger in these books than the tripling of participation in higher education. The White Paper proposes a future with half of youth in higher education, many in institutions that cannot afford to sustain the collegiate tradition and with students who are not attracted to cloisters. Historians must also explicate this world of mass higher education, where English higher education has been fundamentally revolutionized in unexpected ways.

Notes

1. George Orwell, *The Lion and the Unicorn* (Harmondsworth: Penguin Books, 1982 [1941]), 52.
2. Bruce Truscot, *Redbrick University* (Harmondsworth: Penguin Books, 1951 [1943 as *Red Brick*]).
3. Walter Moberly, *The Crisis in the University* (London: SCM Press, 1949).
4. Adolph Lowe, *The Universities in Transformation* (London: Sheldon Press, 1940).
5. F. R. Leavis, *Education and the University* (London: Chatto & Windus, 1979 [1943]).

Review Essay

Encyclopedias as Institutional History

Roger L. Geiger and Christian K. Anderson

Wayne Somers, ed., *Encyclopedia of Union College History* (Schenectady, N.Y.: Union College Press, 2003), 848 pp.

Alexander Leitch, *A Princeton Companion* (Princeton, N.J.: Princeton University Press, 1978), 559 pp.

Martha Mitchell, *Encyclopedia Brunoniana* (Providence, R.I.: Brown University Library, 1993), 629 pp.

If the history of higher education is defined by activities in colleges and universities, its corpus grew appreciably in 2003 with the publication of Wayne Somers' massive *Encyclopedia of Union College History*. With 828 entries in about as many double-column pages, this volume makes accessible an abundance of information about this historically important institution. Founded in 1795 with hopes of uniting Protestant denominations, the college began to thrive shortly after the amazing Eliphalet Nott began his sixty-two-year presidency in 1804. Under Nott Union emerged as one of the major institutions of the era. It sometimes graduated more students than the largest college of the antebellum era, Yale, although with a lower enrollment (as Somers explains, pp. 263–65); and it stood for a time as a kind of anti-Yale in curricular innovation and a more relaxed approach to student discipline. Not by chance, mid-century reformers Francis Wayland and Henry Tappan both graduated from Union. But Nott presided over Union far too long—until his death in 1866 at age ninety-two. By that date the college was in serious decline, plagued by shrinking enrollments, mismanagement and, ironically, a type of inbred conservatism. The college's trials and eventual recovery to become a solid liberal arts college in the twentieth century provide less distinctive but still historically interesting material. Union's history thus has relevance for two eras—as an innovator during the first half of the nineteenth century and as a somewhat representative Eastern liberal arts college in the twentieth. The *Encyclopedia* is enlightening about both these eras, and about far more. Perhaps equally intriguing is the genre itself: an encyclopedia of institutional history.

Not that the genre is likely to inspire a flood of imitators. Serious institutional histories are difficult enough to produce, requiring planning, patience, institutional support, and talented authors.[1] But encyclopedias demand monomaniacal dedication. Wayne Somers, who wrote 726 of the entries, devoted half of his time for over ten years to this volume (which was optimistically commissioned in 1991 for the college's 1995 bicentennial). His model was *A Princeton Companion*, which despite its modest title aspired from the start to be a comprehensive work of reference.[2] That project occupied Alexander Leitch for more than a decade following his retirement as Secretary of the University. He personally authored some 80 percent of 438 entries. Shortly after Somers began, Martha Mitchell published *Encyclopedia Brunoniana*. Having long been the university archivist no doubt helped her compose 667 entries (with some assistance) in only five years.

The genealogy of institutional encyclopedias does not end here. The apparent progenitor of this species is *The University of Michigan: An Encyclopedic Survey*. This project was launched at the 1937 centennial celebration of the university (in Ann Arbor). Editor Wilfred B. Shaw planned a nine-part survey to appear in four volumes. A monument to perseverance, the encyclopedia was published in just this form from 1942 to 1958—2000 pages in all, more than one million words. The work is organized topically rather than alphabetically, making it awkward to use, at least in its original published form. However, the Bentley Historical Library has put the entire work online in electronically searchable form. Moreover, the encyclopedia has been continued online, with three more volumes appearing to date, mostly covering postwar topics.[3]

The University of California also produced an encyclopedic work, again to mark a century of service. Verne A. Stadtman, who also wrote a narrative history of the university, edited *The Centennial*

Record of the University of California.[4] It is organized in an alphabetical format with particularly detailed entries for each of the campuses. The University of California also has an online project for the publication of historical records, managed by the Center for Studies in Higher Education at Berkeley.[5] This review, however, was prompted by the appearance of the Union College volume and we will confine the rest of this discussion to the three most recent works.[6]

Roughly one-third of entries in the Union, Brown, and Princeton volumes are devoted to biographies of (mostly) presidents, administrators and professors. Leitch and Mitchell include biographies of renowned alumni, but Somers felt compelled to omit same for reasons of space. Buildings and grounds claim perhaps half as many entries, although generally short. Organizations and publications are likewise numerous but terse. Academic departments receive more extended treatments. And some of the more interesting entries are items unique to each institution. Students, finally, are an elusive presence in these volumes, although there was clearly a common effort to treat all facets of the curriculum and student activities, including athletics, which are covered amply but not excessively. In total, there is an abundance of material on students, but it has to be ferreted from multiple entries. Much less can be found on teaching and learning, whose history Somers concluded "awaits . . . a whole new discipline" (p. viii).

Such a summary of contents can scarcely convey either the rich material or the value of these volumes. Reading in them, nevertheless, has suggested three possible criteria for both appreciation and comparison. First is historical depth and value, particularly in the longer, synthetic pieces. Second is capacity for critical scrutiny in these obvious labors of love. And third would be the encyclopedic quality of each volume—how much information does each contain and how valuable is it for historians? In any such comparison, it is only fair to note, Somers's volume is the latest, biggest, and best. Coming last has allowed him better to reflect on how to incorporate these qualities into an institutional encyclopedia.

Somers informs us that he considered but rejected a presentist approach to his subject. Instead of focusing on topics that contributed to the modern Union College he has instead chosen to explore the unheralded examples of "discontinuity, failed experiments and extinction" (p. vi). In doing so he has given entries the space needed for full exposition, rather than imposing a word limit. Some delightful surprises are the result. The article on baseball, considered Union's sport in the 1880s, gives a lengthy depiction of the problems stemming from student control, including the hiring of professional ringers. Although these problems existed everywhere, the coverage of baseball at Brown and Princeton provides no such insights, emphasizing the ephemera of players and victories. Another long article describes "Hazing and Class Fights" between freshmen and sophomores, which evolved through various forms from the 1850s to the 1920s, a former rite of passage that has entirely disappeared. This phenomenon did not emerge earlier, the reader is surprised to learn, because so few Union students were admitted as freshmen before 1850. Also, the entry on departments accurately explains the confusing use of that term in the nineteenth century to denote individual subjects. The *Princeton Companion*, in contrast, starts this topic with the creation of the modern type of departments in 1904, and the Brown volume has no such entry.

The longest articles in both the Union and Brown volumes are on curriculum (c. 12,000 and 4,500 words, respectively), and both merit the space. Somers's entry is valuable for both correcting and refining understanding of the stereotypes of Nott's parallel scientific course of 1828, the first successful exemplar of its type. Nott apparently believed that collegiate instruction should serve the needs of a wide variety of students. Union's offerings reflected this belief, although they appear to be rather fluid, changing every few years, perhaps according to the talents of the faculty. Overall, Union probably taught more science to its students than any coeval college. Brown too made its mark in curricular innovation with Wayland's 1850 attempt to design an alternative to the classical course. The *Encyclopedia* describes its revolutionary features, and its subsequent repudiation, but adds nothing to Walter Bronson's 1914 account.[7] In addition, both these entries contain useful descriptions of the quest for formulas for general or liberal education in the postwar era.

A Princeton Companion contains no general discussion of curriculum, although the articles on individual departments are informative. Its longest entry is, regrettably, for football (c. 5000 words). Its most interesting essays (speaking for historians, not Princetonians) are probably the biographies of the Princeton "greats"—Jonathan Witherspoon and Woodrow Wilson—although the coverage of the presidents between them is unduly spare and respectful. The volume in this respect reflects its intended use as a "companion" for devoted Princetonians rather than as a tool for historians.[8]

Wayne Somers begins his preface by disavowing the kind of image burnishing that too often characterizes institutional histories. He enjoined contributors "to esteem honest history and to scorn propaganda" (p. v). He carried this critical perspective even further through conscious attempts to expose the "distortions of college history [as] a venerable and interesting part of that history" (p. viii). On enrollments, for example, Somers sets Union's often-exaggerated record straight. On the career of Eliphalet Nott alone, Somers tackles a mountain of myth, exaggeration and controversy.[9] He is unsparing in presenting the doleful final years and aftermath of Nott's reign. Somers thus sets an unusually high standard of candor and critical judgment, and in so doing he exposes some shortcomings of his predecessors.

Admissions practices provide a litmus test for comparing these three volumes. In the 1920s and 1930s, virtually all of the prestigious Eastern private colleges and universities instituted selective policies that placed social characteristics above intellect and explicitly discriminated against Jewish applicants. Marcia Synnott's study of these practices, published the year after *A Princeton Companion*, demonstrated that social exclusivity was most egregiously upheld at Princeton.[10] Leitch, who was on campus as a student and administrator during those years, could scarcely have been unaware of these practices. Yet his discussion of selective admissions completely omits this overriding social dimension. The Brown entry on Admission is similarly silent, and an article on Jews focuses largely on the difficulties Jewish students had in forming fraternities and other organizations. The handling of this topic exemplifies how both these volumes deal with unpleasant realities: through omission rather than outright misrepresentation.

Somers, in contrast, squarely confronts discrimination in admissions (Admissions, Jews at Union), quoting Synnott to set the context. Union maintained a quota of 8 to 10 percent Jewish students from 1930 until after World War II, when a New York State Law explicitly forbade such practices. The college then accomplished the same purpose by using a geographic quota against the New York City area until the mid-1960s. The persistence of discriminatory admissions into the 1960s is rather shocking; but perhaps it is preferable to have these facts on record in the college's encyclopedia than to have them "discovered" by someone seeking to embarrass the institution.

The history of coeducation at Brown is another example of a topic in which the most interesting material is missing. The education of women was essentially forced on the university in the 1890s by local women's groups, in much the way that Radcliffe was "annexed" to Harvard.[11] The "Women's College in Brown University" operated by the principle that the men came first and that none of their resources would be shared with the women. Mitchell notes that the women's tuition not only had to cover the cost of their instruction, but included a 10 percent premium to Brown as well (p. 422). Women also had to raise the money for their building, Pembroke Hall, which gave its name to Pembroke College only in 1928 (seventeen years after President Faunce had noted that having "no name" was "a real hindrance to the growth of the College," p. 424). Condescension toward the Women's College at Brown was probably greater than that endured by any other coordinate college of the era, but the treatment in the *Encyclopedia* scarcely hints of this relationship.

The question of encyclopedic coverage ought to be linked with the purposes of these volumes, which basically seem to be three. *Institutional memory* is important for any institution, but has special significance to those past the two-century mark. Many people associated with these institutions are simply curious about where things came from and how they got to be the way they are. Moreover, organizations typically pass a good deal of misinformation by word of mouth. Hence, an institutional encyclopedia has the merit of making reliable information of this nature readily accessible.

The *Encyclopedia Brunoniana* above all serves the purposes of institutional memory. The coverage of people, places, and things is quite extensive, even if the entries themselves are succinct. The facts are there for the curious, but there is little of the fascinating trivia that can be discovered in the other volumes.

Alumni identification is a second legitimate goal. Graduates take pride in alma mater, and greater knowledge of its past reinforces that pride. This process tends to promote the kind of feel-good history that Somers condemns, but this need not be entirely the case. Institutions such as these, after all, have accomplished much good in their long existence. Emphasizing those aspects of their histories that exemplify positive institutional images gives meaning and value to this history that is undoubtedly preferable to a state of ignorance.

The silences in such accounts have already been noted, but an institutional encyclopedia by the very obligation of coverage should reveal more than most institutional histories, thus possibly suggesting more searching studies.

A Princeton Companion, by definition, aids alumni in particular to identify with the institution. This purpose seems to carry with it an obligation for interesting, well-written articles—to be a pleasant companion. Alexander Leitch clearly took pains to achieve this goal, and his volume is much the better for them. But one can also perceive the image burnishing in the choice of congenial topics. A good example is Wilson's famous speech of 1896, "Princeton in the Nation's Service." The address itself is fully described and introduces references to twelve other entries on Princetonians as governors, senators, etc. While useful, this theme best fits Princeton before 1800 and after 1900. During the nineteenth century, Princeton might better have been described as in the service of Presbyterianism.[12] Yet, the Presbyterians have no separate entry, nor are they acknowledged in the index! The Princeton Theological Seminary receives the briefest of entries. The role of Presbyterianism naturally is mentioned in many articles, but this image was apparently not one that most alumni would find companionable.

Finally, the approach described by Somers is appropriate for an encyclopedia for the *historical record*—one that aspired to be rigorously critical toward sources, rectify error, and explore at least some of the "cul-de-sacs and meandering cow paths of Union's past—the roads that seem . . . to have led in the wrong direction or nowhere at all" (p. vi). The reviewers may be unfashionable enough to believe that good history does lead somewhere, but this is all the more reason for a different form of publication—an encyclopedia—to record unsuspected cul-de-sacs. The very structure of this encyclopedia draws the reader down some of these cow paths. For anyone seeking to grasp the overall development of the college, the individual entries are rarely sufficient in themselves. For better understanding of the context, or the consequences, one must follow the helpful internal references to additional articles. Keeping track of the Nott dynasty and the roles its members played, for example, requires extended meandering.

Somers acknowledges some shortcomings of his volume, which would apply even more to the other encyclopedias. First, "its approach is not sufficiently comparative" (p. viii). Indeed, this is the bane of almost all institutional histories: they focus so intently on their own institution that they fail to acknowledge or realize that very similar developments were occurring at surrounding institutions. Somers is less culpable than most institutional historians in this respect, but the portrait of Union might have been enriched with material from other published histories of higher education.

Second, "it scants Union's financial history" even though "these factors influenced, sometimes decisively, almost every aspect of the College's history." Somers felt that he lacked the expertise and the additional time that such coverage demanded. But once again, this failing is widespread in institutional histories. Financial matters can be difficult to decipher and soporific to explain. Still, the problem might be substantially improved by including some basic tables containing revenues and expenditures for those few obsessive scholars. In fact, this suggestion can be generalized for all three encyclopedias and most institutional histories: why not include tables with basic institutional data? For anyone laboring in college archives, these data are relatively simple to compile, and they then provide an objective record with which to evaluate allegations of decline or claims of success.[13]

Such cavils aside, the *Encyclopedia of Union College History* is a valuable addition to the history of higher education. Furthermore, having three such encyclopedias (not to mention Michigan and California) is more than three times as valuable as having one. Side by side, they create an instant comparative context, and thus leave students and historians no excuse for not using them in this way. Moreover, the encyclopedias offer relatively painless entry into some otherwise obscure subjects. Curriculum is one. Besides the general articles discussed above, one can trace the appearance and development of specific subjects. Ever wonder when music departments were introduced into male colleges? A partial answer is: 1879 at Union, 1895 at Brown, and 1917 at Princeton. A more challenging topic might be to trace the development of college administration. The various articles on deans and provosts would provide a start, and numerous entries on later offices would further elaborate this picture. If these volumes are employed in this way, they will accomplish far more than furthering institutional memory and alumni identification. And historians of higher education will recognize a debt of gratitude to Alexander Leitch, Martha Mitchell, and especially Wayne Somers.

Notes

1.   See Roger L. Geiger, David B. Potts, and W. Bruce Leslie, "Symposium Report: Exploring Our Professional Backyards: Toward Writing Recent History of American Colleges and Universities," *History of Higher Education Annual* 20 (2000): 79–91.

2.   *The Princeton Companion* is available online: http://etc.princeton.edu/CampusWWW/Companion/.

3.   Wilfred B. Shaw, ed., *The University of Michigan: An Encyclopedic Survey*, 4 vol. (Ann Arbor: University of Michigan Press, 1942, 1951, 1953, 1958); and http://www.hti/umich.edu/u/umsurvey/.

4.   Verne A. Stadtman, ed., *The Centennial Record of the University of California* (Berkeley: University of California, 1967); idem., *The University of California, 1868–1968* (New York: McGraw-Hill, 1970).

5.   "University History Project," Center for Studies in Higher Education, University of California, Berkeley: http://ishi.lib.berkeley.edu/cshe/projects/history/history.html

6.   Interestingly, the private institution volumes fail to acknowledge their public predecessors.

7.   Walter C. Bronson, *The History of Brown University, 1764–1914* (Providence, R.I.: 1914). The failure of an encyclopedia to add any new elements to such well-known episodes strikes us as a lost opportunity.

8.   Unlike Union or Brown, Princeton has received thorough historical coverage for much of its past. Leitch is the only compiler to include a bibliography, since material for the other volumes is largely located in their respective archives. Since 1978, additional historical studies have been published, most notably: three additional volumes of *Princetonians: A Biographical Dictionary* (Princeton: Princeton University Press) extending to 1794; David A. Hoevelar, *James McCosh and the Scottish Intellectual Tradition: From Glasgow to Princeton* (Princeton: Princeton University Press, 1981); Mark A. Noll, *Princeton and the Republic, 1768–1822* (Princeton: Princeton University Press, 1989); Paul C. Kemeny, *Princeton in the Nation's Service: Religious Ideals and Educational Practice, 1868–1928* (New York: Oxford University Press, 1998).

9.   Somers acknowledges the contribution of Union Professor Codman Hislop's renowned *Eliphalet Nott* (Middletown, Conn.: Wesleyan University Press, 1971), but he notes that its literary qualities can detract from its usefulness for historians of the college (p. 384).

10. Marcia Synnott, *The Half-Opened Door: Discrimination and Admissions at Harvard, Yale, and Princeton, 1900–1970* (Westport, Conn.: Greenwood Press, 1979). This study is based on a 1974 dissertation that would have been available to Leitch.

11. Polly Welts Kaufman, ed., *The Search for Equity: Women at Brown University, 1891–1991* (Providence, RI: Brown University Press, 1991).

12. According to W. Bruce Leslie, "Princeton had been reduced to a regional institution by the 1860s," and was "the bastion of Old School 'high church' Presbyterianism": *Gentlemen and Scholars: College and Community in the 'Age of the University,' 1865–1917* (University Park, Pa.: Penn State Press, 1992), 34, 32.

13. Michigan's *Encyclopedic Survey* contains some useful tables, and California's *Centennial Record* has numerous, detailed tables. Most notable in this respect: George W. Pierson, *Yale by the Numbers* (Yale University, 1983); also see Susan R. Richardson, "State Higher Education Database, 1870–1965: An Introduction," *History of Higher Education Annual* 22 (2002): 109–30.

Selected Recent Dissertations in the History of Higher Education

The dissertations listed here are selected from titles supplied by Proquest. Copies of most titles can be ordered by calling 800-521-3042 or via the World Wide Web at www.umi.com. The abstracts have been abridged (with apologies to the authors) to convey the general thrust of the study. Since these titles were compiled from a key word search, some relevant titles may have been overlooked. To achieve more complete coverage, I invite readers to encourage recipients of doctorates in the history of higher education to send the *Annual* an abstract of their dissertations for possible inclusion in this section.

R.G.

Balog, Michael George. *The Creation of the College of Liberal Arts at Texas A&M University, The Decision-Making Process.* Texas A&M University, Ph.D., 2002, 116 pp.

Order No. 3072410

The Aspirations Committee Report, the Century Council Report, the Boards' *Blueprint for Progress*, and the Self-Study Report in 1963 all gave President Rudder the outline to change the Agricultural and Mechanical College of Texas. The Aspirations Committee was the internal study while the Century Council performed the external review of the College. Both of these studies included allowing women to enroll and increasing the support of research activities, particularly those in the School of Arts and Sciences. The Board of Directors took these suggestions and created their "Blueprint" to make the A. and M. College of Texas a premier institution of higher education. The 1963 Self-Study Report reinforced the decree from the Board of Directors. The emergence of the College of Liberal Arts was the culmination of the committee reports of the early sixties that stressed the establishment of a stronger humanities and social science presence at Texas A&M. The limited admission of women in 1963 and making the Corps of Cadets non-compulsory in 1965 occurred near the same time as the creation of the College of Liberal Arts and allowed the liberal arts to pursue their own identity.

Beckham, Leslie Christopher. *Making Good Sons, Useful Citizens, and Christian Scholars: Southern Baptist Higher Education in the Nineteenth Century.* University of Kentucky, Ph.D., 2002, 182 pp.
Order No. 3074490

The main argument of this study is that Southern Baptist colleges and universities were not aggressively sectarian places of higher education in the nineteenth century. Previous studies were largely dismissive of the role of denominational colleges in the history of American higher education, but this is undeserved. Denominational colleges could often be innovative and progressive in their methods and subject matter. Nineteenth-century Baptist colleges were unequivocally Christian in their orientation, but not necessarily "sectarian," a pejorative term. They operated from a theistic worldview, but they did not endeavor to make Baptists out of their students. Their religious orientation did not necessitate an inferior educational endeavor. Generally speaking, strained relations existed between state higher education and religiously controlled higher education. The study begins with the early years of the 1800s and concludes in the 1880s and 1890s. Southern Baptist colleges comprise the subject in Kentucky, Missouri, Alabama, Mississippi, South Carolina, North Carolina, Virginia, Georgia, Texas, and Tennessee. Baptist colleges often viewed themselves as colleges of opportunity for Southern students, and they provided much of the elementary and grammar schooling of the South.

Bradley, Stefan Maurice. *Gym Crow Must Go! The 1968–1969 Student and Community-Protests at Columbia University in the City of New York.* University of Missouri—Columbia, Ph.D., 2003, 280 pp.
Order No. 3091901

This dissertation deals with how community and student activists used race and power to organize at Columbia University, the prestigious Ivy League school adjacent to Harlem. This work also shows how the Civil Rights, Antiwar, New Left, Black Power, and Student Movements interplayed during the controversies. The dissertation concerns Columbia University's intentions to build a gymnasium in nearby Morningside Park, a public space, where the school had already leased five acres of land for softball fields. It also deals with the attempts of black student protesters to enrich the curriculum of the university with a black studies program as well as their campaign to increase the admissions of black students. Some of the main actors in this controversy included an increasingly militant student group, Students' Afro-American Society (SAS), a branch of Students for a Democratic Society (SDS), activists from Harlem, as well as school and city officials. The 1968–1969 protests at Columbia illustrated victories for Black Power against a white institution. The students from SAS, as members of the black intelligentsia, exercised the essence of Black Power by allying themselves with black working-class members of the Harlem community to keep Columbia from building the gymnasium in Morningside Park. The results of the protests were increased power for black students on Columbia's campus and the university's increased respect for the neighboring black community.

Comminey, Shawn Christopher. *A History of Straight College, 1869–1935.* The Florida State University, Ph.D., 2003, 249 pp.

Order No. 3093105

Emancipation left thousands of blacks homeless, unemployed, and without education. Adjusting to new-found freedom, African Americans expressed an intense desire to acquire knowledge that had largely been permitted to whites only. African Americans and white supporters realized the need to establish black institutions of higher learning to train teachers and equip ministers and professionals for leadership. Straight University, later called Straight College, a private, predominantly black institution of higher learning founded in 1869 in New Orleans, Louisiana, by the American Missionary Association (AMA), was the first institution of its kind in the state. Actively involved in black educational work since the beginning of the Civil War, the AMA had established Fisk University, Atlanta University, Hampton University, Tillotson College, and Tougaloo College, as well as Straight College. The AMA realized such institutions could not fully live up to expectations of becoming "colleges" at first. But, it hoped each would work diligently over time to achieve that goal. The purpose of this study is to highlight Straight's origin, growth, and development throughout its existence, and its mission to improve the quality of African American lives spiritually and educationally.

Eden, Timothy E. *Seasons of Change: Catholic Higher Education from the End of the Second World War to the Decade following the Second Vatican Council.* University of San Francisco, Ed.D., 2002, 555 pp.

Order No. 3072268

The study addresses the character, origin, and evolution of the changes that affected Catholic higher education from World War II through the decade following the Second Vatican Council. World War II and its aftermath were seedbeds for new ideas, institutions, and programs that affected both public and private higher education in the United States. As part of that current of change, a group of prominent American Catholic thinkers in the 1940s and 1950s critiqued the state of Catholic higher education and offered a variety of proposals for its renewal. Support for change on Catholic campuses grew in the years before the Council and led to rapid and often radical change in traditional structures of curriculum, governance, religious practice, faculty hiring, and student demographics. The model of the Public Church was used to describe the character of those campus changes. Developed as a description of a significant current of American Church life in the 1970s and 1980s, the Public Church model was a fruitful and accurate description of the reshaping of Catholic higher education from WWII through the postconciliar years. The study includes an extensive historical narrative that covers the period between the end of World War II and the beginning of the Council, the thinking of Catholic educational leaders after the Council, and interviews with three former presidents of Catholic colleges or universities whose tenures covered the 1960s and 1970s.

Evans-Herring, Cassandra Paulette. *An Intersectional Analysis of the Life Experiences of Mary Elizabeth Branch, the First Black Female Senior College President.* Georgia State University, Ph.D., 2003, 331 pp.

Order No. 3082839

In 1930, Mary Elizabeth Branch was part of a small but rising group of African American female leaders of institutions of higher learning and was not only an impressive administrator but also a staunch advocate and an unassuming activist for improving the social conditions and life chances of African Americans. Branch breathed new life into the deteriorating Tillotson College, and it was reborn as a modern institution of higher learning that moved forward a social agenda reflective of Branch's philosophies of community, education, freedom, and leadership. The historical investigation has five research questions, regarding Branch's: (1) familial and educational backgrounds, (2) experiences of race and gender issues, (3) leadership style, (4) personal philosophy, and (5) off-campus relationships. The study contributes to the academy's knowledge and understanding of higher education leadership, both black and women's history, and African American women's endeavors to document their own historical stories.

Gabrielse, David Randall. *Making Men, Colleges and the Midwest: The Building and Writing of Indiana Colleges, 1802–1860.* Michigan State University, Ph.D., 2002, 200 pp.

Order No. 3075006

This work treats the contests between regional and often nationalist and centralizing goals of particular college founders and the particular views of local and regional opposition groups. The core of this work is a study of three colleges established between 1824 and 1840 and the texts they produced first to proclaim their purposes and goals and then to defend them. Indiana College (later Indiana University), Wabash College, and Indiana Asbury University (later Depauw University) are located in an arc to the South and West of Indianapolis. They arose during an early period of institutional development of the region and during the nineteenth-century publishing explosion. The college leaders sought to educate young men to become part of an educated class of ministers, politicians, professionals, and teachers who could provide public and professional leadership and education in an emerging region of the American republic. Neither narrowly sectarian institutions nor merely extensions of a Presbyterian-Congregationalist-Yale axis, they were located in particular towns, but were frequently regionally oriented institutions led by men with regional or national relationships and visions of society. College presidents spoke of providing a "civilizing" function in a region with a population they called "heterogeneous." The colleges published narratives that presented the colleges in the context of a new and growing western region of the American republic and distributed them throughout the region and in the Eastern states.

Henderson-Gasser, Ellen M. *The Evolution of Student Services: An Historical Case Study of a Midwestern, Public, Baccalaureate-Granting University.* University of Kentucky, Ed.D., 2003, 152 pp.

Order No. 3086895

This study follows the evolution of a student services division within a public, baccalaureate-granting, regional institution of higher education in the Midwest. The time frame for this case study begins with the creation of the institution in 1899 and continues to the late 1960s when the organization experienced its last, major restructuring and a vice president of student affairs was appointed. The phrase "student services" had not been coined when institutions of higher education were first formed in the United States. Presidents and faculty members assumed the roles of student services personnel in their daily interactions with students. To prepare young men to assume leadership roles in the community, presidents, with the assistance of faculty members, closely monitored not only academics but also students' lives beyond the classroom. As higher education organizations expanded and became more complex, presidents began delegating complete responsibility for such duties to others within the institution, generally faculty members. The relief offered by faculty members, who had assumed much of the responsibility for discipline and students' out-of-classroom lives, was short-lived. Faculty members, focusing on research and specialization within their academic fields, felt that responsibility for students' moral development was not an appropriate role for academicians. As faculty members focused more narrowly on specializations and research, others were needed to fill the void. Student services divisions were the response to this need.

Huber, Beth Ann. *Manufacturing "Safe" Minds: The Impact of Cold War Rhetoric on the Universities.* University of Missouri at Kansas City, Ph.D., 2002, 262 pp.

Order No. 3071538

This dissertation examines the sources and substance of rhetorical choices made by Cold War foreign policy leaders and explores the impact of those rhetorical paradigms on the culture of the university in general and English studies in particular throughout the 1950s and 1960s. Through detailed rhetorical analysis of seminal early-Cold War foreign policy documents and speeches, loyalty oath laws, and the subsequent academic hearings and conversations on intellectual freedom, the National Defense Education Act, campus activism among students and faculty, and various curricular and professional shifts in English studies, this project documents how the rhetorical patterns created during the inception of international Cold War hostilities were eventually overlaid upon, echoed in, and reversed through subsequent domestic events and crises, leaving English studies, as a profession, radically transformed. As university administrators, faculty, and students were, at the onset, a target audience for much of the propaganda, and later actual targets for attack by patriotic cold warriors, academia was forced to adjust itself in terms of how it envisioned academic freedom, curricular equality, and both professional and humanitarian responsibility. In response to such questions, academics in the humanities, those with the most impetus toward reform, made their own rhetorical choices that resulted in the construction of a reality that was structurally the same as, yet in polar opposition to, early foreign policy leaders. The author concludes that, regardless of extant political pressures, academics have a responsibility to make education relevant and critically evaluate the world in which they live while helping their students to do the same.

Lundquist, Sara Watson. *Achieving Equity and Excellence in 21st Century American Higher Education: The California Master Plan and Beyond*. The Claremont Graduate University, Ph.D., 2003, 379 pp.

Order No. 3065499

The purpose of this research was to investigate California's commitment to broad access to public higher education and to analyze the extent to which this promise has been kept, broken, or modified over the last forty years. This study focused on ways in which access and economic conditions inter-relate and searched for deeper connections between theories of how educational policy is developed, maintained, and changed over time. Among the most troubling findings are the following: (1) The fastest growing and soon to be largest segment of California's population, Latinos, are doing worse today on a variety of higher education indicators than ten years ago. (2) System infrastructure is under-funded and deteriorating in all segments. (3) An outmoded tax structure is unable to produce the revenue required to enable the next generation of students to enter and succeed in college. (4) Numerical increases in student outcomes mask proportional decreases for specific groups in key higher education indicators. The system was found to have tremendous assets and potential but to be in grave danger of deteriorating to the point that it is unable to assure either adequate access or excellence for its current or future students. Recommendations for action are detailed at the conclusion.

Robbins, Jane E. *Solving the Patent Problem: Cognition, Communication, and the National Academy of Sciences in the Evolution of Patent Policy in American Research Universities, 1917-1966.* University of Pennsylvania, 2004.

Order No. Not Available

Though widely practiced and accepted in universities today, the practice of patenting science is not without its critics and conflicts. Two questions overarching contemporary concerns are whether patenting is inhibiting rather than fostering scientific progress, largely due to secrecy, financial conflict, and the costs and difficulty of accessing research tools; and whether universities are at risk of losing their status as sources of independent research and disseminators of knowledge.

This dissertation inquires into the circumstances that led to both the institutionalization of and the contestation over university patenting. Several important patent committees of the National Academy of Sciences/National Research Council, a network hub between universities, government, and industry, provide the lens for a field-level analysis of university patent development. Using a cognitive history approach that rejoins old and new institutional approaches and expands the latter with cognitive analysis, it traces the process of thinking and deciding about university patents in the context of the political and economic pressures of the time. In so doing, it addresses recent critiques of institutional analysis as neglectful of people and process, and offers a more robust approach to understanding change, particularly the seeds of isomorphism.

Early in the twentieth century a strategic campaign was mounted to persuade university administrators of the merits of patent control, despite deep divisions among scientists. Driving this campaign were goals of preserving private control over research; a desire to limit transaction costs and competition in recognition of the growing interdependence of research findings in a changing world of science.

Siepierski, Joel Arthur. *The Politics of Education: The University of Poitiers, 1590–1820.* State University of New York at Buffalo, Ph.D., 2002, 314 pp.

Order No. 3063166

Poitiers began the early modern period as an important center of governmental administration and educational culture. The University of Poitiers was one of the most important institutions in the city, and its professors among the elite of local culture. This dissertation examines the social, intellectual, and political lives of professors of the early modern University of Poitiers, and takes a new look at university life in seventeenth- and eighteenth-century France. Through the examination of all aspects of university culture—publishing, teaching, administrative responsibilities, political action, and family ties—it found university culture to be more active and complex than previously recognized. Four interrelated conclusions have emerged from this analysis. First, university professors represented an urban elite actively engaged in local society and national politics. Second, over the course of the seventeenth century, professors' political style shifted from familial to ideological. By mid-century professors advocated a specific ideology incorporating ardent Gallicanism, anti-Protestantism, and political absolutism and moved away from the family-oriented politics typical of professors in the early part of the century. Third, through this transformation professors gained access to elite patrons based on their use of intellectual skills associated with their education and university position rather than family connections. Finally, by 1700 the University of Poitiers's sphere of influence became more regional than a century earlier. The increasingly local focus of the university, coupled with increasingly acrimonious conflicts between Jesuit and non-Jesuit faculty, initiated a decline in prestige that resulted in the university's inability to recruit students and faculty from outside the immediate geographical area and a less mobile educated elite. The decline of the early modern university came as the result of the political decisions made by faculty rather than an antiquated curriculum or teaching style.

Stiffler, Douglas Alden. *Building Socialism at Chinese People's University: Chinese Cadres and Soviet Experts in The People's Republic of China, 1949–1957.* University of California at San Diego, Ph.D., 2002, 517 pp.

Order No. 3064449

In 1949, the leaders of the victorious Chinese Communist Party decreed the founding of Chinese People's University ["Renda"] as a "new-style, regular university" to absorb the "advanced experience" of the Soviet Union in building socialism. Over seven years, from 1950 to 1957, a contingent of approximately eighty Soviet experts instructed Chinese instructors and graduate students at the new university in such specialties as political economy, factory management, and archives. From 1950 to 1954, Renda occupied a unique, Party-decreed position at the pinnacle of Chinese higher education. By the late 1950s, however, Renda had largely lost this position as the "advanced Soviet experience" the university was called upon to study and transmit was increasingly called into question. In order to understand the fate of the Party's project of creating a new, Soviet-style university, this dissertation analyzes the developmental trajectory of Renda in its formative period of "learning from the Soviet Union." Rather than seeing the 1950s as a relatively uncomplicated and successful period of learning from the Soviet Union, this dissertation shows that difficulties were encountered from the very beginning. One of the main problems the administration of the new university encountered were deep social divisions among poorly educated "old cadres" and "young intellectuals" at the school. Factional divisions in the administration and on the faculty complicated the school's mission in the 1950s. "Study of the Soviet Union" was not uniformly embraced by all in this decade, and this became an issue in the increasingly harsh political campaigns of the 1950s. Chinese People's University did, however, have significant effects on Chinese higher education through its training of a new academic elite and its promotion of a new, Soviet-style academic culture. Certain Soviet-style institutional innovations first introduced at Renda became characteristic features of Chinese academia. The Soviet experts' teaching of a new generation of young academics at Renda helped to inculcate an "orthodox professional academic ethos" characterized by respect for established ideological authority together with professional academic skills. In specialized fields like finance and accounting, young instructors assimilated Soviet templates that remained basic to the fields well past the 1950s. The long-term effects of the "new university" on the formation of a Chinese socialist academia were thus considerable.

Swartout, Lisa Fetheringill. *Dueling Identities: Protestant, Catholic, and Jewish Students in the German Empire, 1890–1914.* University of California at Berkeley, Ph.D., 2002, 316 pp.

Order No. 3082422

This dissertation examines the relations of Protestant, Catholic, and Jewish students in the German Empire, 1890–1914. It explores the Protestant cultural dominance at institutions of higher education and its impact on religious minorities. Catholic and Jewish students created their own organizations, which sheltered them at universities and which by the eve of World War I were among the largest student groups. Part I examines the role of religious identity in student daily life, with individual chapters on Protestant, Catholic, and Jewish students. Part II, focuses on religious prejudice and political culture with three chapters on anti-Catholicism, antisemitism, and conflict within the largest liberal student movement of the Empire, the Free Students. This project is part of a larger trend within German historiography that recognizes the importance of religious faith as a fundamental factor of identity, and focuses on a previously ignored and yet important segment of society, university students. As the site where German adolescents became adults as well as the gateway for society's elites, the universities played an important role in socializing the middle class. The Protestant culture of those environments exacerbated the already sharp divisions between Catholics, Protestants, and Jews, and left a lasting impact on the German middle class. The title of this dissertation, "Dueling Identities," refers both to confessional conflict and to the centrality of the duel within student life. The duel, which to participants symbolized honor and manliness, helped create students' self-conception as an "intellectual aristocracy of the German nation." As opposed to existing literature on student life, this dissertation also demonstrates that liberal currents played a significant role within student subculture. During conflicts at universities, student organizations vied with each other to become the representatives of liberal values like tolerance, academic freedom, the rule of law, the right to associate, freedom of speech, and (even, at certain points) limits on government authority. These insights into the political culture of university life contribute to our understanding of the German middle class and constructions of the German nation.

Tollison, Courtney L. *Moral Imperative and Financial Practicality: Desegregation of South Carolina's Denominationally-Affiliated Colleges and Universities.* University of South Carolina, Ph.D., 2003.

Order No. Not Available

The desegregation of denominational-affiliated colleges and universities forced the white church-going people of South Carolina to confront changes brought about by the civil rights movement. Motivated by either a moral imperative and/or an understanding that continued segregation was financially impractical, select white administrators, trustees, alumni, church leaders, and church members accommodated desegregation in denominationally affiliated colleges and universities over the course of the 1960s. At institutions that desegregated, or attempted to desegregate before the 1964 Civil Rights Act financially forced most institutions to do so, race became a measure of an institution's commitment to academic prominence. At institutions where desegregation prompted conflict between the college or university and the denomination with which it was affiliated, desegregation forced these colleges and universities to reevaluate their institutional identity. Other factors influenced the nature of desegregation at these institutions as well, such as financial stability, student activism and conservatism, African American agency, the organizational structure of the denominations, the power of individual personalities, and federal mandates. This history illustrates the convergence of religion, race, federal law, and higher education.

The case studies that comprise this study include Our Lady of Mercy Junior College and the Catholic Diocese of Charleston; Furman University and the South Carolina Baptist Convention; Wofford and Columbia colleges, both of which are affiliated with the South Carolina United Methodist Conference; and Presbyterian College and the United Presbyterian Church in the United States. Race relations at Bob Jones University, Erskine College, and the historically black colleges and universities in South Carolina are also addressed.

Contributors

Christian K. Anderson is a Ph.D. candidate in higher education at The Pennsylvania State University.

Fred W. Beuttler is associate university historian at the University of Illinois at Chicago, where he is, in association with Robert V. Remini, researching and writing the history of UIC. He is the author of a number of scholarly articles, and the primary author of *The University of Illinois at Chicago: A Pictorial History* (2000).

John Burton is assistant professor and director of American Studies at DePaul University in Chicago.

Roger L. Geiger is distinguished professor of higher education at Penn State and editor of the *History of Higher Education Annual.* His most recent book, *Knowledge and Money: Research Universities and the Paradox of the Marketplace,* appeared in 2004.

John Halsey is a member of the faculty at SUNY College at Brockport. Halsey, a sociologist, directs Brockport's London Program.

Bruce Leslie, a member of the faculty at SUNY College at Brockport, specializes in American social and educational history. With John Halsey he has recently published "A College Upon a Hill: Exceptionalism & American Higher Education," in ed. Dale Carter, *Marks of Distinction: American Exceptionalism Revisited* (Aarhus, Denmark: 2001), and "Britain's White Paper Turns Higher Education away from the EU," *International Higher Education* #32 (2003). Leslie and Halsey are currently writing a book-length socio-historical comparison of British and American higher education.

Courtney L. Tollison received her Ph.D. in history from the University of South Carolina in 2003. She is currently an adjunct professor at Furman University.

Peter Wallenstein teaches history at Virginia Polytechnic Institute and State University. His books include *Blue Laws and Black Codes: Conflict, Courts, and Change in Twentieth-Century Virginia* (2004) and *From VPI to State University: President T. Marshall Hahn Jr. and the Transformation of Virginia Tech, 1962–1974* (2004). He presented an earlier version of this article— "Higher Education and Civil Rights: South Carolina, 1890–1966"—at The Citadel Conference on Civil Rights in South Carolina, Charleston, S.C., March 2003.

Joy Ann Williamson is an assistant professor of the history of American education at Stanford University. Her work focuses on the intersection of social movements and higher educational reform during the middle twentieth century.

For Product Safety Concerns and Information please contact our EU
representative GPSR@taylorandfrancis.com Taylor & Francis Verlag GmbH,
Kaufingerstraße 24, 80331 München, Germany

Batch number: 08158516

Printed by Printforce, the Netherlands